Tom's Thought Provokers

Gems From A Pastor's Heart

By

Tom Younger

ISBN: 1-4140-2026-0 (e-book)
ISBN: 1-4140-2025-2 (Paperback)
ISBN: 1-4140-2024-4 (Dust Jacket)

Library of Congress Control Number: 2003098164

This book is printed on acid-free paper.

Printed in the United States of America
Bloomington, IN

1stBooks - rev. 12/30/03

To our five children:

Brenda, Mark, Peter, Colleen and Lori

Table of Contents

Guest Preface

Long before I ever met Dr. Tom Younger, I had heard stories about his achievements. People told me about how, while serving as senior pastor at Immanuel Baptist Church in Fort Wayne, Indiana, Tom had started a dozen daughter churches. They told about his work as a board member of Cedarville University. They told about his appearances as a guest speaker at Bible conferences and religious retreats. They told me about his tenure as President of Western Baptist College. To me, it sounded as though he was a set of triplets. How could one person get so much done?

Well, I found out the answer to my question within a week after he and I crossed paths for the first time. In 1983 Tom was back in Fort Wayne visiting his son and he happened to sit in on the adult Sunday school class I was teaching at Immanuel Baptist. This was years after he had left Immanuel and he was then pastoring a large church in California.

After class Tom came up and said, "I really, *really* liked your lesson this morning. I'd like you to come out to California and lead a seminar for the teachers at our Christian day school on how to prepare powerful lessons. While you're there, I'd like you to preach in my place that Sunday."

I shook his hand and nonchalantly said, "Yeah, sure. Uh, we'll have to talk about that sometime. That would be nice." I then pretty much forgot about it. People often would make random comments like that to me, but usually nothing came of it.

Well, not so with Tom Younger. I was at home three days later and I got a long distance call from Tom.

"I hope your calendar is clear for March 17 through 19, because I've booked your roundtrip air tickets and I've got our teachers all set to spend a day being trained by you. I told my secretary to type into our bulletin that you'll be preaching that Sunday, too."

And that was that. Next thing I knew, I was on my way to California. It was from this experience that I learned the secret of Tom Younger's success. He was a man of action. He was a true leader. He was short on theory and long on practice. I knew that this fellow and I were going to be life-long friends.

Tom was forever amazing me about how he would seize the moment regarding anything of importance to him. I was visiting his home once, and late one evening as we were relaxing in his living room he said to me, "You're a doctor of English. Give me some advice. I have a lady in our church who has been a very diligent worker. I want to give her a little present to express my appreciation. The woman loves classic mystery stories, but she's read all of the Sherlock Holmes stories, all the Agatha Christie novels, and all the mysteries written by Dorothy Sayers. What could I give her?"

I thought for a moment and then said, "Well, G. K. Chesterton wrote a series of excellent short stories featuring a little country priest named Father Brown who was a detective in England. I think she'd enjoy those books."

Tom nodded, wrote down the information, then went back to reading his newspaper. In about an hour we both turned in for the night. The next morning I got up and came in for breakfast. There on the kitchen table were four Father Brown short story collections by Chesterton. I was amazed.

"Where did these come from?" I asked Tom.

"Oh, I got up around 3 a.m. and went out to an all-night bookstore here in town and bought them. I read four of the stories before dawn. You're right. They're excellent. I'm going to wrap up these books and give them to the lady in our church this morning."

And that is just the way Tom Younger did everything. He never delayed. He always acted. He was a man of achievement.

So it was then that when he told me that he planned to write this book but he was in a race against heart failure, I laughed and said, "I'll bet on *you* rather than the heart failure."

For weeks and months my friend would send me email attachments of devotions and anecdotes and stories he was writing to add to this manuscript. During this process he was losing weight, taking medications, and seeing physicians. But in typical Tom Younger fashion, he charged forward anyway.

Finally, one day he wrote and said, "Dennis, this will probably be the last entry I'll be sending you. I'm very ill and they are putting me in the hospital. I had hoped to come up with an entry for a full year of readings for 365 days. I fell short."

Now, try to imagine if you will what Tom Younger's version of "falling short" was. He had hoped to write 365 entries but because he was dying of heart failure, he ***only*** managed to complete about 350. That made me howl with laughter.

I wrote back and said, "Here's a bulletin for you, pal. You will NEVER be finished with something at the time of your death because once you complete something, you always have to move right into something else. The Lord is just going to have to say one day, 'Good work, Tom, but that's enough. Come home, now.' "

And that is exactly what happened. Tom went to be with the Lord with his book almost finished. Fortunately, he left enough notes, illustrations, and other materials so that his wonderful wife Davina could pull everything together to make Tom's last wish come true—the completion of this book.

Now you, too, can experience the humor, wisdom, and godly depth of one of the finest individuals I ever had the privilege of calling *friend.* Read these pages...and allow Dr. Tom Younger to continue to "live" among us.

Dr. Dennis E. Hensley
Department of English
Taylor University Fort Wayne

Introduction

Reading: Psalm 30

"That my heart may sing to you and not be silent." Psalm 30:12

For many years I have thought about writing brief thought provokers. I almost waited too long to get this work started and finished because of health problems. This all started while fishing for Walleye in the Canadian wilderness. Paul Robbins, my long time friend and fishing buddy, encouraged me to engage in writing. This project took two years to finish. My health has played an integral part in my doing this work for I have always been so active as to neglect the value of waiting, listening and putting thoughts on paper. However, I have been a prodigious reader throughout my career, thanks to the encouragement of Dr. Vernon C. Grounds. This is not a scholarly work – I need not tell you – nor sophisticated. I am deeply indebted to a host of family and friends who have encouraged me to write. I cannot name them, there are so many. I do want to pay special tribute to Dr. and Mrs. James Buchanan, Dr. and Mrs. Robert Edwards, and Dr. and Mrs. David Shaw, whose encouragement and support have meant so much to me. I would be remiss if I neglected to mention Davina, my wife, who has cajoled, prodded and formatted and did the first of several editing wickets, insisting that I show some degree of organization in a mind that has run all over the track.

Last but not least, I am thankful to the Lord for extending my life long enough to finish this work.

Drought

Reading: Job 12

"If he holds back the waters, there is drought; if he lets them loose, they devastate the land" (Job 12:15 NIV).

In the Great Plain section of our country we suffered a drought lasting a decade (1931—1940), known as the dust bowl. "Black blizzards" blocked out the sun and piled dirt in huge drifts. During the 1950s, a seven year drought devastated the Great Plains. A five year drought in the 1960s dried up 25 percent of New York City's reservoirs. Droughts have terrorized humankind for centuries.[1] (from *How Majestic is Thy Name*)

"But blessed is the man who trusts in the LORD, whose confidence is in him. He will be like a tree planted by the water that sends out its roots by the stream. It does not fear when heat comes; its leaves are always green. It has no worries in a year of drought and never fails to bear fruit" (Jeremiah 17:7-9 NIV).

As the water brings growth and fruit to the tree, our daily lives can be refreshed and revitalized by the Word of God.

A Noble Woman

Reading: Proverbs 31

"'Many women do noble things, but you surpass them all.' Charm is deceptive, and beauty is fleeting; but a woman who fears the LORD is to be praised. Give her the reward she has earned, and let her works bring her praise at the city gate" (Proverbs 31:29-31 NIV).

The old lady died a spinster. In her last wishes she insisted that there only be women used as pallbearers. Her reasoning: "Men wouldn't take me out when I was alive; they sure aren't going to take me out after I die." In my career I have frequently met some wonderful women who were single and remained so all their lives. Miss Thompson, one of my Bible teachers in seminary, often said: "It was a testimony to the stupidity of men."

Sure there are some women who pretend to be good persons, but who fail to measure up. But I dare say that there are by far fewer men who don't know enough to come in out of the rain. I am most grateful for a godly woman whose children rise up and call her blessed. If you are married to one, treat her well as God would.

Clouds

Reading: Job 37

"Do you know how the clouds hang poised, those wonders of him who is perfect in knowledge?" (Job 37:16 NIV).

I was flying an airplane for the first time when my instructor asked if I wanted to fly through the dark cloud bank ahead. I assured him that I didn't. He smiled for he wouldn't allow me to do it anyway. I have flown through thousands of cloud banks when experienced airline pilots were in control. It was an interesting bumpy ride sometimes. We often elate that we were on *cloud nine* following some unexpected blessing. "There is no one like the God of Jeshurun, who rides on the heavens to help you and on the clouds in his majesty" (Deuteronomy 33:26 NIV).

"How do you describe a cloud? Do you opt for scientific terms—nimbus, cirrus, stratus, cumulus – or do you lean toward more poetic options like `wispy,' `curly,' `feather like,' `stringy,' or even `puffy'?" [2] (from *How Majestic is Thy Name*) Clouds are important to balance the world's climate. God didn't forget or leave out one detail in His provision for us in this world, did He? If you think you live in a hot climate, what do you think of how much heat you'd bear were it not for the clouds?. I love Oregon's coastal cloud bank where the clouds seem so low; yet they sometimes can rise as high as 45,000 feet in other parts of the country.

Deserts

Reading: Isaiah 41:1-20

"I will put in the desert the cedar and the acacia, the myrtle and the olive. I will set pines in the wasteland, the fir and the cypress together, so that people may see and know, may consider and understand, that the hand of the LORD has done this, that the Holy One of Israel has created it" (Isaiah 41:19-20 NIV).

The Sahara desert covers over 3.5 million miles and holds the record for a blistering heat of 136 degrees. Millions of tons of sand are tossed hundreds of miles across the earth's deserts. Many deserts get less than 10 inches of rain a year.

A British military officer calculated that when the Israelites wandered in the wilderness forty years while escaping Egypt and on their way to the Promised Land, they faced a formidable challenge, but God provided for them. Think of it: 600,000 men on foot, women and children, perhaps 2,000,000 people, plus flocks, herds and cattle. They needed 900 tons of food per day; God provided manna, two full train loads. They needed 2,400 tons of firewood per day to cook food. 100 Persian wheel wells at every halting place to produce 72,000 gallons per hour per 12 hour day. Harnessed they went out of Egypt five in a rank, meaning that 230 hours passed to reach a given point. The first man out of camp would leave 10 days before the last. Camping required 500 square miles each night. All in God's daily work-sheet. The Israelites made it, thanks to an awesome God.

And we sometimes think the logistics of a given circumstance causes a headache! To be sure, we are the headache, for God is able to supply all our needs according to his riches in glory in Christ Jesus.

Hats and Racks

Reading: Hebrews 12

"Do not withhold discipline from a child; if you punish him with the rod, he will not die. Punish him with the rod and save his soul from death" (Proverbs 23:13-14).

Even though Mother went to Heaven ten years ago, I still hear her voice. Now before you draw the conclusion that my theology is gone awry, let me explain. We are often stabbed wide awake by the seemingly innocuous funny sayings of another person close to us. Mom, out of frustration would sometimes say: "Tom, why don't you use your head for something other than a hat rack?" I knew something about rats living in a poor section of Gary, Indiana when I was a kid. I wasn't sure about a rack and its possibilities of use until later in life; however, I knew Mom well enough to duck and get out of sight before she exploded and said something I understood quite well. You never wanted to be near when she interpreted the meaning of a hat rack. Paraphrased it was: "Now, don't you mess with me; I brought you into this world, and I can take you out!" Meanwhile her limited understanding of Greek was quite effective, reflecting on her upbringing in the Rose Children's Home in Terre Haute, Indiana. Even though she never was formally educated except for the first eight grades of school,

Mom knew more about psychology and raising children than a lot of moderns who have acquired degrees trying to figure out how to live. Not to impugn the motives of the study of psychology. Believe me, Mom had a thorough knowledge of the Scriptures, and she weighed man's wisdom against God's and came out preferring to honor Him in raising a family. Even though I no longer use a hat rack nor do I wear hats very often, I still have a special place in my heart when I see one: I think of Mother and thank God for her. My own children benefited from my use of Mother's psychology.

"My son, do not make light of the Lord's discipline, and do not lose heart when he rebukes you, because the Lord disciplines those he loves, and he punishes everyone he accepts as a son. Endure hardship as discipline; God is treating you as sons. For what son is not disciplined by his father? If you are not disciplined (and everyone undergoes discipline), then you are illegitimate children and not true sons. Moreover, we have all had human fathers who disciplined us and we respected them for it. How much more should we submit to the Father of our spirits and live!" (Hebrews12:5-9 NIV).

Earthquakes

Reading: Haggai 2:6-9

"He shakes the earth from its place and makes its pillars tremble" (Job 9:6 NIV).

I got a taste of a devastating earthquake in the San Francisco Bay area in the late 80s. The earth rocked and rolled. I was watching the beginning of the World Series game at the fitness center. That placed emptied of people, fit and fat in nothing flat, something we are warned not to do. I stayed glued to my chair and it danced a jig for almost a minute. A section collapsed on the Oakland Bay Bridge. Fortunately, it collapsed onto a lower highway going the other direction. The Cypress structure of Interstate 880 fell and pan-caked one highway onto another. More than 50 people were killed. Dogs howled; people stopped their cars to look at their tires thinking they had four flats. Apartments in the Marina Bay were reduced to rubble. It was a scary occurrence no one could do anything about, except to wait it out.

The Alaskan quake permanently tilted some 72,000 square miles of land, thrusting it as high as 80 feet at one end and sinking it 9 feet at the other.[3] (from *How Majestic is Thy Name*).

In the future God will use earthquakes in judgment (Ezekiel 38:19; Revelation 6:12; 8:5; 11:13). Christians can be glad to know they will not be the objects of God's judgment. "Therefore, there is now no condemnation for those who are in Christ Jesus, because through Christ Jesus the law of the Spirit of life set me free from the law of sin and death. For what the law was powerless to do in that it was weakened by the sinful nature, God did by sending his own Son in the likeness of sinful man to be a sin offering. And so he condemned sin in sinful man, in order that the righteous requirements of the law might be fully met in us, who do not live according to the sinful nature but according to the Spirit." (Romans 8:1-4 NIV).

Lions

Reading: Revelation 5

"There are three things that are stately in their stride, four that move with stately bearing: a lion, mighty among beasts, who retreats before nothing; a strutting rooster, a he-goat, and a king with his army around him" (Proverbs 30:29-31 NIV).

The lion is a big, powerful cat. It is probably the most famous member of the cat family. People are frightened by the lion's thundering roar and impressed by its strength and royal appearance. The lion is called the "king of beasts," and is a well-known symbol of both beauty and power.

There are no more lions left in the Middle East and northern Africa. Only about 200 lions still live in Asia—all in the Gir Forest in India. Lions still live in the eastern part of central Africa and in southern Africa. But most of these lions live in national parks and areas called *reserves,* where the animals are protected from hunters.

The lion plays a prominent role in prophecy: "The lion has roared- who will not fear? The Sovereign LORD has spoken- who can but prophesy?" (Amos 3:8 NIV) "Then one of the elders said to me, `Do not weep! See, the Lion of the tribe of Judah, the Root of David, has triumphed. He is able to open the scroll and its seven seals".(Revelation 5:5)" Peter wrote to Christians: "Be self-controlled and alert. Your enemy the devil prowls around like a roaring lion looking for someone to devour." (1 Peter 5:8-9 NIV).

Gloves

Reading: Proverbs 15

"But you, man of God, flee from all this, and pursue righteousness, godliness, faith, love, endurance and gentleness" (1 Timothy 6:11 NIV).

TR (Teddy Roosevelt) needed a great deal of exercise, particularly to control a waistline responding to his hearty meals. He played tennis with aides, but he preferred riding and long hikes. On one of the latter, accompanied by some more or less willing diplomats, he encountered a stream that could be forded only by the removal of all clothing. J. J. Jusserrand, the French ambassador and TR's good friend, emulated his host except for a pair of pink gloves. Asked why he retained these, he replied: "In case we should run into ladies." (Louis Aachincloss: *The Biography of Theodore Roosevelt*).

As a kid I was sometimes confronted by my Mother wearing kid gloves, a euphemism I later learned was akin to gentleness. Solomon said: "A gentle answer turns away wrath, but a harsh word stirs up anger" (Proverbs 15:1 NIV). Paraphrased by Eugene Peterson: "A gentle response defuses anger, but a sharp tongue kindles a temper-fire" (Proverbs 15:1 The Message). Think of how often God made use of dealing with us wearing kid gloves, as it were.

Leadership

Reading: Galatians 2

"...this time with Barnabas. I took Titus along also. I went in response to a revelation and set before them the gospel that I preach among the Gentiles. But I did this privately to those who seemed to be leaders for fear that I was running or had run my race in vain" (Galatians 2:1-2 NIV).

"Henry Adams, himself the great-grandson and grandson of presidents as well as the most brilliant of American historians, said the American president `resembles the commander of a ship at sea. He must have a helm to grasp, a course to steer, a port to seek.' The men in the White House (thus far only men, alas) in steering their chosen courses have shaped our destiny as a nation. Great presidents possess, or are possessed by a vision of an ideal America. Their passion, as they grasp the helm, is to set the ship of state on the right course toward the port they seek. Great presidents also have a deep psychic connection with the needs, anxieties, and dreams of people. `I do not believe,' said Wilson, `that any man can lead who does not act ... under the impulse of a profound sympathy with those whom he leads—a sympathy which is insight.—an insight which is of the heart rather than of the intellect.'" Louis Auchincloss: *Theodore Roosevelt.*

This style of leadership is demanded of every leader regardless of who he is leading. The reason so many companies and churches flounder is because the leader thinks he can lead from long distance without knowing his people. To succeed as a leader he must convince the people that it is a port worth seeking.

Eagles

Reading: Obadiah 1

*"Does the eagle soar at your command and build his nest on high? He dwells on a cliff and stays there at night; a rocky crag is his stronghold. From there he seeks out his food; his eyes detect it from afar" (*Job 39:27-29 NIV).

I have great memories of the eagle soaring high above the Gulkana River in Alaska in search of food. Sometimes we would see as many as two dozen on our ten mile float down river. God guides every soaring movement of his flight. Solomon wrote: "There are three things that are too amazing for me, four that I do not understand: the way of an eagle in the sky, the way of a snake on a rock, the way of a ship on the high seas, and the way of a man with a maiden" *(*Proverbs 30:18-19).

There are 59 species of eagles throughout the world, each one adapted to its particular domain. Some weigh more than 20 pounds with a wingspan of 8 feet. They are capable of killing and carting off prey as large as deer and monkeys. Eagles mate for life and use the same nest every year, high in remote places. It's a beautiful sight to see an eagle latching on to fish. The eagle's eyes have sensory cells boasting that of the human retina. If eagles could read, they could absorb a newspaper from a mile away. Some eagles can track a rabbit from up to two miles away.

God used the eagle in a marvelous way to encourage Christians when Isaiah wrote: "but those who hope in the LORD will renew their strength. They will soar on wings like eagles; they will run and not grow weary, they will walk and not be faint" (Isaiah 40:31 NIV).

Energy

Reading: Matthew 28

"His wisdom is profound, his power is vast. Who has resisted him and come out unscathed?" (Job 9:4 NIV).

Feeling pooped; lacking energy? There is enough energy in one raisin to supply energy for New York City in one day. Eat more raisins. No wonder little kids go nuts after eating a little red box of raisins. Ask my little granddaughter, Carly. One little red box of raisins and she can jump all over the house. All day.

"Great is our Lord, and of great power: his understanding is infinite"(Psalm 147:5 NIV). Think of the power available to Christians. "All authority in heaven and on earth has been given to me. Therefore go and make disciples of all nations, baptizing them in the name of the Father and of the Son and of the Holy Spirit, and teaching them to obey everything I have commanded you. And surely I am with you always, to the very end of the age" (Matthew 28:18 - 20 NIV). Matthew uses the word "power" in the sense of ability; privilege, i.e. (subjectively) force, capacity, competency, freedom, or (objectively) mastery (concretely, magistrate, superhuman, potentate, token of control), delegated influence.

The next time you feel down and powerless over a given situation whether it be an addiction or affliction you didn't ask for, think of the mighty power of the Lord to supply the answer and give you power.

Precious Stones

Reading: Revelation 21

"Of greater worth than rubies, topaz, coral, jasper or jewels is God's wisdom. Neither gold nor crystal can compare with it, nor can it be had for jewels of gold. Coral and jasper are not worthy of mention; the price of wisdom is beyond rubies" (Job 28:17-18 NIV).

Pope Clement, who died in 1534, is reported to have pulverized and consumed 40,000 ducats worth of precious stones for medicinal purposes (a ducat was a gold coin). [4] (from *How Majestic is Thy Name*).

Feasting on a bowl of Oyster Stew is like dying and going to heaven. Sans the pearl of course. But there's coming a day (someday when I arrive in heaven) when I will see the preciousness of the pearl: "The twelve gates were twelve pearls, each gate made of a single pearl. The great street of the city was of pure gold, like transparent glass" (Revelation 21:21 NIV). "The future of the world—and the role of God's people in it will shake the world, according to God. The nations will worship at Jerusalem. The Lord will be king over the whole earth." (Zechariah 14:9.from *The Student's Bible*). How foolish is man who seeks precious stones, but ignores the value of God's wisdom, which is far better. God's wisdom is worth more than precious stones.

Thorns

Reading: Proverbs 15:1-19

"In the paths of the wicked lie thorns and snares, but he who guards his soul stays far from them" (Proverbs 22:5 NIV).

I was startled while viewing the Passion Play at Oberammergau when those who crucified Jesus cinched their mockery by slapping a crown on thorns on his head (Matthew 27:29). Their use of thorns was significant because earlier Jesus had said: "The one who received the seed that fell among the thorns is the man who hears the word, but the worries of this life and the deceitfulness of wealth choke it, making it unfruitful." The Apostle Paul had a problem with a thorn he didn't identify, except to say, "To keep me from becoming conceited because of these surpassingly great revelations, there was given me a thorn in my flesh, a messenger of Satan, to torment me. Three times I pleaded with the Lord to take it away from me. But he said to me, 'My grace is sufficient for you, for my power is made perfect in weakness.' Therefore I will boast all the more gladly about my weaknesses, so that Christ's power may rest on me. That is why, for Christ's sake, I delight in weaknesses, in insults, in hardships, in persecutions, in difficulties. For when I am weak, then I am strong" (2 Corinthians 12:7-10 NIV).

We love roses, blackberries, and other types of plants that bear beauty or fruit, but we are careful not to snag our flesh on their thorns. Hurts too much! Now that brings another thorn type to mind that we should avoid at all possible costs, and that is when we become thorns in someone else's life. To remain a principled person with our integrity intact, we develop the wisdom to know when to go along and when to walk away. As Joseph L Badaracco Jr., a business ethics professor at Harvard Business School, points out: "People aren't very effective as thorns."

Mountains

Reading: Psalm 65

"Your righteousness is like the mighty mountains, your justice like the great deep" (Psalm 36:6 NIV).

John Ruskin wrote: "Mountains are to the rest of the body of the earth, what violent muscular action is to the body of man. The muscles and tendons of its anatomy are, in the mountain, brought out with force and convulsive energy, full of expression, passion, and strength." Living in the Northwest affords a spectacular view of numerous mountains in Western Oregon. On a clear day I can see Mount Rainier in the state of Washington. When Mount Saint Helens blew in May, 1980, I was on a plane returning home from California. The awesome power of the volcano was breathtaking. The power of the volcano blasted off more than 1,000 feet of the 9,347 high mountain. Over one hundred square miles of forests were denuded; more than 150 miles of trout and salmon streams were destroyed. An estimated 2 million animals died in the blast. Despite the devastation of the blast, the mountain surged back with new trees, flora and fauna. There is no way to plumb the depths of God's creation.

No doubt that the Psalmist thought about mountains when he wrote: "Where can I go from your Spirit? Where can I flee from your presence? If I go up to the heavens, you are there; if I make my bed in the depths, you are there. If I rise on the wings of the dawn, if I settle on the far side of the sea, even there your hand will guide me, your right hand will hold me fast" (Psalm139:7-10 NIV).

Who Am I?

Reading: Ephesians 1:1-15

"It's in Christ that we find out who we are and what we are living for. Long before we first heard of Christ and got our hopes up, he had his eye on us, had designs on us for glorious living, part of the overall purpose he is working out in everything and everyone" (Ephesians 1:3,4 The Message).

Often through life, unobserved, we search for the answer to the question, "Who am I?" How do I fit into the family? The high school peer group? The freshman class at college? The company that just hired me? Who am I, at that fork in the road when the first real taste of disappointment or defeat or failure hits me?

I noticed one of those "Who am I?" moments of life during Christmas holidays while visiting our daughter, Colleen. Her eight year old son, Aaron, played the piano for us. The family listened as he performed a simple little tune. Later that day Aaron's little brother, Michael, tried to imitate his brother's earlier achievement, but to no avail. He couldn't play a tune; and there was no one to enjoy his effort, nor applaud him. I imagine that what drew Michael to the piano was the "Who am I?" question. "I see how Aaron fits into the family; how do I fit into this family?"

Great people of the past asked, the "Who am I?" question in search of the answer. Moses asked God, "Who am I, that I should go to Pharaoh and bring the Israelites out of Egypt?" (Exodus 3:11) David said to Saul, "Who am I, and what is my family or my father's clan in Israel, that I should become the king's son-in-law?" (1 Samuel 18:18)

Then "King David went in and sat before the Lord, and he said, 'Who am I, O Lord God, and what is my family, that you have brought me this far?" (1 Chronicles 17:16) "But who am I, and who are my people, that we should be able to give as generously as this?" (1 Chronicles 29:14)

During World War II German Gestapo soldiers executed imprisoned pastor, Dietrich Bonhoeffer in 1945. A short while before his death, Bonhoeffer wrote a poem, "*Who am I?*" The last lines were:

"Who am I? They mock me,
these lonely questions of mine,
Whoever I am, thou knowest, O God,
I am thine."

"It's in Christ that we find out who we are and what we are living for." (The Message).

Lightning

Reading: Job 37

"Listen to the roar of his voice, to the rumbling that comes from his mouth. He unleashes his lightning beneath the whole heaven and sends it to the ends of the earth. After that comes the sound of his roar; he thunders with his majestic voice. When his voice resounds, he holds nothing back. God's voice thunders in marvelous ways; he does great things beyond our understanding" (Job 37:2-5 NIV).

My Grandma was struck by lightning while ironing in her home in southern Illinois during a thunderstorm. That meant my mother had to live in a children's home, for her father had a job as a mine inspector in the southeast part of the country requiring him to be away from home a lot. In those days, jobs were so hard to come by that my grandfather felt he had no other choice. Now, living in Oregon, we rarely see lightning unless it is in the mountains or in vast forests. One time our children were awakened by a huge thunderclap and brilliant flashes of lightning. Having rarely seen such, they all jumped out of bed and went outside to see the spectacular fireworks. In the Midwest where I grew up, we ran for the basement until the storm subsided.

"Lightning hits the earth 100 times each second, with 8.6 million strikes per day and over 3 billion each year ... A single bolt of lightning can heat the surrounding air from 15,000 to 50,000 degrees Fahrenheit ... An average bolt packs a wallop of several hundred million volts, with peak currents of up to 20,000 amperes."[5] (from *How Majestic is Thy Name*). If you are playing golf and lightning is imminent run for secure cover; never under a tree. About 80 people in America die each year when struck by lightning. As it turned out in our family, despite the fact my grandmother died while hit by lightning, God placed my mother in a children's home where she learned about Jesus and became a Christian.

Humor

Reading: Genesis 32

"So Jacob was left alone, and a man wrestled with him till daybreak. When the man saw that he could not overpower him, he touched the socket of Jacob's hip so that his hip was wrenched as he wrestled with the man. Then the man said, 'Let me go, for it is daybreak.' But Jacob replied, 'I will not let you go unless you bless me.' The man asked him, 'What is your name?' 'Jacob,' he answered" (Genesis 32:23-27 NIV).

"And when he later chose to write about a character (*Son of Laughter*), he settled on Jacob, the inveterate conniver who challenged God to a wrestling match and got a new name the next morning. Is it any accident that God identified his chosen people as the children of Israel, `the wrestler's children,' the offspring of one who had grappled so fiercely through the night?"[6] (Philip Yancey writing about Frederick Buechner).

Never lose your sense of humor. Recently I made a cross country trip knowing that heart failure looms as a risk. So I asked a dear friend of many years that if I checked out before I returned home, would he be so kind to preach at my funeral. I sent an email with the subject: "Hello", and named my friend, asking him the favor. He returned the email but didn't change the subject so it read: Re: Hello, only the computer inadvertently dropped the O from the title. So it read Re: "Hello" (without the O) "Tom, I would be honored to preach your funeral." While Hell isn't a subject to joke about for it is a real place, it still tickled my funny bone and my friends with whom I shared the story laughed along also. The greatest humor is pointed inwardly making the storyteller the object of the humor. And situations like the one cited are often the funniest, as opposed to telling a joke at someone else's expense. It's also the safest assuring us that we will not be embarrassed by crossing the line at the expense of a friend.

Wind

Reading: Mark 4

"He makes the clouds his chariot and rides on the wings of the wind. He makes winds his messengers, flames of fire his servants" (Psalm 104:3-4 NIV).

Jack Nicklaus of golf fame once said: The older you get the stronger the wind gets—and it's always in your face. Solomon contended that "The wind goeth toward the south, and turneth about unto the north; it whirleth about continually, and the wind returneth again according to his circuits" (Ecclesiastes 1:6). "Why do the swirling walls of a hurricane cause so much damage? Because they store an enormous amount of energy. In one day, a typical hurricane generates the energy equivalent to that released by 400 twenty-megaton hydrogen bombs. If such energy could be harnessed and converted to electricity, it would fuel the electrical needs of the United States for about six months." [7] (from *How Majestic is Thy Name*).

Jesus said to Nicodemus: "You must be born again, the wind blows wherever it pleases. You hear its sound, but you cannot tell where it comes from or where it is going. So it is with everyone born of the Spirit" (John 3:7-8 NIV). It's fascinating to listen to the testimony of those who received Christ into their lives and are therefore "born again." Everybody's story of how they came to Christ is somewhat different; however there is one constant: All of us entered through the same door. The door Jesus said: "I am the door. If anyone enters by me, he will be saved, and will go in and out and find pasture" (John 10:9 NKJV).

Communicating Truth

Reading: Exodus 3:11-17

"Moses said to the LORD, 'O Lord, I have never been eloquent, neither in the past nor since you have spoken to your servant. I am slow of speech and tongue.' The LORD said to him, 'Who gave man his mouth? Who makes him deaf or mute? Who gives him sight or makes him blind? Is it not I, the LORD? Now go; I will help you speak and will teach you what to say'" (Exodus 4:10-12 NIV).

"When I came to you, brothers, I did not come with eloquence or superior wisdom as I proclaimed to you the testimony about God" (1 Corinthians 2:1 NIV)."I came to you in weakness and fear, and with much trembling. My message and my preaching were not with wise and persuasive words, but with a demonstration of the Spirit's power, so that your faith might not rest on men's wisdom, but on God's power" (1 Corinthians 2: 3—5 NIV).

Dave Barry tells of getting on a flight with hands full and no where to put his newspaper, so he sat on it. The fellow next to him said: "Are you reading your paper? David said: "What did you just say?" "Are you reading your newspaper?" Whereupon, Dave stood up and turned the page, placed the newspaper on his seat and sat down again. Now that's communicating!

No teacher fascinates me with his ability to teach truth like Alan Bittel. Alan headed up the Polk County Family Services division for years. Now retired from the State of Oregon, he leads the family services division at Western Baptist College. He has taught our adult fellowship at Perrydale Church more than four years. No one holds my attention and brings me along in his thinking better than Alan. I am sure if you were to talk to him, he would humbly exclaim. "I am slow of speech and tongue," as Moses once said. Not only is Alan not slow of speech, he always has something important to say. His classic sense of humor is spontaneous. He also engages his audience in dialogue as he teaches. They don't come any better than Alan.

Trees

Reading: Isaiah 44

"Then the angel showed me the river of the water of life, as clear as crystal, flowing from the throne of God and of the Lamb down the middle of the great street of the city. On each side of the river stood the tree of life, bearing twelve crops of fruit, yielding its fruit every month. And the leaves of the tree are for the healing of the nations. Blessed are those who wash their robes, that they may have the right to the tree of life and may go through the gates into the city" (Revelation 22:1-2,14 NIV).

"Blessed is the man who does not walk in the counsel of the wicked or stand in the way of sinners or sit in the seat of mockers. But his delight is in the law of the LORD, and on his

law he meditates day and night. He is like a tree planted by streams of water, which yields its fruit in season and whose leaf does not wither.
*Whatever he does prospers" (*Psalm 1:1-3 NIV).

Every living creature depends upon trees that produce carbon dioxide and oxygen. One acre of trees will produce enough oxygen a day for eighteen people. Living in the great northwest, we see thousands of acres of trees. Oregon ships more Christmas trees around the world than any other state. Active ingredients taken from trees can be used in combating anything from asthma to coughs.

An Oregon grown Christmas tree was the choice to be placed at the U. S. Capitol in D. C. It was Christmas, 2002. The tree was transported on a 10-state tour on its way to the White House. A choir from Umpqua Community College sang the Tree's praises at the Toketee Ranger Station prior to its tour to Washington D.C..

The humorist Ogden Nash wrote:

I think that I shall never see
A billboard lovely as a tree
Indeed, unless the billboards fall
I'll never see a tree at all.

Valleys

Reading: Psalm 65

"Then the LORD will go out and fight against those nations, as he fights in the day of battle. On that day his feet will stand on the Mount of Olives, east of Jerusalem, and the Mount of Olives will be split in two from east to west, forming a great valley, with half of the mountain moving north and half moving south" (Zechariah 14:3-4 NIV).

I live in the Willamette valley in Oregon, a beautiful valley about 150 miles long. The Willamette River flows through the valley, enabling farmers and orchardists to raise fruit and grass seed, produce dairy products and lumber. The little country church, of which I am on the pastoral staff, lies in the valley floor between the city of Salem and the Coastal range of mountains. Each Sunday the drive to Perrydale, about 23 miles from home, is worth the effort just to see the rolling hills, beautiful vineyards and other farming interests. A vast valley in North America is the Mississippi River valley. A great treat is to stand high on one of Oregon's many mountains and look down into the Willamette valley, or go for a leisurely drive in the fall along the valley floor to enjoy the spectacular display of the trees as the frost paints them in numerous hues of red, yellow, brown and orange.

Valleys play an important part in the life of Israel and also in the life of Christians, both for God's comforting presence and in the fulfillment of prophecy. For example: "Even though I walk through the valley of the shadow of death, I will fear no evil, for you are with me" (Psalm 23:4 NIV).

"I went down to the grove of nut trees to look at the new growth in the valley, to see if the vines had budded or the pomegranates were in bloom. Before I realized it, my desire set me among the royal chariots of my people" (Song of Solomon. 6:11-12 NIV).

"In that day the mountains will drip new wine, and the hills will flow with milk; All the ravines of Judah will run with water. A fountain will flow out of the LORD's house and will water the valley of acacias" (Joel 3:18 NIV). Christians are to enjoy the beauty of the valleys here and in the future when we get to Heaven.

Gentleness

Reading: Philippians 4

"Rejoice in the Lord always. I will say it again: Rejoice! Let your gentleness be evident to all. The Lord is near. Do not be anxious about anything, but in everything, by prayer and petition, with thanksgiving, present your requests to God. And the peace of God, which transcends all understanding, will guard your hearts and your minds in Christ Jesus. Rejoice in the Lord always. I will say it again: Rejoice! Let your gentleness be evident to all. The Lord is near. Do not be anxious about anything, but in everything, by prayer and petition, with thanksgiving, present your requests to God. And the peace of God, which transcends all understanding, will guard your hearts and your minds in Christ Jesus" (Philippians 4:4-7 NIV).

I have learned more from my son Peter more about gentleness than anybody I know. Not a common thing to observe in families and in the business world. Peter's sympathetic generosity is very effective. He is loved not only for his way with his wife and two sons, but also with those who work for him. People love him because of it.

The powerful effect of gentleness is written about by the Apostle Paul. "But the fruit of the Spirit is love, joy, peace, patience, kindness, goodness, faithfulness, gentleness and self-control. Against such things there is no law" (Galatians 5:22-23 NIV). God is still working with me to perfect that which I need to practice with regard to gentleness.

Rhythm

Reading: Job 5

"To man belongs the plans of the heart, but from the LORD comes the reply of the tongue. ... Commit to the LORD whatever you do, and your plans will succeed. ... In his heart a man plans his course, but the LORD determines his steps" (Proverbs 16:3, 6, 9 NIV).

The greatest leader in my memory, and one from whom I have learned a lot about leadership, is Dr. Paul Dixon, soon to become Chancellor of Cedarville University. In his 25 years as president of a small college and now a formidable university of more than 3,000 students plus hundreds of faculty and support staff, Paul's heartbeat created a rhythm of leadership attained by few of God's chosen leaders. From a career as an evangelist, Paul, who had never led anybody except his own family, assumed an awesome responsibility of leading an educational institution to national prominence. How? By staying close to the Lord and developing a sense of rhythm, exercising a vision that took on only one big project at a time; meanwhile tending to the normal challenges of leading people.

There are many examples in the Bible of leaders who had little sense of timing and the rhythm of God's plans: Peter is an example on one occasion. "With that, one of Jesus' companions reached for his sword, drew it out and struck the servant of the high priest, cutting off his ear" (Matthew 26:51 NIV).

Thank God there are other examples of great leaders in the Bible who had a proper sense of God's timing and rhythm. The bookstores in America contain ubiquitous attempts to define leadership. Nothing yet approaches the wisdom of God available in the Scriptures. We do well who follow the Word of God and observe how God's men carry out lessons of leadership.

Silver

Reading: Exodus 20

"The king, moreover, must not acquire great numbers of horses for himself or make the people return to Egypt to get more of them, for the LORD has told you, 'You are not to go back that way again.' He must not take many wives, or his heart will be led astray. He must not accumulate large amounts of silver and gold" (Deuteronomy 17:16-17 NIV).

My Father-in-law was a champion boxer in the United Kingdom for six years before the Great Depression. In those days money was not given for winning, but silver plates were awarded paying tribute to his boxing skills. We have several billings of prize fights as he fought in and around London.

Silver made possible the creation of the first telegraph in 1832. And were it not for this precious metal, physicians in 1884 would not have invented a vaccine that saved generations of children from a lifetime of blindness. Silver's amazing strength, malleability and ductility make it a precious metal without peer. There's no mystery why mankind has always prized this shiny, costly substance.[8] (from *How Majestic is Thy Name*). Greater yet are the words of the Lord: (Deuteronomy 17:16-17).

"And the words of the LORD are flawless, like silver refined in a furnace of clay, purified seven times" (Psalm 12:6 NIV).

Stars

Reading: Psalm 147

"He determines the number of the stars and calls them each by name. Great is our Lord and mighty in power; his understanding has no limit. The LORD sustains the humble but casts the wicked to the ground" (Psalm 147:4-6 NIV).

"He counts the stars and assigns each a name. Our Lord is great, with limitless strength; we'll never comprehend what he knows and does. God puts the fallen on their feet again and pushes the wicked into the ditch" (Psalm 147, 4,5 The Message)..

Untold millions of stars are in the skies, not the mere thousands we see. The Milky Way is lit up with a hundred billion stars. The one red giant Betelgeuse – is actually up to 500 times larger than the sun.[9] (*How Majestic is Thy Name*). Proxima Centauri, could be reached in 4.3 years if we traveled the speed of light. The Milky Way galaxy is 70,000 light years across. What is all this talk about "near?"

Some people make the mistake of worshiping the stars; something God forbids: "And when you look up to the sky and see the sun, the moon and the stars—all the heavenly array—do not be enticed into bowing down to them and worshiping things the LORD your God has apportioned to all the nations under heaven" (Deuteronomy 4:18-20 NIV). Think about it; who do you worship?

Failure

Reading: Judges 2

"The angel of the LORD went up from Gilgal to Bokim and said, 'I brought you up out of Egypt and led you into the land that I swore to give to your forefathers. I said, 'I will never break my covenant with you, and you shall not make a covenant with the people of this land, but you shall break down their altars.' Yet you have disobeyed me. Why have you done this?'" (Judges 2:1-2 NIV)

"Why have you done this?" A searching question God's people faced. The reason was that they were more interested in compromise than obeying the Lord. God could ask us the same question: "Why?" Often it's very simple: we too prefer to compromise rather than to obey God.

The Apostle Paul wrote: "Therefore, if anyone is in Christ, he is a new creation; the old has gone, the new has come!" (2 Corinthians 5:17-18 NIV). Why do some who trust Christ as Savior fail to show evidence that old things are passed away and new things abound? They have the same mind set of Israel: they would rather all things not become new. Hence God is limited. Little wonder that lives can be shot through with failure. And it's all unnecessary. We need not stay in a failure mode and eat defeat day after day. God is able to cleanse us and bring fruit for all who accept the provision of God for victory. It's never too late to obey God. Failure can be turned into fruitfulness.

Tom Younger

Gentle Whisper

Reading: Isaiah 43

"The LORD said, 'Go out and stand on the mountain in the presence of the LORD, for the LORD is about to pass by.' Then a great and powerful wind tore the mountains apart and shattered the rocks before the LORD, but the LORD was not in the wind. After the wind there was an earthquake, but the LORD was not in the earthquake. After the earthquake came a fire, but the LORD was not in the fire. And after the fire came a gentle whisper. When Elijah heard it, he pulled his cloak over his face and went out and stood at the mouth of the cave" (1 Kings 19:11-13 NIV).

I believe God speaks to us often in a gentle whisper; I know for I have experienced it many times. It was the gentle whisper of the Lord that discovered for me my wife more than 50 years ago; that God wanted me in the ministry at the age of 15 when I was saved; that someday I would pastor the Immanuel Baptist Church in Fort Wayne; that it would include a ministry of church planting; that I should buy a church building in Churubusco, Indiana, for a branch church; that I would someday be invited to be president of a college; that God would silence my critics; that He would take care of our needs when we gave beyond our logical means. Yes, other numerous times it was evident when God spoke to me in a gentle whisper. No, I'm not "nuts" or a mystic; just one who tries to be silent and listen to God when He speaks, often through the Scriptures, often through circumstances and sometimes while asleep.

"When I consider your heavens, the work of your fingers, the moon and the stars, which you have set in place, what is man that you are mindful of him, the son of man, that you care for him?" (Psalm 8: 3, 4 NIV).

Iron Sharpens Iron

Reading: 1 Timothy 4:1-5

"As iron sharpens iron, so one man sharpens another" (Proverbs 27:17 NIV),

Iron sharpening iron always reminds me of my fishing buddy Paul Robbins. Paul, a man of many gifts, is the President of Christianity Today International, the leading force in Evangelical Christianity today. He is likewise a builder, a prodigious reader and writer. We fished Alaska for King Salmon together five separate years. How many trips to Canada for Walleye fishing, I have lost track. The best part of the experience was those times when Paul and I were sitting in a boat, talking, "iron sharpening iron." At those times the force of Genesis 2:18 came to mind: "The LORD God said, 'It is not good for the man to be alone. I will make a helper suitable for him.'"

"Israel went down to the Philistines to have their plowshares, mattocks, axes and sickles sharpened. The price was two thirds of a shekel for sharpening plowshares and mattocks, and a third of a shekel for sharpening forks and axes and for repointing goads" (1 Samuel 13:20-21 NIV).. Why? They recognized the importance of a sharp tool.

It is only as a social being, that a person's powers and affections are fully expanded. Charles Bridges wrote: "So the collision of different minds whets the edge of the other. We owe some of the most valuable discoveries of science to this reciprocity. In the sympathies of friendship, when the mind is dull, and the countenance is overcast, a word from a friend puts an edge upon the blunted energy, and exhilarates the countenance."

I attribute my brief, albeit late, writing career to Paul Robbins, who believed I could succeed in the genre of writing.

Grass

Reading: Psalm 104

"What is the way to the place where the lightning is dispersed, or the place where the east winds are scattered over the earth? Who cuts a channel for the torrents of rain, and a path for the thunderstorm, to water a land where no man lives, a desert with no one in it, to satisfy a desolate wasteland and make it sprout with grass?" (Job 38:24-27 NIV).

David and Christine Brandt are fourth generation on their grass seed farm. Not many farms of that nature are around anymore. Dave and Christine manage to do all the work in a spread that last year yielded 1800 bushels of seed per acre. They also tend to 14 acres of blueberries. It is a beautiful sight to tour their farm, sitting on high ground in the valley before the Coastal range. Dave also leases out 140 acres to a Christmas tree farm operation. They are a vibrant, busy young couple.

An average sized lawn produces enough oxygen for a family of four every year. Grass is a natural filter, purging the air of carbon dioxide, dust, dirt, and other pollutants, while reducing soil erosion. From Poaceae, a commercially valuable grass, we get corn, wheat and rice, food for our tables, feed for our livestock and raw materials for our industries. Ninety percent of all harvested wheat is used to make foodstuffs such as breads, pastas, cakes, crackers, cookies, pastries, and flours.

Giving

Reading: Exodus 36:1-38

"So all the skilled craftsmen who were doing all the work on the sanctuary left their work and said to Moses, 'The people are bringing more than enough for doing the work the LORD commanded to be done'" (Exodus 36: 4, 5. NIV).

"Some commentators estimate that descriptions of the tabernacle make up the largest single subject covered in the Bible. When the time came for construction, the Israelites pitched in with such enthusiasm that they had to be restrained from bringing more offerings (verse 5). Those who could not afford material gifts donated time and labor." (from the Student Bible).

In all my fifty some years in the ministry, I am reminded of the late Reverend Carl Brown who was my predecessor as pastor of the Immanuel Baptist Church in Fort Wayne, Indiana. After Carl died I invited Beryle, his wife to become my secretary. One day she humbly shared with me that when Carl became pastor, the church was in desperate financial straits. "So we took it upon ourselves to spend as little as possible at home and give everything left over back to the church. God was so good to us in providing our needs in those days, both in the church and in our home," said Beryle.

This reinforced my own commitment to give, for God is debtor to no man. Not that I have reached that level of giving, it nevertheless has been the top priority in our home. To God be the glory.

Corkscrews

Reading: Psalm 78

"They were worse, if that's possible, than their parents: traitors – crooked as a corkscrew" (Psalm 78 The Message).

My mother, who was an astute observer of human nature, sometimes commented: "He's as crooked as a corkscrew." It is hard to believe that the children of Israel with all God's blessings at hand should be indicted by God as worse than their parents: crooked as a corkscrew. I have known some corkscrews. Unfortunately, Christians sometimes resort to this kind of behavior to get ahead in life. Eventually they spiral into the ground. One needs to be careful of their influence. They can be con artists. I would hate to think of being indicted as being "crooked as a corkscrew." The best way to assure that that won't happen is to obey the Lord. Then we have nothing to fear concerning our reputation.

Man of Prayer

Reading: Psalm 78

"In spite of all this, they kept on sinning; in spite of his wonders, they did not believe" (Psalm 78:32 NIV).

As a high schooler I delivered mail during World War II. My route covered Emerson Street in Gary, Indiana. On the first day as I approached a mail slot, I noticed a tract rack outside the door. Curious, I took a tract and began reading it. The door opened and older gentleman appeared inviting me in to his home. His name, Fred Johnson. It wasn't long before he took me up in the little tower on the top floor, overlooking the city where there were windows on all sides. There Fred introduced me to his prayer chamber. From that day, we became long time friends and up until he died, Fred often wrote me while I was in seminary and reminded me that he prayed for me "before you got out of bed this morning." Fred was a man of prayer who believed God for great things. I miss him.

"Unbelief" was not in Fred's vocabulary. "Unbelief is characteristic of many of God's people, both in the Bible and in the church today. Jacob's life exemplifies the results of unbelief in the promises of God...Although Jacob knew the promises of God, he prepared his own plans to get what God had already promised – the perfect example of unbelief." John E. Hunter.

Perhaps "Onward Christian Soldiers" should read:
"Like a mighty tortoise
Moves the church of God.
Brethren we are treading
Where we've always trod."

We may be, but for sure God is not.

Depression

Reading: Matthew 6

"Therefore I tell you, do not worry about your life, what you will eat or drink; or about your body, what you will wear. Is not life more important than food, and the body more important than clothes? Look at the birds of the air; they do not sow or reap or store away in barns, and yet your heavenly Father feeds them. Are you not much more valuable than they? Who of you by worrying can add a single hour to his life?" (Matthew 6:25-27 NIV).

"The constant desire to have still more things and a still better life and the struggle to obtain them imprints many western faces with worry and even depression, though it is customarily to conceal feelings." Alexander Solzhenitzyn.

We can choose to be cheerful and choose to be content with what we have. Paul learned how to be content. "I know what it is to be in need, and I know what it is to have plenty. I have learned the secret of being content in any and every situation, whether well fed or hungry, whether living in plenty or in want"(Philippians 4:12 NIV).

Getting more things is like the itch; it always needs scratching. Make it a practice to let the better life come as God wills. It eliminates the need to scratch. "Therefore do not worry about tomorrow, for tomorrow will worry about itself. Each day has enough trouble of its own" (Matthew 6:34).

Moon

Reading: Isaiah 60

"God made two great lights—the greater light to govern the day and the lesser light to govern the night" (Genesis 1:16 NIV).

As a lad I first remember sitting on the banks of the Ohio River fishing for spoonbill in the moonlight. As a teenager I learned that romance is a wonderful experience in the light of the moon. As an old man I learned that writing under cover of the moon during the night is the most creative time for writing.

Of late there are many discoveries and comments about the Moon. **Plaque left behind on the moon's surface** by the crew of Apollo 11 reads:

"Here Men from The Planet Earth
First Set Foot upon The Moon July, 1969 AD.
We Came in Peace for All Mankind"

Picasso, reacting to the first moon-landing said: "It means nothing to me. I have no opinion about it, and I don't care."

Neil Armstrong observed when man first landed on the moon: "That's one small step for a man, one giant leap for mankind."

Russell Baker wrote: "So there he is at last. Man on the moon. The poor magnificent bungler! He can't even get to the office without undergoing the agonies of the damned, but give him a little metal, a few chemicals, some wire and twenty or thirty billion dollars and, vroom! There he is, up on a rock, a quarter of a million miles up in the sky."

God, who created the Moon saw it differently and spoke of a future time: "The sun will no more be your light by day, nor will the brightness of the moon shine on you, for the LORD will be your everlasting light, and your God will be your glory" (Isaiah 60:19 NIV).

Maturity

Reading: Ephesians 4

"Epaphras, who is one of you and a servant of Christ Jesus, sends greetings. He is always wrestling in prayer for you, that you may stand firm in all the will of God, mature and fully assured" (Colossians 4:12 NIV).

The word "firm" is a great word picture. It means "completely filled," The image is of sailing ships driving before the wind, every sail up, billowing out as the wind catches and fills every inch of canvas. That's the picture of the mature Christian, filled with the fullness of Christ. There is no canvas below decks, no clutter of machinery, no man-made power used, just the sound of the wind blowing.

"The wind blows where it pleases. You hear the sound, but you cannot tell where it's coming from and where it's going." John says this is true of those born of the Spirit. (John 3.8.).

Churches weren't built to snuggle in the harbor, tied to their moorings. The tide causes the ship to rise and there is movement. And the ship sails to carry the cargo of the message of God to the nations.

Locusts

Reading: Proverbs 30

*"He spoke, and the locusts came, grasshoppers without number; they ate up every green thing in their land, ate up the produce of their soil" (*Psalm 105:34-35 NIV).

Locusts travel in huge swarms—up to 130 million per square mile. Imagine a locust swarm from Saskatchewan, Canada, all the way to Texas. In 1889 they covered 2,000 square miles near the Red Sea weighing an estimated 42,850 tons. They jump from one green to another. Millions of decaying corpses have derailed railroad trains and caused fatal highway accidents.[10] (from *How Majestic is Thy Name*).

Locusts were referred to as "God's great army." "Surely the LORD has done great things: 'I will drive the northern army far from you, pushing it into a parched and barren land, with its front columns going into the eastern sea and those in the rear into the western sea. And its stench will go up; its smell will rise.' Surely he has done great things. Be not afraid, O land; be glad and rejoice. Surely the LORD has done great things" (Joel 2:20 NIV).

"John's clothes were made of camel's hair, and he had a leather belt around his waist. His food was locusts and wild honey. People went out to him from Jerusalem and all Judea and the whole region of the Jordan. Confessing their sins, they were baptized by him in the Jordan River" (Matthew 3:4-6 NIV).

God showed His power in allowing the locusts to devastate the land. We are happy to know that serving the Lord does not require a diet of locusts!

Rivers

Reading: Psalm 36

"The LORD is my shepherd, I shall not be in want. He makes me lie down in green pastures, he leads me beside quiet waters, he restores my soul" (Psalm 23:1-3 NIV).

There's nothing like spending a cloudy day on the bank of a river, fishing; I have done it many times. My favorite five year experience was to fish for salmon on the Gulkana River in Alaska for a week each summer. What a thrill to wade downstream wrestling with a King Salmon. Nothing like it in my book of memories. The Amazon River in South American carries the most volume of any river in the world. The Nile River is the longest river of 4,132 miles. It would run from New York to Los Angeles. And to think that God on one occasion turned the Nile into blood. (Exodus 7:20). One time God piled up the Jordan River at floodtide, so that the ark of God might cross over on dry land.

"How priceless is your unfailing love! Both high and low among men find refuge in the shadow of your wings. They feast on the abundance of your house; you give them drink from your river of delights. For with you is the fountain of life; in your light we see light" (Psalm 36:7-9 NIV).

His Name

Reading: John 2024-31

"Jesus did many other miraculous signs in the presence of his disciples, which are not recorded in this book. But these are written that you may believe that Jesus is the Christ, the Son of God, and that by believing you may have life in his name" (John 20:30,31 NIV).

Have you thought about what "in his name", means? It doesn't resonate well in English; it doesn't make us stop to think about its meaning. The Amplified Version helps us here: "that is, through what He is". That charges the idea with power. "That you may have life through what He is". Jesus was saying: "He himself is the way, the truth and the life." God wants to be unlimited in our lives, in our daily living. Why limit God? Our bodies are the temple of the Holy Spirit; let the power of God show through in his name, through what he is. God imposes no limits on what we are in Christ Jesus.

Many people don't like their name, so they resort to going by a nickname. For example: An overweight person nicknamed "Skinny." A nickname is the heaviest stone that the devil can throw at a man. It is a bugbear to the imagination, and though we do not believe in it, it still haunts our apprehensions. D.H. Lawrence wrote: "I don't like your miserable lonely single `front name.' It is so limited, so meager; it has no versatility; it is weighted down with the sense of responsibility; it is worn threadbare with much use; it is as bad as having only one jacket and one hat; it is like having only one relation, one blood relation, in the world. Never set a child afloat on the flat sea of life with only one sail to catch the wind." Lawrence needed to be reminded that:

"Salvation is found in no one else, for there is no other name under heaven given to men by which we must be saved" (Acts 4:12 NIV). Bill and Gloria Gaither captured the power of Jesus' name in the song:

Jesus, Jesus, Jesus! There's just something about that name!
Master, Savior, Jesus! Like the fragrance after the rain;
Jesus, Jesus, Jesus! Let all Heaven and earth proclaim:
Kings and kingdoms will all pass away,
But there's something about that name.

The Divine Patience

Reading: Hebrews 6

"Be patient, then, brothers, until the Lord's coming. See how the farmer waits for the land to yield its valuable crop and how patient he is for the autumn and spring rains. You too, be patient and stand firm, because the Lord's coming is near. Don't grumble against each other, brothers, or you will be judged. The Judge is standing at the door!" (James 5:7-9 NIV).

Last week I put 40 garlic bulbs in the ground so we may have plenty of garlic next year for cooking and roasting. What a treat to load up on garlic. This week I found myself out in my back 40 to see how my garlic is growing. I full well know it takes patience to let God and nature do their work, and that the garlic will not be ready for harvesting until summer. Yet there I was inspecting the ground just in case.

The attitude toward my fellow man should be patience, not revenge, never to retaliate. The Greeks prided themselves in refusing to tolerate an injury or insult. To the Greek, the bad man would go all out for vengeance. The Christian is enjoined to engage in the fruit of the spirit and exercise patience toward all men. This is one of the great characteristics of love. We are to be patient with all men just as God is with us. "A man's wisdom gives him patience; it is to his glory to overlook an offense" (Proverbs 19:11 NIV).

Patterns

Reading: 1 Peter 2

"To this you were called, because Christ suffered for you, leaving you an example, that you should follow in his steps" (1 Peter 2:21 NIV).

The Greek schoolboy was taught to write using a pattern. In my generation, we were taught to use a pattern called the "Palmer method." One wouldn't recognize the use of a pattern in most men's handwriting, especially doctors. I am left handed. For some one unexplained reason my teacher suggested that I would do better if I wrote right handed. It didn't take her long to recognize that this wasn't going to work, so I was left to write as I so inclined: left handed. Desks weren't made for left-handers, and I usually turned my paper sideways and curled my hand over the paper so as to write a straight line. That doesn't work too well. But it beats writing left handed with the script slanting backwards. Left handed sports players are a prize and demand a lot of remuneration. So there are some advantages to being left handed. We use a pattern for most everything we make today. I carve ducks from a block of wood and use a pattern to follow. However, the most important pattern we have is to copy Jesus. Just as we learned to write by copying a pattern, so we as Christians copy the perfect pattern which Jesus gave to us.

Sea

Reading: Psalm 93

"Who shut up the sea behind doors when it burst forth from the womb, when I made the clouds its garment and wrapped it in thick darkness, when I fixed limits for it and set its doors and bars in place, when I said, 'This far you may come and no farther; here is where your proud waves halt'?" (Job 38:8-11 NIV).

"Oceans cover more than 70 percent of the earth's surface, to an average depth of 2.3 miles – a volume of water estimated at 329 million miles (11 times the volume of dry land). … the ocean contains a lot more than water. If you were to remove all of its salt, you would harvest 50,000,000,000,000,000 tons of the stuff – enough to cover the entire planet in a layer 150 feet thick. Sea water holds more gold than exists on land, 100 times as much as humans have mined throughout world history."[11] (from *How Majestic is Thy Name*).

Realize the awesome power of the Creator as Jesus calmed the raging sea. "Without warning, a furious storm came up on the lake, so that the waves swept over the boat. But Jesus was sleeping. The disciples went and woke him, saying, Lord, save us! We're going to drown!" He replied, "You of little faith, why are you so afraid?" Then he got up and rebuked the winds and the waves, and it was completely calm. The men were amazed and asked, "What kind of man is this? Even the winds and the waves obey him!"(Matthew 8:24-27 NIV).

We used to sing H.L. Glamour's song: *The Haven of Rest*

My soul, in sad exile, was out on life's sea,
So burdened with sin and distressed,
Till I heard a sweet voice saying,

Make me your choice,
And I entered the haven of rest.

I've anchored my soul in the haven of rest,
I'll sail the wide seas no more;
The tempest may sweep o'er the wild stormy deep –
In Jesus I'm safe ever more.

Is your soul anchored in the haven of rest?

Snakes

Reading: Numbers 21

"The infant will play near the hole of the cobra, and the young child put his hand into the viper's nest. They will neither harm nor destroy on all my holy mountain, for the earth will be full of the knowledge of the LORD as the waters cover the sea" (Isaiah *11:8-9 NIV).*

One day Don Swoverland — the best fly fisherman I have ever been around – and I were fishing in a lake at our church in Auburn, Indiana. Don had a little John boat that we turned over and out slid a big black snake. Immediately Don grabbed a paddle and beat the snake into oblivion. When finished he said: "Tom, that was the only mistake God ever made!" We both laughed. Snakes have often conjured images of evil. The Thread snake prefers sucking the interior of termites while other species diet on birds, fish, frogs, lizards, rabbits, and rats. A Python can devour a 100 pound animal in over an hour. The African cobra can squirt venom into the eyes of an enemy six to eight feet away. The Taipan of central Australia carries venom in a single bit that can kill 250,000 mice. Beware the serpent.

Jesus called the Pharisees snakes: "Woe to you, teachers of the law and Pharisees, you hypocrites! You build tombs for the prophets and decorate the graves of the righteous. And you say, 'If we had lived in the days of our forefathers, we would not have taken part with them in shedding the blood of the prophets.' So you testify against yourselves that you are the descendants of those who murdered the prophets. Fill up, then, the measure of the sin of your forefathers! You snakes! You brood of vipers! How will you escape being condemned to hell?" *(* Matthew 23:33 NIV).

Beware the modern day snakes, the two legged variety; they are still about us today.

Of Strife and Striving

Reading: Ecclesiastes 2

"What does a man get for all the toil and anxious striving with which he labors under the sun? All his days his work is pain and grief; even at night his mind does not rest. This too is meaningless" (Ecclesiastes 2:22-23 NIV).

No venue for dissension and bitter conflict exists like there is among Christians. Most lapse churchmen are victims of dissension, often a fall out of their own conduct or somebody else's. No one likes to admit it, but Christians fall by the wayside and if they ever choose to go back into the fray, they join another congregation. No questions asked: "just glad to see you". "Arguments are like fire-arms which a man may keep at home but should not carry about with him". Samuel Butler.

G. K. Chesterton wrote: "If you do not understand a man you cannot crush him. And if you do understand him, very probably you will not. It's frustrating for as Martin Luther King once said: "Shallow understanding from people of good will is more frustrating than absolute misunderstanding from people of ill-will."

Churches today need to learn what loving one another means, although we talk a lot about it. I know some will read this and ask: "What church is he talking about? Not ours." It sounds good on the bulletin board: "attend here for a peaceful church".

Jesus told his disciples: "Peace I leave with you; my peace I give you. I do not give to you as the world gives" (John 14:26-27 NIV). The problem arises when Christians check peace at the door of the church on Sunday morning and especially in ubiquitous and often unnecessary business meetings. Yes, there are exceptions, of course. I rest my case.

Control

Reading: Proverbs 6

"Whoever loves discipline loves knowledge, but he who hates correction is stupid" (Proverbs 12:1 NIV).

"Discipline must come through liberty. ...We do not consider an individual disciplined only when he has been rendered as artificially silent as a mute and as immovable as a paralytic. He is an individual annihilated, not disciplined". Maria Montessori

One of the greatest issues in the home today is the ability to control the child. Solomon wrote: "The rod and reproof give wisdom: but a child left to himself bringeth his mother to shame;" (Proverbs 29:15). But as Shakespeare expressed: 'O, it is excellent To have a giant's strength, but it is tyrannous To use it like a giant'. William Shakespeare

My wife teaches piano lessons, mostly involving children. There are splendid examples of godly parents who have their children under control and whose children learn self-discipline. It is a pleasure to teach them. On the other hand occasionally there is the exception. A deft use of a paddle would do more to help them than all the lessons in the world. In fact, most such children have mothers who need the paddle also. I know, the threat of a spanking sucks the air out of the modern day moms who think their children are little angels. Mothers reap the whirlwind whose children they fail to control.

Door

Reading: John 10

"I am the gate; whoever enters through me will be saved. He will come in and go out, and find pasture" (John 10:9 NIV).

The German word for door is "gate." Gate could refer to the door of a house; or an outer door leading from the street to a courtyard; a walled sheepfold; a prison cell; or to a temple door. From *New Testament Words in Today's language.*

Jesus referred to himself as the door to the sheepfold and he, the Good Shepherd granted entrance to eternal life. John 10:1-2, 7. Doors create an image for good or ill. Europeans take special care of the door in their homes. Often they paint them red. Doors speak of opportunity. Emerson theorized "though he build his house in the woods, the world will make a beaten path to the door."

George Herbert, a Rector in Bemerton, wrote:

The church with psalms must shout,
No door can shut them out:
But above all the heart
Must bear the longest part.

Youngsters often sing:

One door and only one,
And yet its sides are two;
I'm on the inside,
On which side are you?

A good thought to ponder.

Reading

Reading: Acts 8:31-40

"Then Philip ran up to the chariot and heard the man reading Isaiah the prophet. 'Do you understand what you are reading?' Philip asked. 'How can I,' he said, 'unless someone explains it to me?' So he invited Philip to come up and sit with him. The eunuch was reading this passage of Scripture" (Acts 8:30-32 NIV).

Theodore Roosevelt once said, after reading *Anna Karenina*: "It was true, ... that with me reading is a disease." More than 40 years ago I read about a Supreme Court Justice who was the least educated formally, but spend his lunch hours in the Library of Congress reading different subjects about which he knew nothing. From that day on I have endeavored to do the same, though not necessarily at the expense of missing lunch. I did not acquire an education in the prescribed formal way, but endeavored to do so day after day. My father, a blue collar steel worker, who went to work in the third grade never learned to read until he was forty years old. Self taught he was a knowledgeable and humble man. I learned a lot from him.

"A great book should leave you with many experiences, and slightly exhausted at the end. You live several lives while reading it". (William Styron)

Resting On the Greatness of God

Reading: Romans 8

"Do not be anxious about anything, but in everything, by prayer and petition, with thanksgiving, present your requests to God. And the peace of God, which transcends all understanding, will guard your hearts and your minds in Christ Jesus" (Philippians 4:6-7 NIV).

Vernon C. Grounds is a splendid example of a man who rests on the greatness of God. A scholarly man in his own right, he never rests on his scholarship; an outstanding seminary professor, he never rests on his laurels as a teacher; a counselor in great demand, he never rests on his own wisdom; he rests on the greatness of God. I have known him and been close to him for more than 50 years. Never have I seen him trust in his own greatness; it was simply resting on the greatness of our God.

The poet Sidney Lanier put this into beautiful images;

As the Marsh-hen secretly builds on the watery sod,
Behold I will build me a nest on the greatness of God;
I will fly in the greatness of God as the marsh-hen flies
In the freedom that fills all the space `twixt the marsh and the skies:
By so many roots as the marsh-grass sends in the sod
I will heartedly lay me a-hold on the greatness of God.[12]

(from Dallas Willard: *Renovation of The Heart*).

Determination

Reading: Acts 27

"Because the hand of the LORD my God was on me, I took courage and gathered leading men from Israel to go up with me" (Ezra 7:27-8:1 NIV).

"So keep up your courage, men, for I have faith in God that it will happen just as he told me" (Acts 27:25 NIV).

Teddy Roosevelt gave a campaign speech with a bullet in his chest. Campaigning in Milwaukee in 1912, he was shot by an anti-third term fanatic. Biographer Nathan Miller recounts, "He'd once been told when he was in the army to [try to] cough up blood to see if he'd been wounded internally. ...He did not cough up blood, so he knew that it was not a very serious wound. He immediately demanded to be taken to the hall and stood for ninety minutes giving the speech while he had a bullet in his chest. Blood was pouring over the front of his shirt. (Brian Lamb; C-Span).

Hebrews 11 lists the brave exploits of courage and faith that provided the seed of the Martyrs. In spite of everything these men never lost their vision and their hopes. We need to press on with faith, never losing the vision and hope, to reach the goal that is set before us in Christ.

Culture

Reading: Acts 19:13-20

"So the word of the Lord grew and prevailed mightily" (Acts 19:20).

We don't know what went wrong with the Ephesian Church, but we do know the culture of its day took over.

What is culture? It is the totality of socially transmitted behavior patterns, arts, beliefs, institutions, and all other products of human work and thought. These patterns, traits, and products considered are the expression of a particular period, class, community or population. *Edwardian culture:* A development of the intellect through training or education. Enlightenment resulting from such training or education. Such as: *The books and paintings in her library reflect her considerable cultivation.*

Breeding is revealed especially in good manners, poise, and sensitivity to the feelings of others: *"The test of a man's or woman's breeding is how they behave in a quarrel"* (George Bernard Shaw).

A man should be just cultured enough to be able to look with suspicion upon culture at first, not second hand. Samuel Butler. (from *The Bookshelf 2000*).

"Most of us, no matter how wonderful a place we enter into, are going to find ourselves in the middle of a mess sooner or later. For the Christian faith is always lived out in the conditions of the world; try as we may, we cannot isolate our Christian lives from the world in which we make our living. And this culture seeps into the church, just as it seeped into the Ephesian church. (The distressing thing is when we invite it in.) This is what we are faced with continuously. This culture seeps into the church through the pores of our congregations: a religion without commitment, spirituality without content, aspiration and talk of longing fulfillment and needs, but not much concern about God." Eugene Peterson.

Curses

Reading: Psalm 109

"He who gives to the poor will lack nothing, but he who closes his eyes to them receives many curses. If a man curses his father or mother, his lamp will be snuffed out in pitch darkness" (Proverbs 28:27; 20:20 NIV).

Cursing can be the use of slang words or phrases. I am thinking of the curse that is an appeal or prayer for evil or misfortune to befall someone or something. The evil or misfortune that comes in or as if in response to such an appeal: bewailed the curse of ill health.

The Psalmist speaks of evil men dressed up in curses, an apt picture of a vain person who sees nothing good in anybody. Paradoxically, some people wear the finest of clothing, dress as we might say, "fit to kill", yet all the while dressed up in curses. They seldom are aware of how they appear to other people, thinking they are astute in judging other people.

"...With their mouth they bless, but in their hearts they curse" (Psalm 62:4 NIV). Others may see only the good in a person, but the Lord looks on the heart.

The Young Ox

Reading: Acts 26: 1-18

"On one of these journeys I was going to Damascus with the authority and commission of the chief priests. About noon, O king, as I was on the road, I saw a light from heaven, brighter than the sun, blazing around me and my companions. We all fell to the ground, and I heard a voice saying to me in Aramaic,'

Saul, Saul, why do you persecute me? It is hard for you to kick against the goads.'
"Then I asked, 'Who are you, Lord?'
"'I am Jesus, whom you are persecuting,' the Lord replied.' Now get up and stand on your feet. I have appeared to you to appoint you as a servant and as a witness of what you have seen of me and what I will show you. I will rescue you from your own people and from the Gentiles. I am sending you to them to open their eyes and turn them from darkness to light, and from the power of Satan to God, so that they may receive forgiveness of sins and a place among those who are sanctified by faith in me.'" (Acts 26:12-18 NIV).

Paul gives his testimony before King Agrippa. He had been on a mission of persecuting the Christians when he saw the light from heaven and heard the voice of Jesus.

The Risen Christ tells Paul it's hard to kick against the pricks. Young oxen kick hard to get out from under the yoke. Yoked to a one handed plow the plowman held in his hand a long staff sharpened end which he held close to the ox' heels so that every time it kicked, it was jagged with the spike. The young ox had to learn submission to the yoke the hard way. So also Paul.

This is what Christ does for men: He opens our eyes; He turns us from the darkness to light; He transfers us from the power of Satan to the power of God; He gives forgiveness of sins.

Swamps

Reading: Isaiah 51

"The LORD will surely comfort Zion and will look with compassion on all her ruins; he will make her deserts like Eden, her wastelands like the garden of the LORD. Joy and gladness

will be found in her, thanksgiving and the sound of singing" (Isaiah 51:3 NIV).

Many of our most beautiful wildflowers grow in swamps. In the southwest tip of Indiana, where the Wabash River flows in the Ohio, there is the Twin Swamps Nature Preserve. In order to save the state's dwindling population of bald cypress trees, this 500 acre site is home to other plants, including prized Virginia Bluebells.

New Orleans is a low-lying island surrounded by swamp land, second only to Death Valley as the lowest area in the country. The bayou is often considered a dark, foreboding territory which offers some of the wildest nature to be found on earth. There are several swamp tours offered in New Orleans. Recommended is — a professional wetlands ecologist who takes you on a personalized narrated nature tour of one of the wildest swamps in America. The size of the boats used allows you greater access into the interior of the swamp.

Let the declaration of God concerning swamps filter through your mind. "Cursed is the one who trusts in man, who depends on flesh for his strength and whose heart turns away from the LORD. He will be like a bush in the wastelands; he will not see prosperity when it comes. He will dwell in the parched places of the desert, in a salt land where no one lives" (Jeremiah 17:5-6 NIV).

God promises His people "The Lord will guide you always; he will satisfy your needs in a sun-scorched land and will strengthen your frame. You will be like a well-watered garden, like a spring whose waters never fail" (Isaiah 58:11 NIV).

Focused

Reading: Colossians 3

"Whatever you do, work at it with all your heart, as working for the Lord, not for men, since you know that you will receive an inheritance from the Lord as a reward. It is the Lord Christ you are serving. Anyone who does wrong will be repaid for his wrong, and there is no favoritism" (Colossians 3:23-25 NIV).

I have never been close to anyone more focused in carrying out his call to the ministry than David Jeremiah whom I knew from those early days of his childhood. I was just beginning the ministry when I first met him. I was planting a church in Arcanum, Ohio, at the time. His Dad often invited me to come over to Dayton on Monday morning to visit and busy ourselves binding past copies of the Sword of the Lord. I often arrived just as the Jeremiah kids were leaving for school.

Later, while pastoring in Fort Wayne, Indiana, and drawing up plans to start the Blackhawk Baptist Church. My attention turned to David, and I invited him to become its first pastor. David came, and within a span of a few years, he led Blackhawk Church into the leading voice for evangelism in the city. He carried on a radio-television ministry as well and became a nationally famed author who has written many books. Presently, David is pastor of the Shadow Mountain Church, and founder and Chancellor of Christian Heritage College in San Diego.

Baggage

I Samuel 10

"Samuel went back to God; `Is he anywhere around?' God said, `yes, he's right over there—hidden in that pile of baggage.'" (1 Samuel 10:22. The Message).

Saul was to be chosen as king. On one occasion he was nowhere to be found, but God knew where he was: "God said, `yes, he's right over there—hidden in that pile of baggage.'"

I have often seen Christians hiding in a pile of baggage of bad decisions; of an unfortunate circumstance over which they had no control or as a result of their own indecision. There they wallow a lifetime in the pile of baggage, pitying themselves every inch of the way. Rather than getting up and moving on, they prefer the comfort of the baggage pile. How is it that some climb over the top of the baggage and move on? Like a single mother who is left with four children to raise and little money or skills to accompany her but finds a way to support her family; like the preacher who endures criticism of people but does not forsake his calling: like the fellow who loses his job but refuses to be defeated. Some of the most heroic people I have known have overcome the baggage scene and went on to great things. I have a friend who was a klutz when it came to athletics, but took interest in the game of handball and through arduous and long hours of practice, became a master at the game and won many tournaments against those blessed with athleticism. I have a preacher friend who showed little skill in communication when it came to preaching, but he persisted and became a dearly loved pastor parishioners loved and respected.

Everybody I know could hide in a pile of baggage if they chose to do so, but many never look back and they move on to fulfill the expectations God had for them. You can do the same. What will it be?

Irony

Isaiah 58

"'For my thoughts are not your thoughts, neither are your ways my ways,' declares the LORD" (Isaiah 55:8 NIV).

Our friends, Dave and Sharon went their separate ways for a few days; he to the mountains in search of a deer; she to a business conference. He is an expert outdoorsman and hunting guide; she is an accomplished executive secretary at a prominent West Coast university. During the three days they were apart, Dave did not see a deer at all. Sharon, while attending the conference, on her off time, saw several deer. Sharon commented to a local friend: "I wish I had brought my gun, I have a deer tag." Her friend suggested that they go to a nearby farm her parents owned and borrow one of their guns. She did. In a short time Sharon sighted a deer and brought it down in one shot. The women field dressed the deer, quartered it and packed it out so Sharon could return home with it. Upon arriving at home, she discovered that Dave had not even seen a deer, while she saw many and of them had proof of her Annie Oakley sharp shooting expertise. What irony there is in the humorous story! Irony is an incongruity between what might be expected and what actually occurs. It is a form of paradox, what is good and great at the same time.

Reading the Bible we run across irony in many different stories. Satan sought to defeat God, but Jesus, in whom is all power, prevailed at the Cross and defeated Satan. The Pharisees were looking for a king; Jesus came as their Savior. The world looks for one who might accomplish its purposes; God chose many, who were neither noble nor mighty, to accomplish His purposes. These are just a few ironical accounts of which there are many in the Scriptures. The fact that God has called you, saved you and is using you for his glory is an incongruity; who would have thought it?

Relativism

Reading: Jeremiah 6

"Thus says the Lord: 'Stand in the ways and see, and ask for the old paths, where the good way is, and walk in it; then you will find rest for your souls'" (Jeremiah 6:16 NIV).

Eugene Peterson paraphrases verse 16 and 17 "Go stand at the crossroads and look around. Ask for directions to the old road. Then take it. Discover the right route for your souls. But they said 'nothing doing. We aren't going that way.'" (Jeremiah 6. The Message).

"The late Professor Allan Bloom, author of *The Closing of the American Mind,* told about asking his undergraduate class at the University of Chicago to identify an evil person. Not one student could do so. 'Evil' simply did not exist as a category in their minds. The inability to recognize and identify evil, said Bloom, is a perilous sign in our society." (Philip Yancey).

We live in a society now that shows no shock when Playboy pinup Shannon Doherty refers to herself as "just a nice, southern Baptist, Republican girl." Not an indictment of the southern Baptists only but the whole of society. The word "relativism" that says nothing is always right or wrong" and sentimentalism that says "because I love you, I will let you" has displaced the Bible's moral absolutism and genuine love that cares enough to correct.

How did Christians succumb to such a low level of living where relativism has displaced moral absolutism? The answer is in the neglect or ignoring of sound doctrine. Search out the Scriptures. We are all born into the world, therefore, without spiritual ability to save ourselves, and we are deserving of God's wrath (Romans 8:7, 8; Ephesians 2:1-3). God is not willing to let the whole human race go to hell, and has from before the foundation of the world, chosen individual sinners to be saved. This choice is not based on any merit or justification found in the individual, but is sovereignly exercised by God solely out of His grace and love (John 17:6; Ephesians 1:4; 2 Thessalonians 2:13). Those who are elected by God were given to Jesus Christ before the foundation of the world so that he should redeem them from sin (Matthew 1:21; John 6:37-40; 10:11, 14, 15 cf. 26-28). (From *"The Foundation Journal"* Issue 19/20 Winter/Spring 1995).

Once we have the foundation for sound doctrine, then we can live with God's absolutes and give no truck with relativism.

Comfort

Reading: Job 7

"My bed shall comfort me; my couch shall ease my complaint". (Hebrew Bible. in Job 7:13).

"If I say, `I'm going to bed, then I'll feel better. A little nap will lift my spirits.'" Job 7 (The Message).

"I quoted some passages at David's funeral, for at that time AIDS patients were hearing a steady stream of judgment from the church. Like Donne (John), I found comfort in the fact that not once did Jesus turn on a suffering person with a `You deserve it!' accusation. He offered instead forgiveness and healing." (Philip Yancey).

On one occasion a dear friend accused me of being soft on sin. I examined my attitude toward such and concluded that I have spent more than fifty years trying to emulate Jesus (sometimes without knowing it) by offering forgiveness and healing (God's healing of course). I have some friends who specialize in preaching the judgment of God, and I don't like the trail of bodies my friends leave in their wake. On the contrary, I have seen God do wonders among many who have sought God's forgiveness and healing. I suppose everybody has their calling and are bent accordingly when it comes to what they emphasize in ministry.

Coming Out

Reading: Acts 7

"Get out from your country and from your kindred and come here to a land which I will show you. Then he came out from the land of the Chaldeans and took up his residence in this land where you now live." (Acts 7:3.4 Wm. Barclay paraphrase).

Abraham answered God's summons to come out, not knowing where he was going. (Hebrews 11:8). He had an adventurous spirit. Leslie Newbigin, Scottish minister, talks about a union of churches in South India: "Negotiations were proceeding towards that union, but they were often held up by demands of where he is going." Whereupon someone said: "A Christian has no right to ask where he is going." While Abraham, a man of faith and of hope, even to the end never doubted it would be so.

In recent years we have seen the phrase "coming out" as a pejorative description of Gay People. There is a much higher use of the phrase. Faith often involves risk. Abraham answered God's call to come out, not knowing where he was going.

Weapons of Mass Destruction

Job 38

"Have you entered the storehouses of the snow or seen the storehouses of the hail which I reserve for times of trouble for days of war and battle?" (Job 38:22,23 NIV).

God's heavenly arsenal includes the mighty drip of water known as hailstones. Hail is usually accompanied by thunderstorms. It has been known to be as large as golf balls, baseballs and even grapefruit. Hail hurtles to the ground at the speed of 90 miles per hour. The Palmist declared that God hurls hail like pebbles. (Psalm 147:17). Why is it a part of God's arsenal? Isaiah says God used hail to "cause men to hear his majestic voice; to make them see his arm" (Isaiah 30:30). God asked Job if he had "seen the storehouses of the hail, which I reserve for time of trouble for days of war and battle?" (Job 38:22, 23).

The Israelites were freed from Egyptian bondage by hail (Exodus 9:19-25). God will use enormous hailstones in future judgment. (Revelation 16:21). Thank God that those who trust him have nothing to fear: "My people will live in peaceful dwelling places, in secure homes, in undisturbed places of rest. Though hail flattens the forest and the city is leveled completely, how blessed you will be, sowing your seed by every stream, and letting your cattle and donkeys range free."[13] (Isaiah 32: 18-20 NIV). (Excerpted from the book *How Majestic is Thy Name*).

Judgment

Reading: Psalm 1, 2

"Therefore the wicked will not stand in the judgment, nor sinners in the assembly of the righteous. For the LORD watches over the way of the righteous, but the way of the wicked will perish" (Psalm 1:5,6 NIV).

"You're not at all like the wicked, who are mere windblown dust—Without defense in court, unfit company for innocent people" (Psalm 1 The Message).

Philip Yancey and his wife befriended a young man dying of AIDS. His name was David. David's partner asked Philip if he would speak at his funeral. Philip recounts the conversation: "When David finally died, his distraught partner had one request—please don't preach judgment. Most of the people who will come haven't been in church in years. They've heard nothing but judgment from the church. They need to hear about a God of grace and mercy—the God that David worshiped. They need hope."[14]

Granted that we need to preach about a God of grace and mercy, but we also are commissioned to preach about the judgment of God. I suspect the churches referred to by David's partner also preached mercy and hope, but David was probably not interested in what the preachers said because he didn't want to hear about the judgment of God. Judgment relating to God occurs more than 100 times in the Bible. Of course, we don't like to hear about it because it challenges us to quit sinning and obey God, something we don't like to think about for we are too busy thinking about ourselves being happy. Some of the apparently happy folks I know are on their way to hell because they refuse to listen to God.

Where we get into trouble in our preaching about judgment is when we resort to our own observations, not knowing all that is involved in another person's life. We are to leave judgment to God. But that doesn't excuse us from preaching about the concept. We'd best be busy repenting of the sin of judging others; that would keep us all busy.

Common

Reading: Luke 8

"Do not store up for yourselves treasures on earth, where moth and rust destroy, and where thieves break in and steal. But store up for yourselves treasures in heaven, where moth and rust do not destroy, and where thieves do not break in and steal. For where your treasure is, there your heart will be also" (Matthew 6:19-21 NIV).

Someone could refer to you as a part of a community or as a common person. Like an "old shoe." I have a dear pastor friend, Wayne Smith, who is a common person; he wears like an "old shoe." That is a great compliment. I have never met a pastor who better wore like an "old shoe" than Wayne. One always was made to feel comfortable when he was around. Then, like many words, common has many other connections. It could be companion. Greek was the common language of New Testament times.

The early church held possessions in common for use of other believers. There is reference to common faith among believers. Peter was taught by the Lord that no meat is common or profane. Believers held to a common hope. That believers held all things in common was different from the use of the Communist word for common. For believers it wasn't Communism because what they shared was temporary, voluntary and Christian. For Communists it was permanent, enforced and atheistic. Dr. Kenneth Kinney preached a sermon on the New Testament practice of Communism using the story of the early church as an example. He hammered away that it was a failure. Kinney was wearing his smoky glasses that day as he tore into Communism with a vengeance, Joe McCarthy style, as preachers were wont to do during the 1950s.

Contempt

Reading: Job 5

"Remove from me scorn and contempt, for I keep your statutes" (Psalm 119:22 NIV).

Men at ease have contempt for misfortune as the fate of those whose feet are slipping. I have often marveled about Job whose anger never shifted into high gear of what we know as contempt. The Psalmist's prayer could well have been Job's.

We get the word contempt from the word despise: according to the dictionary it is the state of being despised or dishonored; disgraced. Open disrespect or willful disobedience of the authority of a court of law or legislative body. Lord Chesterfield once said: "There is nothing that people bear more impatiently, or forgive less, than contempt: and an injury is much sooner forgotten than an insult."

Christians need to be on guard in their attitude toward others with whom they disagree, lest they slip into contempt, a disaster in the in the making. "Or do you show contempt for the riches of his kindness, tolerance and patience, not realizing that God's kindness leads you toward repentance?" (Romans 2:3–5 NIV).

A Cheerful Heart

Proverbs 17

"A cheerful heart is good medicine, but a crushed spirit dries up the bones" (Proverbs 17:2 NIV).
"A cheerful disposition is good for your health; gloom and doom leave you bone tired" (Proverbs 17 The Message).

"Humor is a rubber sword. It allows you to make a point without drawing blood." (Mary Hirsch). My Sister, Dorothy is the one who makes me laugh the most. She could have been another Irma Bombeck, except for a higher calling. W. H. Auden said: "Among those whom I like or admire, I can find no common denominator, but among those whom I love, I can: all of them make me laugh." We can learn a lot about the healthy aspect of humor by reading about the trials of Black folks, who once were slaves. They are the best comics in my judgment. Many a person has endured poverty by the cultivation of a humorous spirit. Alas, there are some who only see life as a glass half empty rather than half full. It is risky to try making them laugh and see the humorous side of life. Interesting that God gave man a sense of humor when he created him, but he did not give laughter to the animal kingdom. There is nothing like discovering, after the fact, the humor of an unfortunate circumstance. "Humor is not a mood but a way of looking at the world. So if it is correct to say that humor was stamped out in Nazi Germany. That does not mean that people were not in good spirits, or anything of that sort, but something much deeper and more important." (Ludwig Wittgenstein).

I love to listen to Minnesota Public Radio's Prairie Home Companion. Garrison Keillor, a great humorist who once said: "Humor, a good sense of it, is to Americans what manhood is to Spaniards and we will go to great lengths to prove it. Experiments with laboratory rats have shown that, if one psychologist in the room laughs at something a rat does, all of the other psychologists in the room will laugh equally. Nobody wants to be left holding the joke."

Humor at its best is expressed by James Thurber: "The wit makes fun of other persons; the satirist makes fun of the world; the humorist makes fun of himself, but in so doing, he identifies himself with people—that is, people everywhere, not for the purpose of taking them apart, but simply revealing their true nature." In many respects we take ourselves too seriously; lighten up.

Partnerships

Reading: Philippians 1:1-11

"I thank my God every time I remember you. In all my prayers for all of you, I always pray with joy because of your partnership in the gospel from the first day until now" (Philippians 1: 3- 5).

Paul blessed us with the privilege of being in partnership with him in the Gospel. One of the greatest joys in life is to be in partnership with God. It's a whole lot better than living the life of a couch potato. Partnerships give us a new lease on life; places us in God's immediate presence; teaches us to relate to others; gives us access to Jesus who raises the dead; keeps our minds active; delivers us from boredom. Couch potatoes lose their endurance; forego a dynamic journey.

Ecclesiastes says: "Two are better than one; because they have a good reward for their labour. For if they fall, the one will lift up his fellow: but woe to him that is alone when he falleth; for he hath not another to help him up. Again, if two lie together, then they have heat: but how can one be warm alone? And if one prevail against him, two shall withstand him; and a threefold cord is not quickly broken." (Ecclesiastes 4:9–12 KJV).

Two such as you with such a master speed
Cannot be parted nor be swept away
From one another once you are agreed
That life is only life forevermore
Together wing to wing and oar to oar. — Robert Frost

Boasting

Reading: 1 Samuel 2

"I'm walking on air. I am laughing at my rivals. I'm dancing my salvation. Nothing and no one is holy like God. Don't dare talk pretentiously—not a word of boasting, ever!" (I Samuel 2:3 The Message).

There is something in the human psyche that finds solace in boasting. Not boasting about another person, but ourselves. As Logan Pearsall Smith reminded us: "We need two kinds of acquaintances, one to complain to, while to the others we boast." I remember my late friend, Fred Brown, who once said: "Nothing we have to brag about in our lives but that there is enough to make us weep." Why do we think we have to boast about ourselves? It could be just to draw simple attention or to get a better position in the minds of others. Certainly it is an ego trip to boast. We see so much crass boasting of those who doctor their resume to make themselves appear more qualified for a job. Most of what we hear in that regard, we see through quite quickly for we are not dumb, but rather perceptive about what we smell. "Conceit spoils the finest genius. There is not much danger that real talent or goodness will be overlooked long; even if it is, the consciousness of possessing and using it well should satisfy one, and the great charm of all power is modesty." (Louisa May Alcott)

When Hannah gave birth to a son, she prayed "I'm walking on air. I am laughing at my rivals. I'm dancing my salvation. Nothing and no one is holy like God. Don't dare talk pretentiously—not a word of boasting, ever." (1 Samuel 2:2,3 The Message).

Witnessing

Reading: Matthew 28

"But you will receive power when the Holy Spirit comes on you; and you will be my witnesses in Jerusalem, and in all Judea and Samaria, and to the ends of the earth" (Acts 1:8)

A witness is a man who says I know this is true. In a court of law a man would tell his own story. Evidence carried the story. In the days of his uncertainty John Bunyan wasn't sure. He was worried that the Jews would think their religion the best religion. If a man embraces a "think so" religion he can't say: "I know." When the light broke, Bunyan could say, "I know; I know." Real witnessing comes by deeds. A fellow spent time with David Livingstone. He said: "If I had been with him any longer I would have been compelled to become a Christian and he never spoke to me about it at all."

I have been involved in seeing many people come to Christ. I dare say, it was not because of my words. There was something about the witness of being with people and living for the Lord that meant the difference. "If he has faith, the believer cannot be restrained. He betrays himself. He breaks out. He confesses and teaches this gospel to the people at the risk of life itself." Martin Luther

---

Absolutism

Hebrews 13

"Appreciate your pastoral leaders who gave you the Word of God. Take a good look at the way they live, and let their faithfulness instruct you, as well as their truthfulness. There should be consistency that runs through us all. For Jesus doesn't change—yesterday, today, tomorrow, he's always totally himself" (Hebrews 13:7,8 The Message).

"Every country has its own constitution; ours is absolutism moderated by assassination". (Anonymous Russian. Quoted in: Count Munster, *Political Sketches of the State of Europe 1814—1867 (1868)*

"Religious systems, said Tolstoy, tend to promote external rules: Judaism did so, as did Buddhism, Hinduism, and Islam. But Jesus introduced a different approach by refusing to define a set of external rules which his followers could then abide by with a sense of self-righteousness".

In a pivotal passage, Tolstoy made this distinction between Christ's approach and that of all other religions: "A man who professes an external law is like someone standing in the light of a lantern fixed to a post. It is light all round him, but there is nowhere further for him to walk. A man who professes the teaching of Christ is like a man carrying a lantern before him on a long, or not so long, pole: the light is in front of him, always lighting up fresh ground and always encouraging him to walk further." [15](As quoted by Philip Yancey).

We do well to consider the difference and walk as Jesus instructed us. Therein lies both our freedom and accountability.

Dedication

I Samuel 1:21—28

"After the child is weaned, I'll bring him myself and present him to God – and that's where he'll stay, for good" (1 Samuel 1 The Message).

Baby dedications are a happy event for parents who are committed to raise their children in the fear and admonition of the Lord. Occasionally I am asked to speak at such events. Calculations are made each year about how much it takes to raise a child. There are a lot of intangibles for Christians to consider also.

Unconditional love is just one of them; a love that helps the child understand that he is a sinner by nature and needs to be born again by trusting Christ as his Savior. Then there is the matter of ethics – character. Personal character is not a secret. Those who associate with us know our character. We need to listen to their testimony and be ready to make necessary changes. God demands of parents that they "do not offer the parts of your body to sin, as instruments of wickedness, but rather offer yourselves to God, as those who have been brought from death to life; and offer the parts of your body to him as instruments of righteousness (Romans 6:12, 13. NIV). Children do not always do as we expect them to do; neither do Christians. Paul writes the Corinthians and says: "And they did not do as we expected, but they gave themselves first to the Lord and then to us in keeping with God's will" (2 Corinthians 8:5 NIV). This reference is back to the act of giving on the part of the Macedonians, explained in verses 3 and 4. It makes this more explicit by repeating the verb: "and they gave in a way that we did not expect."

Yes, dedicating a child is a lifelong pursuit that requires a great deal from us in addition to the actual out of pocket costs until they are on their own.

But

Reading: Psalm 3

"Though the LORD is on high, he looks upon the lowly, but the proud he knows from afar" (Psalm 138:6 NIV).

One of the best epitaphs I've read is that which was carved in the cemetery stone of a man which said: "He was a good husband, a good father and an honest man; But..."

There are many instances in the Bible that the conjunction "but" is used. Solomon makes use of the conjunction more than 150 times in Proverbs such as: "The wise inherit honor, but fools he holds up to shame." "But the way of the wicked is like deep darkness; they do not know what makes them stumble;"..." But a man who commits adultery lacks judgment; whoever does so destroys himself" (Proverbs 3:35; 4:19 6:32 NIV). In Ecclesiastes Solomon uses the conjunction more than 30 times. For example: "Words from a wise man's mouth are gracious, but a fool is consumed by his own lips" (Ecclesiastes 10:12 NIV).

The wise person pays attention to the conjunction "but" for God has an important message in it. May our lives honor the Lord and show the positive side of the "but".

Tom Younger

Ethics

Reading: Psalm 89—91

"Flee the evil desires of youth, and pursue righteousness, faith, love and peace, along with those who call on the Lord out of a pure heart" (2 Timothy 2:22 NIV).

"Flee from sexual immorality. All other sins a man commits are outside his body, but he who sins sexually sins against his own body. Do you not know that your body is a temple of the Holy Spirit, who is in you, whom you have received from God? You are not your own; you were bought at a price. Therefore honor God with your body". (1 Corinthians 6:18-20 NIV).

Bill Moyers: "So what's the mandate for an ethical person?" Michael Josephson: "The mandate is that an ethical person ought to do more than he's required to do and less than he's allowed to do."

Ethics, principles or standards of human conduct, are sometimes called morals, and the study of such principles, sometimes called moral philosophy. This article primarily concerns ethics in the second sense in Western civilization, although every culture has developed an ethic of its own.

The English churchman, Joseph Butler, published *Fifteen Sermons*, in which he defends Christianity against Deism and provides a moral system that (unlike many ethical positions of the period) stresses the role of benevolence in human motivation.

The 16th-century Protestant Reformation caused a return to basic principles within the Christian tradition. According to the German theologian Martin Luther, goodness of spirit is the essence of Christian piety. Moral conduct, or good works, is required, but salvation comes by faith alone. In general, individual responsibility was considered more important than obedience to authority or tradition. This change of emphasis indirectly led to the development of modern secular ethics.

Shadows

Reading: Acts 5:12-16

"Yet because the wicked do not fear God, it will not go well with them, and their days will not lengthen like a shadow" (Ecclesiastes 8:13 NIV).

My hat's off in tribute to the Reverend Marvin Troyer. He spent a career casting a shadow that ministered to literally hundreds of hurting people. If a parishioner was in the hospital scheduled for surgery at six a.m. Marv was there to pray with him; if a child was struck by an automobile, Marv was there before the ambulance arrived; if a marriage was falling apart, Marv was present to counsel; if a fellow pastor needed help, Marv was the first to offer help; if a person was at death's door, Marv was there to comfort as the Psalmist said: "Even though I walk through the valley of the shadow of death, I will fear no evil, for you are with me;" He cast a long shadow. No one was a stranger to Marvin.

"As a result, people brought the sick into the streets and laid them on beds and mats so that at least Peter's shadow might fall on some of them as he passed by" (Acts 5:15 NIV).

All Christians cast a shadow. Does our shadow fall upon those in need to whom we minister?

Tom Younger

The Second Chance

Reading: Acts 10:9-23

"Then the word of the LORD came to Jonah a second time" (Jonah 3:1 NIV).

One night I received a phone call from a long time friend whom I had not seen for 20 years and talked rather infrequently during these years. A believer, he kicked over the traces, experienced bankruptcy because of greed, raised a dysfunctional family, went through a divorce and held many jobs mostly business ventures. The whole scene was utter chaos for years. Then the word of the Lord came to him a second time as it did Jonah. He remarried a Christian woman, his life straightened out, and he lives for the Lord to this day. He has a thriving business that is growing out of sight; a little boy, the delight of his life, who is four years old; is deeply committed to his church and has seen his entire family turn around and live for the Lord. To be sure there are issues he has to face daily in his walk with the Lord. I marvel when I see a turn of events like this, for I am preconditioned to think that when a life is so messed up, there is little God can do to get a person's attention and send his word to him a second time. I don't know why I marvel at such. The grace of God is not stunted, nor stymied; neither is God's arm shortened that he cannot reach down and rescue people like that. This leads me to realize, where would we be were it not for the word of the Lord coming a second time. Or third. The working of God's grace shuts my mouth when it comes to judging others.

"The voice spoke to him a second time, 'Do not call anything impure that God has made clean'" (Acts 10:15 NIV).

Alternatives

Reading: 2 Corinthians 6:1-13

""For he says, 'In the time of my favor I heard you, and in the day of salvation I helped you. .I tell you, now is the time of God's favor, now is the day of salvation" (2 Corinthians 6:2 NIV).

We have the choice between two mutually exclusive possibilities. One of a number of things from which one must choose. We may choose the way of the world or we may choose the way of Christ. David wrote: Choose life and not death!

Is that not one of the finest pictures of the Church? As a parallel society, we gather together on Sunday mornings for the only thing the culture cannot do – worship! We pray our prayers; we sing our songs that speak a different language from the world's; we read our story, the grand master narrative of the promising God.

Of all the thirty-six alternatives, running away is best. Chinese Proverb.

I shall be telling this with a sigh
Somewhere ages and ages hence:
Two roads diverged in a wood, and I—
I took the one less traveled by,
And that has made all the difference.— Robert Frost

"How could a man be satisfied with a decision between such alternatives and under such circumstances? No more than he can be satisfied with his hat, which he's chosen from among such shapes as the resources of the age offer him, wearing it at best with a resignation which is chiefly supported by comparison." George Eliot

I shall forever be thankful that by the prompting of the Holy Spirit, I chose to follow Jesus Christ as Lord and Savior.

Dealing With People

Reading:1 Timothy 5:1-8

"I am writing you these instructions, so that, if I am delayed, you may know how people ought to conduct themselves in God's household, which is the church of the living God, the pillar and foundation of the truth" (1 Timothy 3:14 &15 NIV).

We must deal with people the way Jesus deals with them. We cannot treat organizationally or functionally, but personally. The Bible says that where two or three are gathered together, Jesus is in the midst. Culture says where two or three together we must have a chairperson, a secretary and a committee. It is no wonder that we are confused about our place in the culture of our day. We cannot deal with people effectively by looking upon them organizationally or functionally. Culture knows nothing about community to be lived rightly. When we deal with people we take a page from the Psalmist:

> Quick God, I need your helping hand!
> The last decent person just went down,
> All the friends I depended on gone.
> Everyone talks in lie language,
> Lies slide off their oily lips,
> They doubletalk with forked tongues.
> (Psalm 12:1-4 The Message).

"On the other hand, in the Word, Jesus creates community. The Gospel that takes care of our eternal destiny plunges us into community relationships. Culture knows nothing about community; salvation requires community." Eugene Peterson.

Hurry

Reading: Luke 14:25-35

"Suppose one of you wants to build a tower. Will he not first sit down and estimate the cost to see if he has enough money to complete it? For if he lays the foundation and is not able to finish it, everyone who sees it will ridicule him, saying, 'This fellow began to build and was not able to finish'" (Luke 14:28-30 NIV).

Nine times out of ten my reason to hurry led to a bad decision. Occasionally one reads a story about hurrying and it benefits others as well as themselves. Marva Dawn tells this about her husband. "On our way to the doctor, we were stopped by a red light on a four lane road. When the light turned green, the car in front of us didn't move. I kept saying, 'Myron, you can go around now. It's clear Myron, it's open; why don't you go?' Nagging is what I was doing. Finally, Myron in his gracious, good, generous self leaned over to me and said, 'I am looking to make sure the woman in that car in front of us is all right.'"

My story was not so beneficial. I bought a new Buick in Fort Wayne on one of our trips to the Midwest. Taking possession of the car, Mark, our son, gave me five sets of keys: "Dad, this is the first time you have owned a car with automatic door locks. Take these keys and place them in ways that you have a spare key when you lock yourself out of the car." Wouldn't you know I threw the keys, all five sets, in the glove box of the car and headed off to Dallas where our daughter Colleen lived. We were going to see a Texas Ranger ball game the next evening. During the seventh inning stretch as we all stood to cheer the Rangers, I slipped my hand in my pocket and realized my five sets of car keys were safely in the glove box locked tight. To add to my dilemma in our hurry to get into the ball park, I had left the engine running. Woe is me! After the game a generously tattooed park attendant drove me around to my parked car which by now was out of gas. In a matter of a few seconds, the attendant left a small tattoo on the door frame of the car, but the doors opened and alas I had found my five sets of keys safely tucked away in the glove box. From that day on I had car keys squirreled away in places that protected me when I am in a hurry. That is, if I can remember where I hid the keys.

Years ago, a high premium was placed on rushing people into the Kingdom for the Lord's coming is near. In retrospect we failed in our hurry to see that the people we witnessed to would count the cost of following Jesus and to make sure they understood the issues of salvation.

Desperate

Reading: Ephesians 2:1-10

"As for you, you were dead in your transgressions and sins, in which you used to live when you followed the ways of this world and of the ruler of the kingdom of the air, the spirit who is now at work in those who are disobedient. All of us also lived among them at one time, gratifying the cravings of our sinful nature and following its desires and thoughts. Like the rest, we were by nature objects of wrath" (Ephesians 2:1-3 NIV).

"But because of his great love for us, God, who is rich in mercy, made us alive with Christ even when we were dead in transgressions—it is by grace you have been saved. For it is by grace you have been saved, through faith-and this not from yourselves, it is the gift of God, not by works, so that no one can boast. For we are God's workmanship, created in Christ Jesus to do good works, which God prepared in advance for us to do"*(*Ephesians 2:4-5,8-10 NIV).

The passage shows that we are not really bad because of sin. In our sin we are dead. Many in the church don't know how dead they are. We prefer to talk of brokenness. More palatable; seems not our fault. Something else caused us to be broken. So we never take responsibility for our self centeredness, faults, and blatant evil.

The problem is if we never acknowledge that we are sinners, we cannot be forgiven. So we turn into our pillow out of our guilt and make the best of it. That is why we can relate to Romans 7:15-20. We keep on doing what we want to do. We wallow in our despair. We miss the joy that comes in worship to confess our sins. Until we know how dead we are, we will never know how desperate we are for forgiveness.

Clean House

Reading: 1 Samuel 7

"Then Samuel addressed the house of Israel: 'If you are truly serious about coming back to God, clean house. Get rid of the foreign gods…'" (1 Samuel 7:3 The Message).

Samuel addressed the nation Israel with the sobering message: "Clean house!" Are you serious about coming back to God? Get rid of your false gods, goddesses, and the images of Baal and Ashtoreth. They did, believe it or not, and gave exclusive attention to God. Israel gathered at Mizpah and Samuel prayed for them. They poured water before God, a ritual of cleansing, fasted all day and confessed: "We have sinned against God."

Periodically with our propensity to stray away from God's precepts, we need to clean house. Personally and in our churches. God has too much riff-raff to wade through in order to bless his people. We get careless and fail to give our full attention to God.

The people prayed that God would save Israel from the boot of the Philistines. Prayer and confession of sin had a major part in Israel's turn around. The same principles apply to us today. It is not possible to clean house and get back into the place God wants us, without prayer and confession of sin.

Offense

Reading: 1 Corinthians 13

"A man's wisdom gives him patience; it is to his glory to overlook an offense" (Proverbs 19:11 NIV).

An offense is the act of causing anger, resentment, displeasure, or affront. The state of being offended.

"Love is patient, love is kind. It does not envy, it does not boast, it is not proud. It is not rude, it is not self-seeking, it is not easily angered, it keeps no record of wrongs. Love does not delight in evil but rejoices with the truth. It always protects, always trusts, always hopes, always perseveres". (1 Corinthians 13:4-8 NIV)

Bantering among people is a form of pleasure that produces a smile and makes life more tolerable. The problem is some people need to lighten up and enjoy a good laugh, even when it is at their own expense. The greatest humorists poke fun at themselves with abandon, which is the safest form of humor. But let's not live so uptight we can't laugh as others laugh at us and with us. Unfortunately, there are those who keep a record of being offended and carry it to their grave just to spite others. Hence we should always be alert as to whom we are laughing at and avoid offending them for when we have offended someone it is always appropriate to apologize sincerely, even if it doesn't do any good. Ambrose Bierce wrote: "To apologize is to lay the foundation for a future offense."

Just listen in on a conversation of some folks and you learn that the subject of conversation is people remembering when they were offended and rather enjoy being miserable in their anguish. We don't need to be like this for it does no good for our own soul nor for the souls of others.

Insignificance

Reading: Romans 12:1-13

"For by the grace given me I say to every one of you: Do not think of yourself more highly than you ought, but rather think of yourself with sober judgment, in accordance with the measure of faith God has given you" (Romans 12:3 NIV).

Insignificance looks upon itself as lacking in importance; not trivial; worthy of little regard. Small in size or amount. Spurgeon wrote: "It needs more skill than I can tell to play the second fiddle well."

"If we are fascinated by the statistics of magnitude, we are no less fascinated by the statistics of insignificance. We never tire of repeating the communizing figures of population and population growth. We are entranced to think of ourselves as specks on the pages of our own overwhelming history. I remember that my high school biology text dealt with the human body by listing its constituent elements, measuring their quantities, and giving their monetary worth – at the time a little less than a dollar. There was a bit of the typical fodder of the modern mind, at once sensational and belittling – no accidental product of the age of Dachau and Hiroshima". Wendell Berry

I admire longtime friend and pastor of Lakewood Park Church in Auburn, Indiana. He has an air of insignificance that ingratiates people to him and allows him to minister to their needs. Wayne knows every crook in the winding roads of Dekalb County and the people who live there. The County is his parish. Wayne, is called upon to bury the dead and to bind the wounds of the living with those whom he considers his friends. He has ministered in Auburn more than forty years and been loved by all of us.

Weariness

Reading: Galatians 6:1-10

"Like cold water to a weary soul is good news from a distant land".(Proverbs 25:25 NIV). *"Let us not become weary in doing good, for at the proper time we will reap a harvest if we do not give up"*. (Galatians 6:8-9 NIV)

"Weariness can snore upon the flint, when resting sloth finds the down pillow hard". Wm. Shakespeare.

Thomas Traherne wrote: "The soul is made for action, and cannot rest till it be employed. Idleness is its rust. Unless it will up and think and taste and see, all is in vain."

Lord Chesterfield looked upon indolence as a sort of suicide.

"A lazy person, whatever the talents with which he set out, will have condemned himself to second-hand thoughts and to second-rate friends". Cyril Connolly.

"Go to the ant, you sluggard; consider its ways and be wise" (Proverbs 6:6 NIV).The ant is not lazy.

I have often shaken weariness by moving into action.

Ambivalence

Reading: Proverbs 16:1-17

"How much better to get wisdom than gold, to choose understanding rather than silver!" (Proverbs 16:16 NIV).

"Since they hated knowledge and did not choose to fear the LORD, since they would not accept my advice and spurned my rebuke, they will eat the fruit of their ways and be filled with the fruit of their schemes. For the waywardness of the simple will kill them, and the complacency of fools will destroy them; but whoever listens to me will live in safety and be at ease, without fear of harm" (Proverbs 1:29-33 NIV).

Ambivalence is the coexistence of opposing attitudes or feelings, such as love and hate, toward a person, an object, or an idea; uncertainty or indecisiveness as to which course to follow.

Adrienne Rich wrote: "My children cause me the most exquisite suffering of which I have any experience. It is the suffering of ambivalence; the murderous alternation between bitter resentment and raw-edged nerves, and blissful gratification and tenderness. Sometimes I seem to myself, in my feelings toward these tiny guiltless beings, a monster of selfishness and intolerance."

Her children must have been in the terrible two syndrome.

There are those who waffle between two courses of action so that the waffle tastes like hard pan. They simply cannot make a decision. They will drive up to a gas pump and then pull away looking cross town for gas a cent cheaper. When they find it they still can't make up their mind to buy gas for their car. Others who engage in writing hit the wall and rewrite until they are blue in the face and never want to see their work again. Ambivalence is a deadly game.

"But if serving the LORD seems undesirable to you, then choose for yourselves this day whom you will serve, whether the gods your forefathers served beyond the River, or the gods of the Amorites, in whose land you are living. But as for me and my household, we will serve the LORD" (Joshua 24:15 NIV).

Meanwhile those who are not overwhelmed with ambivalence get a day's work in and move on, leaving the indecisive person standing at the gate.

Kindness

Reading: Job 10

"But when the kindness and love of God our Savior appeared, he saved us, not because of righteous things we had done, but because of his mercy. He saved us through the washing of rebirth and renewal by the Holy Spirit, whom he poured out on us generously through Jesus Christ our Savior, so that, having been justified by his grace, we might become heirs having the hope of eternal life. This is a trustworthy saying. And I want you to stress these things, so that those who have trusted in God may be careful to devote themselves to doing what is good. These things are excellent and profitable for everyone" (Titus 3:3-8 NIV).

Kindness is a quality of character that enhances good relationships. Mary Webb wrote: "If you stop to be kind, you must swerve often from your path."

Kindness is its own motive. We become kind by being kind toward others. Willa Cather observed that "when kindness has left people, even for a few moments, we become afraid of them as if their reason had left them. When it has left a place where we have always found it, it is like shipwreck; we drop from security into something malevolent and bottomless".

The love and kindness of God reaches out to us. It is not because we deserve it. Our sin would separate us from God, but because of the love of God and Jesus taking our place and dying for our sins, the kindness of God takes over and permits us to become His children as we believe in Him.. Because of His kindness to us, we should be showing kindness to others.

Young people often think kindness is their right. While it's not a right, it is a highly prized characteristic.

Neglect

Reading: Nehemiah 10:35-39

"The people of Israel, including the Levites, are to bring their contributions of grain, new wine and oil to the storerooms where the articles for the sanctuary are kept and where the ministering priests, the gatekeepers and the singers stay. `We will not neglect the house of our God'" (Nehemiah10:39 NIV).

"I delight in your decrees; I will not neglect your word" (Psalm 119:16 NIV).

Neglect is to pay little or no attention to; fail to heed; disregard; to fail to care for or attend to properly; to fail to do or carry out, as through carelessness or oversight. G.K. Chesterton defines a saint as one that exaggerates what the world neglects, and what is neglected today is the art of paying attention.

"What is a neglected child? He is a child not planned for, not wanted. Neglect begins, therefore, before he is born." Pearl S. Buck.

Stephan was chosen so as not to neglect the Word of God in the early church.. "It would not be right for us to neglect the ministry of the word of God in order to wait on tables. Brothers, choose seven men from among you who are known to be full of the Spirit and wisdom. We will turn this responsibility over to them and will give our attention to prayer and the ministry of the word." This proposal pleased the whole group. They chose Stephen. Acts 6:2-5.

We are reminded "not to neglect your gift, which was given you through a prophetic message when the body of elders laid their hands on you." (1 Timothy 4:13-14 NIV).

What needs our attention today?

Pleasure

Reading: Ecclesiastes 2

"'Go up into the mountains and bring down timber and build the house, so that I may take pleasure in it and be honored,' says the LORD". (Haggai 1:8 NIV).

Pleasure: The state or feeling of being pleased or gratified. A source of enjoyment or delight: Amusement, diversion. "Do not bite at the bait of pleasure, till you know there is no hook beneath it." Thomas Jefferson

"More and more, we take for granted that work must be destitute of pleasure. More and more we assume that if we want to be pleased we must wait until evening, or the weekend, or vacation or retirement. More and more, our farms and forests resemble our factories and offices, which in turn more and more resemble prisons – why else should we be so eager to escape them? We recognize defeated landscapes by the absence of pleasure from them. We are defeated at work because our work gives us no pleasure. We are defeated at home because we have no pleasant work there. We turn to pleasure industries for relief from our defeat, and are again and again defeated, for the pleasure industries can thrive and grow only upon dissatisfaction with them." Wendell Berry

As a society we have settled for a perverse sense of pleasure most often sensual. We spend millions of dollars on books, but seldom read them. We are functionally illiterate. We have nothing to meditate upon except our sensual thoughts. We watch television by the hour each day and pollute our minds with worthless and harmful stuff. We need to turn off the television, learn to read and think once again. That's real pleasure.

So many times the scriptures state that we are to be joyful. There are so many pleasures to enjoy in knowing God and being in His family.

When You're Hard Pressed

Reading: 2 Corinthians 4

"But we have this treasure in jars of clay to show that this all-surpassing power is from God and not from us. We are hard pressed on every side, but not crushed; perplexed, but not in despair; persecuted, but not abandoned; struck down, but not destroyed. We always carry around in our body the death of Jesus, so that the life of Jesus may also be revealed in our body" (2 Corinthians 4:7-12 NIV).

Ministry is a hard choice when you're working in darkness and besieged on all sides by opposition. It's understandable that we stress out. What then do we do? Paul gives us several clues on what to do when we're hard pressed. He writes: "We have this treasure in jars of clay; we always carry around in our body the death of Jesus; we believe therefore we speak; we do not lose heart; we fix our eyes on Jesus for he brings light out of darkness. We are renewed day by day. Therefore we need not be crushed, perplexed, persecuted or in despair. Recognizing our options, we see all this as temporary for what is unseen is eternal."

Concentrate on the goodness of God. Count your blessings. Trust in the Lord. "For God did not give us a spirit of timidity, but a spirit of power, of love and of self-discipline" (2 Timothy 1:7 NIV).

Ability

Reading: Mark 6

"On the Sabbath, he gave a lecture in the meeting place. He made a real hit, impressing everyone. 'We had no idea he was this good!' they said. 'How did he get so wise all of a sudden, get such ability?'" (Mark 6:2 The Message).

They were referring to Jesus. What the religious leaders didn't realize was Jesus is wisdom. He created it

God is the dispenser of ability and never expects of us more than our ability. "The disciples, each according to his ability, decided to provide help for the brothers living in Judea. This they did, sending their gift to the elders by Barnabas and Saul." (Acts 11:29-30 NIV).

Relating to suffering hardships, Paul wrote: "We do not want you to be uninformed, brothers, about the hardships we suffered in the province of Asia. We were under great pressure, far beyond our ability to endure, so that we despaired even of life. Indeed, in our hearts we felt the sentence of death. But this happened that we might not rely on ourselves but on God, who raises the dead" (2 Corinthians 1:8 NIV).

When it came to giving, Paul wrote: "For I testify that they gave as much as they were able, and even beyond their ability" (2 Corinthians 8:2 NIV). It's always according to our ability. "To one he gave five talents of money, to another two talents, and to another one talent, each according to his ability" (Matthew 25:14 NIV).

"According to their ability they gave to the treasury for this work 61,000 drachmas of gold, 5,000 minas of silver and 100 priestly garments" (Ezra 2:68-69 NIV).

Amends

Reading: 2 John

"...I ask that we love one another. And this is love: that we walk in obedience to his commands. As you have heard from the beginning, his command is that you walk in love" (2 John 5-6 NIV).

What does one do when you have insulted someone and seek to make amends? Apologize? Not according to G.K. Chesterton who insists, "A stiff apology is a second insult. ... The injured party does not want to be compensated because he has been wronged; he wants to be healed because he has been hurt".

"There is nothing that people bear more impatiently, or forgive less, than contempt: and an injury is much sooner forgotten than an insult". Lord Chesterfield

"The only gracious way to accept an insult is to ignore it; if you can't ignore it, top it; if you can't top it, laugh at it; if you can't laugh at it, it's probably deserved." Russell Lynes. "A fly, Sir, may sting a stately horse and make him wince; but one is but an insect, and the other is a horse still." Samuel Johnson

There are several ways to make amends upon dealing with an insult: overlook it, let time heal the wound, and treat the offender with love and acceptance. Harboring an insult is a canker sore that won't heal. It destroys relationships and eats one's vitality out. And how does one make amends in his relationship with someone he has insulted. Treat that person with the respect due them and let time bring reconciliation.

Compromise

Reading: 2 John

"If anyone comes to you and does not bring this teaching, do not take him into your house or welcome him. Anyone who welcomes him shares in his wicked work. I have much to write to you, but I do not want to use paper and ink. Instead, I hope to visit you and talk with you face to face, so that our joy may be complete. The children of your chosen sister send their greetings" (2 John 10-13 NIV).

Compromise is a loaded word. John is talking about out and out heretics in this passage; enemies of the gospel. Today we tend to become Pharisaical and accuse others of compromise that causes hurt to the body of Christ. A lot of people have been wounded in recent years by the careless interpretation their brethren put on the word compromise. Christians often treat others like a tractor treats dirt. Polycarp met Marcion, a heretic once. Marcion said: "Do you recognize me?" "I recognize Satan's firstborn," answered Polycarp. There is a difference between a mistaken fellow believer and a heretic. C. H. Dodd said a good humored tolerance can never be enough. [16]William Barclay.

John was soon to come to see his brethren, face to face, as he writes the book of 2 John. The actual meaning is "mouth to mouth." John knew that a letter was often given to false interpretation and looked forward to a heart to heart talk with his fellow brethren. Cromwell disliked John Fox, but met him one day. He said: "If you and I had had but an hour together, we would be better friends today". That's why it's better to speak "mouth to mouth" rather than write letters.[17] William Barclay. Speaking face to face is a more sure way to avoid being labeled a compromiser.

Greatness

Reading: Romans 1

"Do not exalt yourself in the king's presence, and do not claim a place among great men; it is better for him to say to you, "Come up here," than for him to humiliate you before a nobleman" (Proverbs 25:6-7 NIV).

"First, I thank my God through Jesus Christ for all of you, because your faith is being reported all over the world. God, whom I serve with my whole heart in preaching the gospel of his Son, is my witness how constantly I remember you in my prayers at all times; and I pray that now at last by God's will the way may be opened for me to come to you. I long to see you so that I may impart to you some spiritual gift to make you strong; that is, that you and I may be mutually encouraged by each other's faith. I do not want you to be unaware, brothers, that I planned many times to come to you (but have been prevented from doing so until now) in order that I might have a harvest among you, just as I have had among the other Gentiles. I am obligated both to Greeks and non-Greeks, both to the wise and the foolish. That is why I am so eager to preach the gospel also to you who are at Rome" (Romans 1:8-15 NIV).

The Apostle Paul was a great man. How do we know this? By watching how he treated other people. He commenced with a compliment; he prayed for them; he was willing to receive not just give; he saw himself as a debtor to them. It was their kindness to him that caused him to say, I am under an obligation to preach to them.

Battle Of The Mind

Reading: 1 John 2

"Dear children, this is the last hour; and as you have heard that the antichrist is coming, even now many antichrists have come. This is how we know it is the last hour. They went out from us, but they did not really belong to us. For if they had belonged to us, they would have remained with us; but their going showed that none of them belonged to us" (1 John 2:18-19 NIV).

"Many will come in my name, claiming, 'I am he,' and will deceive many" (Mark 13:5-6 NIV).

The process at work for the battle of the mind is the same as it was in Biblical times. Men will take an idea and repeat it over and over again until it is accepted as truth in men's minds. They accept it for they have heard it so many times. Music and philosophy are good examples. The force of evil invades the mind of man. The Media deliberately alters the minds of men in its advertising philosophy.

Speaking of the mind: "It is eminently a *weariable* faculty, eminently delicate, and incapable of bearing fatigue; so that if we give it too many objects at a time to employ itself upon, or very grand ones for a long time together, it fails under the effort, becomes jaded, exactly as the limbs do by bodily fatigue, and incapable of answering any further appeal till it has had rest". John Ruskin

"Then make my joy complete by being like-minded, having the same love, being one in spirit and purpose...Your attitude should be the same as that of Christ Jesus..." (Philippians 2:2 & 5 NIV).

"You will keep in perfect peace him whose mind is steadfast, because he trusts in you" (Isaiah 26:3 NIV).

Anointed

Reading: Romans 12

"For by the grace given me I say to every one of you: Do not think of yourself more highly than you ought, but rather think of yourself with sober judgment, in accordance with the measure of faith God has given you" (Romans 12: 3 NIV).

Every so often a hotshot springs forth out of no where to announce he is God's anointed. The gullible public falls in line to worship the person. Once ensconced in the minds of people, the anointed one wants their money. That's the bottom line to scams. When people wake up to the fact that they were duped, they say it was beautiful and simple and truly great. All swindles are.

A lot of politicians fall into this category, thinking they are God's anointed. As Ogden Nash observed:

> Whether elected or appointed
> He considers himself the Lord's anointed,
> And indeed the ointment lingers on him
> So thick you can't get your fingers on him.

The American public is the smartest judge of human nature, but occasionally they call such anointment scams for what they are and the anointed commits suicide: "And one of his partners asked "Has he vertigo?" and the other glanced out and down and said "Oh no, only about ten feet more." Ogden Nash

---

Callused

Reading: Romans 11

"But encourage one another daily, as long as it is called Today, so that none of you may be hardened by sin's deceitfulness" (Hebrews 3:12 NIV).

The Jews were so secure, so self-satisfied, so at ease in their confidence of being the Chosen People, that that very idea of being the Chosen People had become the thing that ruined them, Their hearts were hardened. Hardened is a medical term and means a callus. A callus had grown over their hearts. They became insensitive.

This can happen to any of us. As Burns wrote:

I waive the quantum of the sin,
The hazard o' concealing;
But och! It hardens a' within,
And petrifies the feeling.

"To be callused is a tragedy, but out of tragedy comes hope. Recognizing the callus, something that we see or sense and we can change and God can effect that change"[18] William Barclay

---

Careful to Listen

Reading: Mark 4

"He who answers before listening—that is his folly and his shame" (Proverbs 18:13 NIV).

"Men listened to me expectantly, waiting in silence for my counsel. After I had spoken, they spoke no more; my words fell gently on their ears" (Job 29:21-22 NIV).

It takes a lot of patience and careful listening to understand what another is trying to communicate. Douglas Steere wrote: "A friend suggested that there are always at least six people present. What each person said are two; what each person meant to say are two more; and what each person understood the other to say are two more. There is certainly no reason to stop at six, but the fathomless depth of the listener who can go beyond, who can go beyond the conscious meanings behind words and listen with the third ear what is unconsciously being meant by the speaker, this fashion of attentive listening furnishes a climate where the most unexpected disclosures occur that are in the way of being miracles in one sense, and the most natural and obvious things in the world, on the other."

Attorneys are taught to listen in depth for the meaning behind the words. Some day I hope to sit down with friend, Judge Bob Thomas, and discuss this matter. One thing we are sure of, God sees behind our rhetoric and understands what we are trying to communicate. I think mothers are pretty good at this also.

Anticipation

Reading: 1 John 3

"How great is the love the Father has lavished on us, that we should be called children of God! And that is what we are! The reason the world does not know us is that it did not know him. Dear friends, now we are children of God, and what we will be has not yet been made known. But we know that when he appears, we shall be like him, for we shall see him as he is.

Everyone who has this hope in him purifies himself, just as he is pure" (1 John 3:1-3 NIV).

The anticipation of an event or happening in our lives often out shines the reality of it. Not so with the anticipation of being with Christ some day.

"Such is the state of life, that none are happy but by the anticipation of change: the change itself is nothing; when we have made it, the next wish is to change again. The world is not yet exhausted; let me see something tomorrow which I never saw before." Samuel Johnson. The blessing of knowing God personally is that we not only anticipate being with Him, but we are happy in this life also, knowing Him.

What greater anticipation than to be like Christ. William Barclay tells the story of a poor and simple man who often would go into a cathedral to pray; and he would always be kneeling in prayer. His lips never moved and he never appeared to say anything. Someone asked the man what he was doing kneeling like that. The man answered simply; "I look at Him and He looks at me."[19]

This is the simplest vision of God a man can have. He who looks long enough at Jesus Christ must ultimately become like Him. John is anticipating the second coming of the Lord Jesus in this passage. The man who knows that God is at the end of the road will make all life a preparation to meet God.

The Devout

Reading: Luke 8

"'Still other seed fell on good soil. It came up and yielded a crop, a hundred times more than was sown.' When he said this, he called out, 'He who has ears to hear, let him hear.' His disciples asked him what this parable meant. He said, 'The knowledge of the secrets of the kingdom of God has been

given to you, but to others I speak in parables, so that, though seeing, they may not see; though hearing, they may not understand'" (Luke 8:7-10 NIV).

"The devout of all times have been aware of these resources of domineering appeal and have therefore mobilized other forces against them. Above all, they have meditated upon the Scriptures and prayed. But how the great ones in the kingdom of God did that! For then every reading of the Bible was a battle and every prayer a sword stroke. Why is it that so often our prayers do not help us? Why is it that they scarcely rise to the ceiling of room and fall back with broken wings? Why is it that the Word of God becomes a mere jingle of words that simply bore us? Because we read it and because we pray as if we were skimming through a picture magazine or chatting with a neighbor. We simply do not wrestle with the text in deadly earnest. When a person is reading his Bible in the morning or just beginning to pray, sometimes the thought of bingo or numbers, the next business letter, or the coming meeting enters his mind. He has already blown an inaudible supersonic whistle and summoned whole flocks of birds which one—two—three snap up the poor little seeds.

"In other words, the Word of God is demanding. It demands a stretch of time in our day—even though a modest one—in which it is our only companion. We can't bite off even a simple `text for the day' and swallow it in one lump while we have our hand on the doorknob. Such things are not digested; they are not assimilated into one's organism. God simply will not put up with being fobbed off with prayers in telegram style and cut short like a troublesome visitor for whom we open the door just a crack to get rid of him as quickly as possible."[20] Helmut Thielicke

We need to stop and ponder the thoughts of the Word of God, and meditate upon it, in order to practice what being devout means. Then apply it to ourselves. This will come to pass only as we learn to pray as the devout prayed.

Tom Younger

Catching Up

Reading: Psalm 71

"King David grew old. The years had caught up with him. Even though they piled blankets on him, he couldn't keep warm" (1 Kings 1:1 The Message).

"So Elihu son of Barakel the Buzite said: I am young in years, and you are old; that is why I was fearful, not daring to tell you what I know. I thought, 'Age should speak; advanced years should teach wisdom.' But it is the spirit in a man, the breath of the Almighty, that gives him understanding. It is not only the old who are wise, not only the aged who understand what is right".(Job 32:6-9 NIV).

A lot of agers are afraid of growing old. They do everything they can, sometimes stupid things, to appear young. Many weary the treadmill into exhaustion. True, we all wish to live long enough to accomplish unfinished tasks and see our grandchildren grow up. On the other hand, there are those who booze themselves into oblivion in an effort to escape old age.

Age wins and one must learn to grow old. ... I must learn to walk this long unlovely wintry way, looking for spectacles, shunning the cruel looking-glass, laughing at my clumsiness before others mistakenly condole, not expecting gallantry yet disappointed to receive none, apprehending every ache or shaft of pain, alive to blinding flashes of mortality, unarmed, totally vulnerable.

Forty years on, growing older and older,
Shorter in wind, as in memory long,
Feeble of foot, and rheumatic of shoulder
What will it help you that once you were strong?
E. E. Bowen

Old Age and Aging

I dread no more the first white in my hair,
Or even age itself, the easy shoe,
The cane, the wrinkled hands, the special chair:
Time, doing this to me, may alter too
My anguish, into something I can bear.
Edna St. Vincent Millay

The aging factor has never bothered me. I am quite willing to accept the fact that every day past three score and ten is a bonus. Why kick against the inevitable.

That Which is Certain

Reading: 1 John 5

"We know that anyone born of God does not continue to sin; the one who was born of God keeps him safe, and the evil one cannot harm him. We know that we are children of God, and that the whole world is under the control of the evil one. We know also that the Son of God has come and has given us understanding, so that we may know him who is true. And we are in him who is true—even in his Son Jesus Christ. He is the true God and eternal life" (1 John 5:18-20 NIV).

We live in a world of uncertainty; however there are eternal certainties we take hold of. We are liberated from the power of sin. What does that mean? It doesn't mean that the Christian never sins. We may sin, but our normal condition is resistance to evil. F. W. H. Myers speaks of Paul's battle with the flesh:

"Well, let me sin, but not with my consenting,
Well, let me die, but willing to be whole:

Never, O Christ — so stay with me from relenting –
Shall there be truce betwixt my flesh and my soul."

The reason we are liberated from the power of sin is we have the new birth from God that keeps us. As Westcott has said: "The Christian has an active enemy, but he also has a watchful guardian." The Christian is also on the side of God against the world. It is not that we never fall, but we get up and go on every time we fall. Our source of being is God; the world's source of being lies in the power of the evil one. While the world guesses and gropes we enter the knowledge of reality. God is on our side.

Habit

Reading: 1Timothy 5

"Let us not give up meeting together, as some are in the habit of doing, but let us encourage one another-and all the more as you see the Day approaching" (Hebrews 10:25 NIV).

Good habits are worth developing. Paul practiced the habit of going where sinners were in order to teach the truths of the Gospel of Jesus Christ. "As his custom was, Paul went into the synagogue, and on three Sabbath days he reasoned with them from the Scriptures, explaining and proving that the Christ had to suffer and rise from the dead. 'This Jesus I am proclaiming to you is the Christ,' he said. Some of the Jews were persuaded and joined Paul and Silas, as did a large number of God-fearing Greeks and not a few prominent women" (Acts 17:1-4 NIV).

Mark Twain believed that good habits were developed one step at a time. "Habit is habit, and not to be flung out of the window by any man, but coaxed downstairs a step at a time." How does one coax good habits downstairs one step at a time?

Salvatore Satta speaks of orderliness: "His vocation was orderliness, which is the basis of creation. Accordingly, when a letter came, he would turn it over in his hands for a long time, gazing at it meditatively; then he would put it away in a file without opening it, because everything had its own time." Are you accustomed to developing good habits?

Confidence

Reading: 2 Corinthians 5

"Therefore we are always confident and know that as long as we are at home in the body we are away from the Lord. We live by faith, not by sight. We are confident, I say, and would prefer to be away from the body and at home with the Lord. So we make it our goal to please him, whether we are at home in the body or away from it" (2 Corinthians 5:6-9 NIV).

Lord Melbourne wrote: "I wish I was as cocksure of anything as Tom Macaulay is of everything." And William Pitt the Elder, Lord Chatham gives insight to confidence, "I cannot give them my confidence; pardon me, gentlemen, confidence is a plant of slow growth in an aged bosom: youth is the season of credulity".

Culture is constantly in search of confidence. The best it can come up with is self-confidence. The King of Assyria asked Hezekiah, "On what are you basing this confidence of yours? You say you have strategy and military strength—but you speak only empty words. On whom are you depending, that you rebel against me? Look now, you are depending on Egypt that splintered reed of a staff, which pierces a man's hand and wounds him if he leans on it! Such is Pharaoh King of Egypt to all who depend on him" (Isaiah 36:4-6 NIV).

"Such confidence as this is ours through Christ before God. Not that we are competent in ourselves to claim anything for ourselves, but our competence comes from God" (2 Corinthians 3:4-5 NIV).

If you are looking for peace, engage in the fruit of righteousness; find peace; "…the effect of righteousness will be quietness and confidence forever." (Isaiah 32:17 NIV).

"…blessed is the man who trusts in the LORD, whose confidence is in him. He will be like a tree planted by the water that sends out its roots by the stream. It does not fear when heat comes; its leaves are always green. It has no worries in a year of drought and never fails to bear fruit." (Jeremiah 17:7-8 NIV). .

The writer of Hebrews encourages us not to throw away our confidence; for it will be richly rewarded. Persevere so that when we have done the will of God, we will receive what he has promised. Hebrews 10:35-37

Giftedness

Reading: Romans 12

"For by the grace given me I say to every one of you: Do not think of yourself more highly than you ought, but rather think of yourself with sober judgment, in accordance with the measure of faith God has given you. Just as each of us has one body with many members, and these members do not all have the same function, so in Christ we who are many form one body, and each member belongs to all the others. We have different gifts, according to the grace given us. If a man's gift is prophesying, let him use it in proportion to his faith. If it is serving, let him serve; if it is teaching, let him teach; if it is encouraging, let him encourage; if it is contributing to the needs of others, let him give generously; if it is leadership, let him govern diligently; if it is showing mercy, let him do it cheerfully" (Romans 12:3-8 NIV).

It is a pity that some Christians go through life not knowing anything about giftedness, so they plod along trying to find themselves in the body of Christ. Often they are given to trying to do what they are not equipped to do and therefore spend their time here on earth spinning their wheels. The Greeks were big on a man to know himself. They found it essential to a useful life. They also learned to accept themselves and to use to the fullest the gift God has given them. There is nothing worse than a man trying to do what he is not equipped to do. The Greeks saw their gift as a gift from God. It was not something they attained by themselves. God expects his own to use the gift he's given them. His motive is not to be for personal aggrandizement. It is his duty and God-given privilege to use the gift. Then Paul lists the gifts God has given. I for one, know that I was given the gift of encouragement. I am at my best when I concentrate on using that gift. If I get down in the dumps, the one sure way for me to emerge from a state of depression is to exercise the gift of encouraging others in their walk with God. I have also the gift of giving to share what God has given me. I find great satisfaction in giving others a boost with a monetary gift. Interesting that the well never runs dry for God is debtor to no man.

The Hard Path

Reading: Luke 8

"While a large crowd was gathering and people were coming to Jesus from town after town, he told this parable:' A farmer went out to sow his seed. As he was scattering the seed, some fell along the path; it was trampled on, and the birds of the air ate it up. Some fell on rock, and when it came up, the plants withered because they had no moisture'" (Luke 8:4-6 NIV).

First let us get the scene itself clearly before us. The path, which is spoken of here, is not intended to receive seed; its function is to enable people to walk upon it. It is beaten down and quite smooth. There are even asphalted paths and there are asphalted hearts too. They are smooth and often they look quite presentable. In human intercourse they play their part. Paths and streets also have names; you must know them if you want to get somewhere. And there are a great many people whom you must know—just as you must know these streets—if you want to get somewhere. They hold key positions, they are influential, and only through them will you get somewhere. This is good and quite in order. Nobody is to blame a person for being influential. And nobody will blame a path for not being a field or for being hard. On the contrary! But that which is an advantage in one way can be a hindrance in another. The fact is that seed cannot very well take root on a much-traveled and smooth—beaten path.

"A person who is only a path through which the daily traffic passes, who is no more than a busy street where people go rushing by hour after hour and where there is never a moment of rest, will hardly provide the soil in which the eternal seed can grow. People who are always on the go are the most in danger."[21] Helmut Thielicke.

There are a lot of people on the path that is hardened. You can spot them by listening to their criticisms. They know how to run a college for example and criticize everyone who has tried his best to honor God by being involved in college administration. Generally, they are people whose pockets are lined with money and become influential in areas of which they know little. This is true of any enterprise, especially in the field of medical science. Better to listen to doctors who are trained and know what they are talking about than to listen to all other voices of those who are ignorant and know little of what they are talking about.

Hands

Reading: Acts 11

"I spread out my hands to you; my soul thirsts for you like a parched land" (Psalm 143:6 NIV).

Barnabas was a giant in the church. He took the Gospel seriously. His name means "Son of exhortation." Rich in wisdom and optimism, he inspired confidence in those near him. Paul owed Barnabas lot. One time, Saul, who later was named Paul, went to Jerusalem. The disciples did not believe Saul was a disciple. But Barnabas took Saul with him. The phrase, "Barnabas took him with him" is a verb, the same verb that Jesus used when Jesus takes Peter's hand when he is about to sink in the lake during the storm (Matthew 14:31). What compassion. Barnabas takes Saul by the hand and says: "Come with me, I'll go with you and introduce you." That was typical of Barnabas in his love for Paul.

Take my hand, O Father, and lead thou me,
Until I end my journey, and heaven see,
Alone I would but wander one single day;
Be Thou my true compassion and with me stay.
Katharina Hausmann

Chance

Reading: Psalm 141

"Sovereign LORD, you are God! Your words are trustworthy, and you have promised these good things to your servant" (2 Samuel 7:28 NIV).

During the course of years, we have often developed friendships from what appears to have been a chance meeting of two people. But we must remember that God is sovereign and with God there are no such meetings as chance, even though it may appear to be.

"Yet more astonishing is the Holy Fellowship, the Blessed Community, to those who are within it. Yet one can be surprised at being *at home*? In wonder and awe we find ourselves already interknit within unofficial groups of kindred souls. A `chance' conversation comes, and in a few moments we know that we have Community. Sometimes we are thus suddenly knit together in the bonds of love far faster than those of many years' acquaintance. In unbounded eagerness we seek for more such fellowship, and wonder at the apparent lethargy of mere members." William C. Braithwaite.

Now what do we do with those so called chance meetings with scoffers? First, we must be alert and on our guard. Then we recognize God has a purpose in our meeting. Finally, we share the truths of the Gospel of Jesus Christ with the person, love him and pray for him. "But, dear friends, remember what the apostles of our Lord Jesus Christ foretold. They said to you, 'In the last times there will be scoffers who will follow their own ungodly desires.' These are the men who divide you, who follow mere natural instincts and do not have the Spirit" (Jude 17-21 NIV).

Love Abides

Reading: Revelation 2

"Yet I hold this against you: You have forsaken your first love" (Revelation 2:4-5 NIV).

> "[Love] Puts up with anything,
> Trusts God always,

Always looks for the best,
Never looks back,
But keeps going to the end." (1 Corinthians 13. the Message)..

Love gives a stable foundation to relationships, —family and friends. For the believer, we are one in the bond of love. Wherever we are when we meet other believers there is a connection in Christ.

Soren Kierkegaard wrote: "Love abides – it never wastes away. That a certain spontaneous good nature, a certain benevolent cooperativeness and helpfulness still has time to give in affectionately waiting. We certainly appreciate with rejoicing; that it becomes weary as time stretches out or moves slowly and therefore drags – this is only too clear. Duration, duration of time is indeed the demand which brings the majority into bankruptcy. In the commercial world it is more customary for an establishment to go under because in a single stroke too great a demand is made upon it, but in the world of the spirit it is the duration which does this with so many. People have strength enough for a moment; on the long haul, however, they become insolvent. But love endures. O, what ability the poets and the orators have to characterize the changeableness of everything, to show the power of time over something which comes into time, over the wonders of the world, which in time have become almost unrecognizable ruins, over the most imperishable name, which in time ends in vagueness of legends."[22]

Love perseveres. Accept God's will and move ahead with joy trusting that God does all things well. Most of us are better starters than finishers.

Thanksgiving

Reading: Psalm 28

"Thanks be to God for His unspeakable gift" (2 Corinthians 9:15 NKJV).

Thanks for prayers that Thou has answered,
Thanks for what Thou dost deny!
Thanks for storms that I have weathered,
Thanks for all Thou dost supply!
Thanks for pain and thanks for pleasure,
Thanks for comfort in despair!
Thanks for grace that none can measure,
Thanks for love beyond compare.
August Ludwig Storm

"Open for me the gates of righteousness; I will enter and give thanks to the LORD. This is the gate of the LORD through which the righteous may enter. I will give you thanks, for you answered me; you have become my salvation" (Psalm 118:19-21 NIV).

Thanksgiving is a special day set aside in our American tradition for which I am grateful. It's family time for us as we gather from all parts of the world to celebrate God's goodness. We traditionally roast a big turkey, throw in a batch of homemade dressing and smother it with turkey gravy. On the side, I will bake up a big helping of Oyster Dressing. There is whole cranberry sauce, mashed potatoes and a vegetable. Condiments adorn the table as well as generous glasses filled with Sparkling Grape Juice. To top it off we will drink coffee while we devour a homemade pumpkin pie. Afterward, we relax and watch the Chicago Bears football game or the Detroit Lions. Conversation takes us into the night celebrating God's goodness to us this year and the years gone by. The next morning, the fellows will go out to breakfast, read the newspapers and continue the man talk. The women will rest after a hard day's work.

It's only once a year that we do this, and we make a special effort to show ourselves available to appreciate family and especially to express our thanks for God's goodness.

Character

Reading: Acts 17:10-12

"We also rejoice in our sufferings, because we know that suffering produces perseverance; perseverance, character; and character, hope. And hope does not disappoint us, because God has poured out his love into our hearts by the Holy Spirit, whom he has given us" (Romans 5:3-6 NIV).

"Do not be misled: Bad company corrupts good character." (1 Corinthians 15:33 NIV)

"Nothing astonishes men so much as common sense and plain dealing"**.** Ralph Waldo Emerson.

What is character? It is moral or ethical strength. A description of a person's attributes, traits, or abilities. We use an idiom: someone in character, meaning consistent with behavior: that was totally in character. Or out of character: Inconsistent with someone's general character or behavior: We have heard someone say, "a response so much out of character that it amazed me."

F. Scott Fitgerald wrote: "No such thing as a man willing to be honest—that would be like a blind man willing to see."

What does our character reveal about us?

Inadequacies

Reading: Romans 7

"We know that the law is spiritual; but I am unspiritual, sold as a slave to sin. I do not understand what I do. For what I want to do I do not do, but what I hate I do. And if I do what I do not want to do, I agree that the law is good. As it is, it is no longer I myself who do it, but it is sin living in me. I know that nothing good lives in me, that is, in my sinful nature. For I have the desire to do what is good, but I cannot carry it out. For what I do is not the good I want to do; no, the evil I do not want to do-this I keep on doing. Now if I do what I do not want to do, it is no longer I who do it, but it is sin living in me that does it. So I find this law at work: When I want to do good, evil is right there with me. For in my inner being I delight in God's law; but I see another law at work in the members of my body, waging war against the law of my mind and making me a prisoner of the law of sin at work within my members. What a wretched man I am! Who will rescue me from this body of death? Thanks be to God-through Jesus Christ our Lord!" (Romans 7:14-25 NIV).

Despite our position in the body of Christ we all have to deal with inadequacies in our walk with the Lord. Ovid, the Roman poet, had penned the famous tag: "I see the better things, and I approve them, but I follow the worse."

This testimony of Paul's demonstrates the inadequacy of human knowledge. A good man is not made by knowledge itself. Try playing golf if you doubt it. Knowing how it should be played does not mean we are able to play it. Paul's testimony also demonstrates the inadequacy of human resolution. Resolving to do something and doing it are two different aspects of our condition. Furthermore, Paul's testimony demonstrated the inadequacy of diagnosis. Like a doctor capable of diagnosing a disease but who is quite powerless to prescribe a cure.

Cleavage Between God And The World

Reading: 1 John 4

"You, dear children, are from God and have overcome them, because the one who is in you is greater than the one who is in the world. They are from the world and therefore speak from the viewpoint of the world, and the world listens to them. We are from God, and whoever knows God listens to us; but whoever is not from God does not listen to us. This is how we recognize the Spirit of truth and the spirit of falsehood" (1 John 4:4-6 NIV).

The world rejects the truth. How can a man understand when his watchword is competition? How can a man understand a life lived for living is love, when he is consumed by self-exaltation? How can a man understand that living is in the light of eternity when he thinks material things are the only thing that matters? A man can hear what he is fitted to hear and can unfit himself to hear the message of truth? Some men's source and origin is the world and they are incapable of hearing the truth.

On the other side is the man whose origin is God and he hears the truth. He sees there is no limit to the grace of God. He knows that the love of God can break apart every barrier. He believes Christ is knocking at the door of every heart and that the voice of God can be heard above all other voices.

Not Good Men; Sinners

Reading: Romans 5

"For Christ died for sins once for all, the righteous for the unrighteous, to bring you to God" (1 Peter 3:18 NIV).

Jasmin killed a Turkish tax collector and fled to the desert. Someone said: "Look, Jasmin's camel has no rider." "Someone has shot him on the march", said another. Someone else said: "He is not strong in the head, perhaps he is lost in mirage perhaps he has fainted and fallen off his camel. What does it matter? He's not worth half a crown."

The Arabs rode on, but Lawrence turned around and rode back. At the risk of his life, he braved the desert heat to find Jasmin, blind and mad with thirst. Lawrence gave him his last drops of water and lifted Jasmin to his camel to take him back to his company. The Arabs looked on in amazement. "Here is Jasmin," they said, "saved at his own risk by Lawrence our Lord." Looked upon as a parable, it was not good men Christ died to save; it was sinners. It wasn't God's friends Christ died to rescue; it was men who were at enmity with God.[23] William Barclay.

"For if, when we were God's enemies, we were reconciled to him through the death of his Son, how much more, having been reconciled, shall we be saved through his life!" (Romans 5:10 NIV).

How great is the grace of God that he should save such as us.

Seeing Ourselves

Reading: Psalm 104

"May the words of my mouth and the meditation of my heart be pleasing in your sight, O LORD, my Rock and my Redeemer" *(Psalm 19:14 NIV).*

Helmut Thielicke makes an important point about reading the Bible. "A landscape painter moves about from one spot to another until he discovers the right perspective for his picture. There is no value in his pedaling through the high country until he spies the outline of a snow-capped peak between two treetops and then says, `This is the Santis,' and immediately dismounts and sets up his easel. No. From this point the outline of the Santis is so undefined that it might just as well be some other mountain. The artist must rather search for a long time until he has found the spot from which he can see all the characteristic features of this mountain. This is the only way it will be recognized and the only way to avoid the danger of people's saying that his picture is an imaginary landscape or confusing the painted Santis with some other mountain."[24]

So we too must search for the right vantage point from which we see the Lord rightly and without distortion, and not in such a way that he can be confused with all kinds of other people, heroes, moral teachers, or founders of religions. Now, the best thing to do is always to take up your position from the Scriptures at exactly the same spot where one of the persons who meet Him or appear in the parables stands; to stand, for example, where John is in prison, addressing the doubting questions to Him, or the Canaanite woman, who desires nothing of him but the crumbs that fall from the Lord's table, or the rich young ruler, who will not forsake the god of Mammon and so goes away unblessed.

When we observe these people we make a remarkable discovery: and suddenly see ourselves and find a ground plan for our own life. Obviously, this exercise takes time for contemplation and meditation. It's not a five minute exercise while reading on the fly at the beginning of a day.

Returning Home

Reading: Luke 15

"I'm going back to my father. I'll say to him, `Father, I've sinned against God, I've sinned before you, I don't deserve to be called your son. Take me on as a hired hand.' He got right up and went home to his father" (Luke 15:18-20 The Message).

Helmut Thielicke writes: "And now the son arises and goes home. In all his rags he dares to approach the father's house. How will the father receive him? But, more important, what will he himself say when suddenly he is there before the father again? Will he say, `Father, I grew up more mature in the far country. Father, I've grown up, I have suffered and atoned for all my sins; I have a claim on your acceptance. I accepted the risk of life and in good and evil I have been a man. Now you must take me in; I'm at the end of my resources!` Is this the way the lost son will speak when he meets his father?

"Andre' Gide, the French writer (along with many other thinkers), takes this point of view. He invents another ending to the parable and has returned prodigal sending his brother out into the far country so that he, too, can `grow up' and mature. What Gide is really saying is that it was good for the lost son to be lost for a while. It was good for him to sin. After all, a person has to go though this kind of thing. And one must have the courage to renounce God in order that one may be accepted by him afterward. The son has simply experienced to the full the fruitful polarity of life.

"But Jesus' parable says nothing about all this. The son who came home says only, `Father, I have sinned against heaven and before you.' What he is saying is, `Father, I have no claim on you whatsoever.'" Helmut Thielicke

The French writer's example of twisting Scriptures is what gets us into trouble. The Scripture ends up meaning nothing more than man's fanciful and erroneous thinking. What the son did in returning home was not easy, but more than that, to repent of his sin and take responsibility for it is refreshing in a day when we love playing the victim (The Devil made me do it).

Good Books

Reading: Ecclesiastes 12

"Of making many books there is no end, and much study wearies the body. Now all has been heard; here is the conclusion of the matter: Fear God and keep his commandments, for this is the whole [duty] of man. For God will bring every deed into judgment, including every hidden thing, whether it is good or evil" (Ecclesiastes12:12-14 NIV).

Philip Yancey has observed as he has looked at people's Bibles that there is a band of white on the paper edges just over the halfway mark. He reasons that it is because there are seventeen books of the Old Testament, the Prophetic books, which tend to go unread. Some people seem to think the prophets,—Isaiah, Jeremiah, and Ezekiel— may be considered manic, depressive and psychotic in their explanations of the prophets message. He has a point.

But the seventeen books of prophecy help us know what God is like—His anger, His justice, and sometimes His silence. Many questions the prophets ask are our questions. I recommend that this is a book you ought to buy and read along with your Bible over and over again until the prophets make sense is *The Bible Jesus Read,* by Philip Yancey, published

1999 by Zondervan Publishing House. Try it; you'll not regret the outlay of money.

The Regions Beyond

Reading: Matthew 28

"so that we can preach the gospel in the regions beyond you. For we do not want to boast about work already done in another man's territory, but, 'Let him who boasts boast in the Lord.' For it is not the one who commends himself who is approved, but the one whom the Lord commends". (2 Corinthians 10:16-18 NIV).

Larry Armstrong, veteran missionary of more than 40 years, has a heartbeat for the regions beyond, unlike most people I know. Now a missionary at large, Larry awaits the sound of the alarm to go to any part of the world that needs help, whether it be Bosnia, Mongolia, Italy, Nepal or Bangkok. He never sees a stray book but that he sends it to a third world country to aid pastors. He will take a worn out computer, have it rehabbed and ship it to a missionary pastor. You will recognize him disguised in a Francis Schaffer goatee and clothes garnered out of the missionary closet of some church. His heartbeat, along with his wife Jacqui form a team. All they need is a bed to sleep in to get them to go to the world that needs Christ. They are truly dedicated to the regions beyond.

I'm reminded of Rudyard Kipling's poem, "*The Explorer.*"

"'There's no sense in going further – it's the edge of cultivation,'
So they said, and I believed it – broke my land and sowed my crop –

Built my barns and strung my fences in the little border station
Tucked away below the foothills where the trails run out and stop.

"Till a voice, as bad as Conscience, rang interminable changes
On one everlasting Whisper, day and night repeated – so:
`Something hidden. Go and find it. Go and look behind the ranges –
Something lost behind the ranges. Lost and waiting for you. Go!"

Little People

Reading: 1 Chronicles 23

*"The duty of the Levites was to help Aaron's descendants in the service of the temple of the Lord; to be in charge of the courtyards, the side rooms, the purification of all sacred things and the performance of other duties at the house of God" (*1Chronicles 23:28 NIV).

God never overlooked the importance of little people and thanked them for their diligent service; neither should we. Little people lack position and status; they are unpretentious, modest, helping the cause in their own small way. When they walk into a room, someone may ask: "Who is he?" They may not be loud and forceful. Yet they are indispensable to the cause of Christ. They often go unnamed in the credits. The little people never are invited to sit at the head table, nor deliver a speech even though they have something to say. It's the little people who know what's going on behind the scenes that make the wheel turn. "There is a small boy here with five loaves and two fishes." John 6:9.

They are the first to suggest how to improve what is going on. God looks out for them "Do not be afraid, O worm Jacob, O little Israel, for I myself will help you," declares the LORD, your Redeemer, the Holy One of Israel"(Isaiah 41:14 NIV)..

See how God honored and cared for little children. "Then little children were brought to Jesus for him to place his hands on them and pray for them. But the disciples rebuked those who brought them. (Matthew" 19:13 NIV). Like the disciples, we often neglect them.

In the harvest field now ripened,
There's a work for all to do;
Hark, the voice of God is calling,
To the harvest calling you.
Little is much when God is in it,
Labor not for wealth or fame;
There's a crown and you can win it,
If you go in Jesus' name.
Mrs. F. W. Suffield

Love and Confidence

Reading: Exodus 15

"In your unfailing love you will lead the people you have redeemed" (Exodus 15:13 NIV).

Many Christians suffer from lack of confidence and thereby think there is no other recourse but to live life as such. What they fail to recognize is that within each person God has made provision for them to love others. Loving another helps them to be confident. It's not necessary to live life a cripple because of a lack of confidence.

Soren Kierkegaard addresses this issue:

"When we say, `Love makes for confidence,' we thereby say that the lover by his own makes others confident; wherever love is, confidence propagated; people readily approach the lover, for he casts out fear. Whereas the mistrustful person scares everyone away; whereas the sly and cunning disseminate anxiety and painful unrest around them; whereas the presence of the domineering oppresses like the heavy pressure of sultry air—love makes for confidence." [25]

Overcomers

Reading: Romans 5

"Therefore, since we have been justified through faith, we have peace with God through our Lord Jesus Christ, through whom we have gained access by faith into this grace in which we now stand. And we rejoice in the hope of the glory of God. Not only so, but we also rejoice in our sufferings, because we know that suffering produces perseverance; perseverance, character; and character, hope. And hope does not disappoint us, because God has poured out his love into our hearts by the Holy Spirit, whom he has given us" (Romans 5:1-5 NIV).

Philip Hensley was asked by someone: "Sorrow fairly colors life, doesn't it?" Hensley consented that it does but insisted that he chose the color. He was in seminary in Edinburgh at the time recovering from leg amputation. The other leg might also be taken off. During this time Hensley wrote: I*nvictus.*

Out of the night that covers me,
Black as the Pit from pole to pole,

I thank whatever gods may be
For my unconquerable soul.

That is the spirit that doesn't lie down and let happen that which will happen; but the spirit that meets things face to face and overcomes them. This is fortitude; fortitude produces character. The word for character is used for metal that has passed through the fire. Character produces hope.

Lord Reith wrote: "I do not like the crisis, but I do like the opportunities they provide." Only God can give the hope that turns dust and ashes into the love of God. Sterling metal, if you will.

Dew

Reading: Job 38

"Does the rain have a father? Who fathers the drops of dew?" (Job 38:28 NIV).

"Sweet day, so cool, so calm, so bright, The bridal of the earth and sky, The dew shall weep thy fall tonight; For thou must die." George Herbert.

"Total annual dew precipitation ranges from about .5 inches in cold climates to about 3 inches in semi-humid, warm climates. In Israel and parts of Australia, sufficient dew can be trapped for use in irrigation. Wherever it appears, we marvel at the beauty these little droplets of water can lend to an otherwise remarkable landscape"[26] (from *How Majestic is Thy Name*).

"It is as if the dew of Hermon were falling on Mount Zion. For there the LORD bestows his blessing, even life forevermore" (Psalm 133:3 NIV).

How refreshing to the land is the morning dew. God completed every detail in creation in order that we might enjoy the earth.

Paul, the Leader

Reading: Romans 1

"First, I thank my God through Jesus Christ for all of you, because your faith is being reported all over the world. God, whom I serve with my whole heart in preaching the gospel of his Son, is my witness how constantly I remember you in my prayers at all times; and I pray that now at last by God's will the way may be opened for me to come to you. I long to see you so that I may impart to you some spiritual gift to make you strong; that is, that you and I may be mutually encouraged by each other's faith. I do not want you to be unaware, brothers, that I planned many times to come to you (but have been prevented from doing so until now) in order that I might have a harvest among you, just as I have had among the other Gentiles. I am obligated both to Greeks and non-Greeks, both to the wise and the foolish. That is why I am so eager to preach the gospel also to you who are at Rome" (Romans 1:8-15 NIV).

The Apostle Paul had never been to Rome. He was not involved in the founding of the church there. He knew the Romans would be suspicious of his leadership. He was challenged not to interfere where he had no right to intervene. So he had to get alongside the Romans in order for that strangeness and suspicion to be broken down. This required of Paul the use of emotional intelligence. Some call it "temperament;" Max Weber labeled it the "taming of the soul." It was the handling of his emotions and his relationships with the Romans. This is a display of excellent leadership on Paul's part.

Great leaders are distinguished from average ones by this capacity to understand the importance of emotional intelligence. Paul understood the Romans because he understood their emotions. As Paul "Bear" Bryant, great football coach at Alabama said: "I know my players better than they know themselves."

Our Western culture glories in the traditional cognitive skills putting a premium of IQ. Do you think IQ is more important than emotional Intelligence? Why do you believe such? Paul demonstrated in his approach to win the Romans over that he engaged their emotional intelligence.

Limits

Reading: Joshua 15

"It was you who set all the boundaries of the earth; you made both summer and winter" (Psalm 74:17 NIV).

"Artists learn to love limits: a poet respects the fourteen-line limit on the sonnet as a form of freedom; a painter respects the limiting frame of the canvas as a check on endless subjectivism and so a freedom to deal with *this* piece of reality; a performing musician respects the limitations of the score as freedom to participate in another and usually larger world of music; a composing musician respects the limits of a key signature in order to be free to explore *that* tonality without interference from all the others.

"And all men and women learn to respect their deaths, both their own and others', as limits, the boundaries of the human. It's *within* these boundaries, not by transgressing them, that we become human." Philip Yancey.

We are indebted to those who reached to the boundaries, else we would not have the Micro Wave that many of us use so much for cooking; the use of the modern airplane;

clothing that is comfortable; automobiles that enable us to get around more quickly; and a host of other inventions we all enjoy having.

Spiritually, there are many who never develop the gifts God has given them because of fear of failure. Some folks right out of the chute miss the blessing of using their gifts and fail to realize that they will never know what they can accomplish, for they think they can never do whatever they are asked to do when it falls within the scope of God's enablement. Other folks think they have a certain gift but fail to realize that even after years of practice they are boring people to death.

Splits

Reading: John 4:1-26

"God is spirit, and his worshipers must worship in spirit and in truth" (John 4:24 NIV).

Baptists are known for their splits. Oh we don't like to talk about it. But we will split a church over the drop of a hat. Sometimes it is because of doctrine or Theology, but usually we dress up the wording disguising that it is in fact, a split. Most of the time it is over personality conflicts. Some pastors are like lawyers chasing the fire engine on its way to a fire; they chase church splits and make a living as Senior Pastor of splits. They make a lifetime of it. Now we are into splitting over worship forms. "We need to rewrite `neither Jew nor Greek' to say `neither Boomer nor youngster, neither lover of hymns nor lover of jazz, neither guitarist nor organist.'" Marva Dawn.

It's too much a stretch to think we can worship as we once did. Granted I am tough on the Baptists here; it's because I am more familiar with them.

How refreshing it is to worship the Lord in peace and not have to contend with the swirling winds of controversy, swords and daggers.

The Other Brother

Reading: Luke 15

"Meanwhile, the older son was in the field. When he came near the house, he heard music and dancing. So he called one of the servants and asked him what was going on. 'Your brother has come,' he replied, 'and your father has killed the fattened calf because he has him back safe and sound.' The older brother became angry and refused to go in. So his father went out and pleaded with him. But he answered his father, 'Look! All these years I've been slaving for you and never disobeyed your orders. Yet you never gave me even a young goat so I could celebrate with my friends. But when this son of yours who has squandered your property with prostitutes comes home, you kill the fattened calf for him!'
'My son,' the father said, 'you are always with me, and everything I have is yours. But we had to celebrate and be glad, because this brother of yours was dead and is alive again; he was lost and is found.'"(Luke 15:25-32 NIV).

"The second part of the parable, on the other hand, in which the elder brother has the center of the stage, seems by contrast to be a bit dull and humdrum. The story actually has no proper ending at all. It seems—first reading at least to run somewhat forlornly and endlessly.

"The man who occupies the center here does not live `dangerously.' Nor does he get what Sartre calls `dirty hands.' When a man is good and remains faithful to the father he has played it safe.

"Undoubtedly, there are many people today, young and old, who live their lives quite differently from the elder brother and therefore would much more readily recognize themselves in the image of the younger brother. Perhaps they have no time, or in any case think they have no time to devote to the ultimate things of our life. Each day they ride the carrousel of their round of business, disposing of this and calculating that. And when evening comes they hardly know where there heads are. And therefore, they do not know where God is either; for to know this, one must have some time to spare for him."[27] Helmut Thielicke

The reason we have so much easy believeism in evangelism today in the Western world is that people want to take on Jesus as it were, along with all the other baggage they carry about and take no time to contemplate who God is and what it means to follow Him.

Lessons from History

Reading: Jude 11

"They've gone down Cain's road. They've been sucked into Balaam's error by greed; they're cancelled out in Korah's rebellion. These people are warts on your love feasts as you worship and eat together. They're giving you a black eye – carousing shamelessly, grabbing anything that isn't nailed down" (Jude 11,12 The Message).

To ignore history is to ignore the lessons of life. Balaam taught Israel to sin. Balaam is remembered for two things. He is a picture consumed with covetousness, prepared to sin for what there is in it for him. He also is a picture of the evil man, guilty of teaching others to sin. To sin is bad enough; Balaam robbed someone else of their innocence when he taught them to sin.

George Walden wrote: "A country losing touch with its own history is like an old man losing his glasses, a distressing sight, at once vulnerable, unsure, and easily disoriented."

Every time we ignore history, the price goes up for as Henry Miller observed, "All history is the record of man's single failure to thwart his destiny—the record, in other words, of the few men of destiny who, through the recognition of their symbolic role, made history.

We ought to learn from history how to live better. From the history in scriptures we should learn to serve the Lord better.

The Far Country

Reading: Luke 15

"I will set out and go back to my father and say to him: 'Father, I have sinned against heaven and against you. I am no longer worthy to be called your son; make me like one of your hired men.' So he got up and went to his father" (Luke 15:18-20 NIV).

So the son wants to go back home. He is so desperate to have a place again in his father's house, that he is willing to take the place of a hired servant. He plans to make this his plea to his father. The hired servant was the lowest of the slaves. Because he was hired he could be dismissed at a day's notice. He was not one of the family at all. The son has learned the hard way that the way of sin leaves him destitute.

The prodigal son does not act like he is home. He honestly despairs when he speaks of being in the far country. If he could only know that the Father is waiting for him and lovingly wants him back.

"Every age has is own peculiar `far country,' and so has ours." Helmut Thielicke

We have the far country in our Western world, as seen by the squandering of inheritances, profligate, dysfunctional families and suit happy in order to bleed others of their money.

Uncertainty

Reading: Matthew 11

"Vindicate me, O LORD, for I have led a blameless life; I have trusted in the LORD without wavering. Test me, O LORD, and try me, examine my heart and my mind; for your love is ever before me, and I walk continually in your truth" (Psalm 26:1-3 NIV).

"But when he asks, he must believe and not doubt, because he who doubts is like a wave of the sea, blown and tossed by the wind. That man should not think he will receive anything from the Lord; he is a double-minded man, unstable in all he does" (James 1:6-8 NIV).

As we get older some Christians become more certain of their eternal destiny, while others waver. It is a human condition for as Ernest Hemingway wrote "Hesitation increases in relation to risk in equal proportion to age." That is why we must anchor our thoughts in the Word of God and trust Him for our salvation, believing and accepting Jesus as our Savior, knowing in him we have a sure foundation. The hymn writer had it right: "I've Anchored My Soul in The Haven of Rest."

Shame

Reading: 1 Peter 2

"My head is high, God, held high; I'm looking to you, God; No hangdog skulking for me. I've thrown in my lot with you; You won't embarrass me, will you? Or let my enemies get the best of me?" (Psalm 25:1,2 The Message).

Shame is a painful emotion caused by a strong sense of guilt, embarrassment, unworthiness, or disgrace. We sometimes question the capacity for such a feeling: *Have you no shame?* We define shame as one that brings dishonor, disgrace, or condemnation.

Bernard Mandeville wrote: "Ashamed of the many frailties they feel within, all men endeavor to hide themselves, their ugly nakedness, from each other, and wrapping up the true motives of their hearts in the specious cloak of sociableness, and their concern for the public good, they are in hopes of concealing their filthy appetites and the deformity of their desires."

"The basis of shame is not some personal mistake of ours, but the ignominy, the humiliation we feel that we must be what we are without any choice in the matter, and that this humiliation is seen by everyone". Milan Kundera

We've lost our sense of shame in our culture. Parents erasing the notion that there is such a matter as shame who will go "to the wall" to defend the wrongdoing of their offspring; criminals who see nothing to be ashamed over while they bilk the public of heir hard earned dollar; Christians who are ashamed of the Cross of Jesus.

"Am I a soldier of the cross, a follower of the Lamb?

And shall I fear to own His cause or blush to speak his name?"

Isaac Watts

For in Scripture it says: "See, I lay a stone in Zion, a chosen and precious cornerstone, and the one who trusts in him will never be put to shame. Now to you who believe, this stone is precious. But to those who do not believe, 'The stone the builders rejected has become the capstone'" (1 Peter 2:6,7 NIV).

Technique

Reading: Ephesians 6:11- 5

"...and with your feet fitted with the readiness that comes from the gospel of peace" (Ephesians 6:15 NIV).

Years ago pastors used to vie for who could grow the fastest growing and biggest VBS in the country. Never mind the promotional tools. It fostered greed; championed "consumerism, offering a bicycle as the prize for bringing the most children with them to VBS. Follow up be hanged afterward. A dangerous method. It pulled children away from other Sunday Schools and denied the opportunity to practice honest evangelism, witness and hospitality. We must admit that it is engaging in diabolical methods. Gimmicks were used to raise money. Jacques Ellul designated such measures "Technique." We used "Pony Express riders", carrying saddlebags to collect pledges to finance our "Technique." Marketing became the watchword. We forgot Paul's admonition:

"Put on the full armor of God so that you can take your stand against the devil's schemes. For our struggle is not against flesh and blood, but against the rulers, against the authorities, against the powers of this dark world and against the spiritual forces of evil in the heavenly realms. Therefore put on the full armor of God, so that when the day of evil comes, you may be able to stand your ground, and after you have done everything, to stand. Stand firm then, with the belt of truth buckled around your waist, with the breastplate of righteousness in place" (Ephesians 6:11-14 NIV)

Understanding God

Reading: Acts 1

"He said to them: 'It is not for you to know the times or dates the Father has set by his own authority. But you will receive power when the Holy Spirit comes on you; and you will be my witnesses in Jerusalem, and in all Judea and Samaria, and to the ends of the earth'" (Acts 1:7,8 NIV).

What can we know about the nature and being of God? "The God that can be fully understood is not really God." Hudson T. Armerding. "For my thoughts are not your thoughts, neither are your ways my ways, declares the Lord. As the heavens are higher that the earth, so are my ways higher than your ways and my thoughts than your thoughts" (Isaiah 55:8,9 NIV).

Do words mean anything? An example: The billboard message says, "Thou shalt not steal?" "What is it you don't understand?" God makes many things plain to us in His Word. It is not the things we don't understand that causes trouble; it is the things we do understand and don't believe. Yet we see all about us Christians who are bent on knowing everything God knows.

We don't live in a perfect world nor do we live in a black and white mode. You can't make God explain all there is to his grace or sovereignty. To see everything black and white when we sin misses what God may do in bringing repentance in His time, not necessarily ours. It is vain to try to understand everything about God. We must keep in mind to let God be God while we practice those things we do understand.

Useless Discussion

Reading: Titus 3

"Avoid a contentious and opinionative man, after giving him a first and a second warning, for you must be well aware that such a man is perverted and stands a self-condemned sinner" (Titus 3:9-11 The Message).

One day I approached a businessman about whether he would be interested in a Bible study. I suggested meeting in a hotel which was a neutral place. He responded enthusiastically although he was not a churchman. He gave me a $100 bill with a promise for more when needed to cover the breakfast meetings. Six other businessmen agreed to attend. On the first morning, it became apparent that the fellow who funded the effort was not interested in learning about Jesus and the Bible; all he was interested in was to argue why the Bible wasn't true and why the passage didn't say what it said. He was a gentleman but carried on his monologue no end. I sensed the other men were shocked and disappointed. Afterward I spoke with my friend about how his arguments were not well conceived, neither were they received by the other men. We met a second time and it was more of the same. Again, I pointed out to my friend that unless he was willing to honestly look at the Scriptures with an interest in learning about Jesus, this study would not meet again. We didn't meet again as it turned out. Of course I felt badly about it, but my attempt to practice good deeds fell flat on that occasion. I did everything I knew to stand in front of the men with the claims of Christ, but it was not received because of the useless discussions my friend engaged in.

Those circumstances I find rare, but they do happen. There comes a time when in such a meeting, one must decide which hill he wants to do battle over. Even though we parted that second day, we remained good friends, and I hoped for another day to reach out to the unsaved.

Worship

Reading: Ecclesiastes 3

"Woe to those who go to great depths to hide their plans from the LORD, who do their work in darkness and think, 'Who sees us? Who will know?' You turn things upside down, as if the potter were thought to be like the clay!. Shall what is formed say to him who formed it, 'He did not make me'? Can the pot say of the potter, 'He knows nothing'?" (Isaiah 29:15-16 NIV).

Real worship of the Lord is accomplished when we guard our step, go near to listen, are not quick with our mouth, neither hasty in heart, and keep our vows. Our mouth leads us into sin. Why did Israel need to worship God? Had they not, they would have turned to idol worship which is what they often did. The heart is deceitful; we are not strong enough to fight the desperate depths of sin that lead to idol worship.

"Do not worship any other god, for the LORD, whose name is Jealous, is a jealous God." (Exodus 34:14 NIV). Jealousy is a neutral word and can be good or bad jealousy depending on the context in which the word is used. Jealousy means: a feeling of intolerance toward a rival. The fact that our God is a jealous God is an indication that he will not tolerate a rival. Israel got into trouble by allowing other gods to rival God. That, God will not tolerate.

Visualize This

Reading: Luke 15

"The older brother became angry and refused to go in. So his father went out and pleaded with him. But he answered his father, 'Look! All these years I've been slaving for you and never disobeyed your orders. Yet you never gave me even a young goat so I could celebrate with my friends. But when this son of yours who has squandered your property with prostitutes comes home, you kill the fattened calf for him!' "My son,' the father said, 'you are always with me, and everything I have is yours. But we had to celebrate and be glad, because this brother of yours was dead and is alive again; he was lost and is found'" (Luke 15:28-31 NIV).

Just visualize this situation. This elder brother has lived from his childhood and every day since, from morning till night in the atmosphere and protection of his father's house. Naturally he *loves* the father and his environment. But the fact that he loves his father and is loved in return is so taken for granted, that he is hardly conscious of it, neither does anyone speak about it. To him it would have seemed ridiculous to go up to his father and say, `Father, today I love you quite specially.' We do not reflect upon what is normal, and near as the air we breathe. Nor do we give thanks for it. It is the same way with so many married couples. They are accustomed to each other. It would not occur to them to express in words what they mean to each other. Each is hardly aware of what the other means until he or she has gone on a journey or one is left forlorn at an open grave. Something like this is the elder son's relationship to his father.

"Is not the Christianity of many people very much like this relationship? From childhood on they have heard that there is a `loving God.'"[28] Helmut Thielicke.

When last did you express to your spouse that you love him or her? Your God, when last have you told him how much you love him?

Sitting Up Straight

Reading: Job 4

"A spirit glided past my face, and the hair on my body stood on end" (Job 4:15 NIV).

When I was 7 years old, we couldn't afford a barber so my Mom let a friend come in to cut my hair. He was ancient and knew nothing about barbering, but he owned a pair of hand shears that were as old as he. He'd take me to the basement of our home and place me on a chair under a basement window sized one foot by two so as to shed some light on the shearing. The window was dirty with coal dust. Between the shady window and this old man's failing eyesight, he went to work on my head. He was shaky to boot. The results of his barbering were disastrous. Especially when he ran the clipper up from the bottom of my head toward the crown. The clipper was balky and it caught me where the hair was short. Wow! Did it hurt.

After a while I garnered a little money and went down to Alessandro, the corner barber. "Give me a butch haircut." He said, "Does your mother know you want a butch?" "My mother knows nothing about it, just give me a butch." So he did, and I paid for a good ragging in my ear from my dear mother who thought I was going to the dogs.

I learned two things from that experience. One, never scrimp on paying a barber to get a real haircut; two, sit up straight for one never knows when the clipper may pull where the hair is short. Two lessons worth the price. Fortunately, the old man never quit his day job. Since then, I always sit up straight when I am getting a haircut.

One should always sit up straight when God's clippers are at work. You never want to miss the lessons learned where the hair is short. "Does not the very nature of things teach you that if a man has long hair, it is a disgrace to him" (1 Corinthians 11:13-14 NIV).

Winter Kill

Reading: 1 Corinthians 4

"If a man dies, will he live again? All the days of my hard service I will wait for my renewal to come. You will call and I will answer you; you will long for the creature your hands have made" (Job 14:14-15 NIV).

"A medical doctor once refused to give a bed-ridden college professor patient of his a most helpful book, saying it would serve no purpose, because he would only tear it to pieces with his critically poised mind.

"For every plant there is a degree of frost beyond which it will winter-kill, and the tender plant of vocal ministry is no exception. It is when the worshipping group is open and loving, it is when it is abandoned to the inner exercise that may take place in it, when there is a movement at its heart expressed Guy Butler's lines, `We wait, we wait, we wait,' that becomes possible for one member to arise and express the very moving which half dozen others my have felt, albeit not in their own words. In such an atmosphere when ministry is brief and does not try to exhaust the insight, others may rise and add to it until something grows that no single speaker could have presented, and the meeting closes with a feeling of blessing and unity." Douglas Steere.

We are a lot like Margaret Thatcher who wrote: "I am extraordinarily patient provided I get my own way in the end."

We have a difficult time waiting forty seconds for the traffic to turn green so we can hurry to the next light. We switch check-out lanes at the super-market only to wait. We have developed a `road rage' mentality if someone passes us at an inopportune time. We think bad things when we are put on voice mail, but the recorder voices run us through high jinks before we can talk to the person we called. We want our pay raise now not later. We think ill thoughts of a doctor who schedules surgery a week later. Let's face it. We are not trained to wait. "Be still before the LORD and wait patiently for him; do not fret when men succeed in their ways, when they carry out their wicked schemes" (Psalm 37:7 NIV).

What We Think of Ourselves

Reading: Psalm 144

"For by the grace given me I say to every one of you: Do not think of yourself more highly than you ought, but rather think of yourself with sober judgment, in accordance with the measure of faith God has given you" (Romans 12:3 NIV).

Society has put a false face on what man thinks of himself. Today in the sexual context in which we live, men are judged by many as truly men by all the women they have conquered. Wealth has also been a false measure of a man's estimation of who he truly is. Status is an example.

"The question that always interested me most was whether and to what extent a whole new understanding of life comes to expression in the Christian faith. For me the leitmotiv became Luther's dictum, *Presona facit opera,*"'It is the person that performs the works.' In everything that man thinks, wills, and does, no matter in what province of his life, he is realizing himself. I was never interested in political, economic, and cultural programs and performances as such; but I have been extremely concerned with the question of what the person looks like in all these areas. I cannot even see a movie or watch a tightrope dancer without asking myself what this person, who is here manifesting himself, really thinks of himself, and to what extent therefore all these things are fragments of a great confession. Correspondingly, I have been interested in the theological question of what takes place in a man, and naturally also in the forms in which he expresses himself, when he finds God and so finds himself. For one thing I was always sure, that when a man seeks himself, he fails to find himself, and that he gains and realizes himself only when he loses his life in God." (J. W. D.; translator of Helmut Thielicke's *The Waiting Father.)*

The Hurry Up Sickness

Exodus 14

"Be still, and know that I am God; I will be exalted among the nations" (Psalm 46:10 NIV).

Archibald Hart, clinical psychologist wrote: "I grew up in Southern Africa and know something of life in a more primitive culture. African culture has always fascinated me because, in many respects, it has taught me a number of important lessons about my preoccupation with time. It has helped me, for instance, to put my Western culture in proper perspective and has pointed the way to a more balanced life."

I have been in few third world countries myself and can attest to Hart's testimony. Church services begin when they begin. Clocks are non existent. The service lasts for hours crammed with long sermons, and sometimes they run another speaker in and let him preach when one drops by the wayside. The hurry up sickness has been an integral part of my ministry. Of late – perhaps – too late, I have been forced to slow down. It had been my custom to divide my days into fifteen minute segments and then race to see how much I could pack in a day. Of course it took its toll on my adrenalin and stress system in my body. Now I am fortunate, because of ill health brought on by stress, I have slowed down. I had never heard anything about a type A personality until I was hit by a heart attack, and it's been downhill now for twenty years.

Don't misunderstand what I am saying though, because all of the past twenty years has had its blessings, and God has shown me lessons about life. I may not have learned any other way. Even though I don't feel well (all of the time), I begin each morning choosing to be happy and thankful to God for his blessings.

Villainy

Reading Romans 1

"Furthermore, since they did not think it worthwhile to retain the knowledge of God, he gave them over to a depraved mind, to do what ought not to be done. They have become filled with every kind of wickedness, evil, greed and depravity. They are full of envy, murder, strife, deceit and malice. They are gossips, slanderers, God-haters, insolent, arrogant and boastful; they invent ways of doing evil; they disobey their parents; they are senseless, faithless, heartless, ruthless. Although they know God's righteous decree that those who do such things deserve death, they not only continue to do these very things but also approve of those who practice them" (Romans 1:28-32 NIV).

Villainy is worse than badness; which hurts only the person concerned. It is thoughtlessly cruel activity in order to do someone harm. It is not always deliberate, but pursues its own interest. A woman of ill repute deliberately seduces the innocent. The man who is this bad wants to make everybody as bad as he is. It is destructive and involves the curse of wanting to have more. It is an aggressive vice in order to bring someone down to his level. It is vicious, deceitful and comes from the heart filled with jealousy. Villainy hates God because he knows he is defying God. It is indolent, arrogant and filled with bragging about it. It is disobedient to parents, senseless and without natural affection.

Only God can measure up to change a villainous heart. He can make a new creature out of a sinful man, when that person accepts Jesus Christ as Savior.

Stephen, an Example

Reading: Acts 7

"While they were stoning him, Stephen prayed, 'Lord Jesus receive my spirit.' Then he fell on his knees and cried out, 'Lord, do not hold sin against them.' When he had said this, he fell asleep'" (Acts 7:59,60 NIV).

Stephen was a man to be emulated: he was a man of courage; he followed the Lord's example; he possessed a strange peace, the peace which comes to a man who has done the right thing even if it kills him. Stephen's blood became the seed of the church.

The stoning of Stephen made an impression on Saul. He was at the scene.. Witnesses laid their clothes at the feet of Saul. (Acts 7:58) No doubt the example of Stephen led Paul to be ready for salvation when he heard the Lord's voice.

Few things are harder to put up with than the annoyance of a good example, so said Mark Twain. Satire at its best. Example is a bright looking-glass, universal and for all shapes to look into. "He preaches well that lives well." Miguel de Cervantes. "This, then, is the test we must set for ourselves; not to march alone but to march in such a way that others will wish to join us." Hubert H. Humphrey

Too many Christians operate on the maxim: "Don't do as I am; do as I say. We underestimate the power of a good example. God does not call many of us to be martyrs as Stephen, but we are to be living examples.

The Chamber

Reading: 1 Timothy 2

"But godliness with contentment is great gain. For we brought nothing into the world, and we can take nothing out of it. But if we have food and clothing, we will be content with that. People who want to get rich fall into temptation and a trap and into many foolish and harmful desires that plunge men into ruin and destruction. For the love of money is a root of all kinds of evil. Some people, eager for money, have wandered from the faith and pierced themselves with many griefs" (1 Timothy 6:6-10 NIV).

Vernon Grounds, Chancellor of the Denver Seminary, epitomizes the example of godliness like no other man I have known in my time. He gave himself unstintingly to others in order to help them, drawing from a reservoir of godliness in his chamber of the Lord. I have known Vernon for more than fifty years and never have I seen him live outside that chamber.

The Christian philosopher and scientist Blasé Pascal commented, "I have discovered that all the unhappiness of men arises from one single fact that they cannot stay quietly in their own chamber." I owe a lot to Dr. Grounds who has been a mentor as it were to me for all these years. Not to say, I have reached much past the threshold of that chamber he so ably lived.

Dallas Willard puts it another way: "A well- known Methodist evangelist used to say that a dancing foot and a praying knee do not grow on the same leg. This might prove to be a fairly good empirical generalization. It may be that as a matter of fact few prayerfully bent knees are on legs with a dancing foot at the end. Still, just *not* dancing would hardly prove that you had abandoned your life to God." At the advanced age of 88, Vernon Grounds is still on bent knee and dancing.

To Play the Corinthian

Reading: Acts 18

"When Silas and Timothy came from Macedonia, Paul devoted himself exclusively to preaching, testifying to the Jews that Jesus was the Christ. But when the Jews opposed Paul and became abusive, he shook out his clothes in protest and said to them, 'Your blood be on your own heads! I am clear of my responsibility. From now on I will go to the Gentiles'" (Acts 18:5-6 NIV).

"To play the Corinthian" was to give your life over to the practice of debauchery.

Goncourt Edmond de wrote of debauchery: "How utterly futile debauchery seems once it has been accomplished, and what ashes of disgust it leaves in the soul! The pity of it is that the soul outlives the body, or in other words that impression judges sensation and that one thinks about and finds fault with the pleasure one has taken."

"Corinthian" described in regency times a reckless, town drunk. The Acropolis was located in Corinth. Dominating the city was the temple of Aphrodite. Sacred prostitutes by the thousands plied their trade in the streets. It was said that "not every man could afford a journey to Corinth."

Paul lived and worked there and saw some of his greatest triumphs in that city.

His message? “Do you not know that the wicked will not inherit the kingdom of God? Do not be deceived: Neither the sexually immoral nor idolaters nor adulterers nor male prostitutes nor homosexual offenders nor thieves nor the greedy nor drunkards nor slanderers nor swindlers will inherit the kingdom of God. And that is what some of you were. But you were washed, you were sanctified, you were justified in the name of the Lord Jesus Christ and by the Spirit of our God” (1 Corinthians 6:9-11 NIV).

Millions of Americans “Play the Corinthian.” We need the Gospel here as well as there.

Brain Dead

Reading: Acts 8:30-35

“May the words of my mouth and the meditation of my heart be pleasing in your sight, O LORD, my Rock and my Redeemer” (Psalm 19:14 NIV).

Marva Dawn wrote: “By the time they graduate from high school, youth in the United States have spent more hours watching television commercials than they have spent in school. A high school senior who watches the average amount of programming has seen 500,000 commercials.” What about the Internet? “Which controls the most hours of young people’s lives? If they get one hour per week of Christian education and perhaps a few minutes each day of family or personal devotions and then watch the average four and a half hours per day of television with all its violence, greed, sexual immorality, and passivity training, what has the greatest chance of forming their values and attitudes and behaviors and goals?”

Little wonder that we are concerned about the “dumbing down of America.” One thing I admire about the required discipline of the “Home School” industry. Families are much better off spending their time reading, writing and doing other intellectual things than watching television. And the children love it when they see the payoff in good grades and intellectual stimulus.

Handicapped

Reading: 2 Corinthians 12

"To keep me from becoming conceited because of these surpassingly great revelations, there was given me a thorn in my flesh, a messenger of Satan, to torment me. Three times I pleaded with the Lord to take it away from me. But he said to me, 'My grace is sufficient for you, for my power is made perfect in weakness.' Therefore I will boast all the more gladly about my weaknesses, so that Christ's power may rest on me" (2 Corinthians 12:7-9 NIV).

All his life Paul struggled against a serious physical handicap. Paul traveled about 6,000 miles under difficult circumstances in contrast to how we travel today. Wherever Paul went he walked; imagine walking 6,000 miles. He tramped all over Asia Minor and half of Europe. His handicap held him back, yet he refused to give in. The word "thorn" should be translated "stake", implying that it was not merely a pricking of the skin, but a twisting and turning stake in his flesh.

"To be blind is not miserable; not to be able to bear blindness, that is miserable." John Milton. We miss the opportunity for meaningful ministry if we overlook the benefits of a handicap.

Great souls are those who overcome handicaps of one sort or another. They recognize that God has a purpose in our handicaps. Why? That we may know that God's grace is sufficient for us, for His power is made perfect in our weakness.

"Therefore I will boast all the more gladly about my weaknesses, so that Christ's power may rest on me."

Hidden Out of Sight

Reading: Ecclesiastes 9

"We always thank God, the Father of our Lord Jesus Christ, when we pray for you, because we have heard of your faith in Christ Jesus and of the love you have for all the saints" (Colossians 1:3,4 NIV).

Never overlook what God is doing in little places. Colossae at the time of the early church was a small town in the Province of Asia. It was tucked away out of sight in the Lycus Valley. It was a little "nowhere" inhabited by little "nobodies." Laodicea was an important center for commerce and more importantly judged by the world's standards. We look at some tiny church hidden in the hinterlands as insignificant. However, a church lost in the hills can still be true and successful.

I am a member of such a church now and find it a place where God is at work. Case in point, the church is in Perrydale, Oregon, where you have to want to drive through that part of country on purpose. It's a little white building built in 1889 by the Christian Church and purchased by our congregation for a dollar. There is seating for 125 with a congregation of 100 or so. We only meet once a week since most of the people drive a far piece to get there. The Bible School is staffed by competent men and women. The adult fellowship is taught by the able Alan Bittel, whose understanding of the Word is excellent, and in imparting those truths each Sunday, he is without equal. Pastor Greg Trull, who happens to have a PhD. in Old Testament exegesis, is without a doubt one of the most able young man I have listened to in my time. Hymn singing is featured during the worship service. One Sunday a month, the folks celebrate "Fat Sunday" where refreshments are served in between Bible School and Worship. Occasionally there is a potluck lunch after church, featuring all kinds of food from chicken to deer and elk sausage. Children and young people participate in the worship service. Tithes and offerings are placed in a box in the little foyer. A business meeting is held once a year where a report is given of income, expenditures and budget to be adopted. There is no Bible School during the three months in the summertime in order to give the Bible School staff a time to reload. One might ask: "What then do you do?" We worship the Lord, encourage one another and spend time in prayer and praise. We support missionaries generously, take care of the needs of those in the congregation, whether physical or financial, and care for the widows. The emphasis is put on family growth and life.

It is a pleasure to drive 25 miles to get to church when you have something to look forward to like we do at Perrydale.

Longevity

Reading: 1 Corinthians 10

"Those who have served well gain an excellent standing and great assurance in their faith in Christ Jesus" (1 Timothy 3:13 NIV).

Two men stand out in my mind who were great leaders who stayed by the stuff, pastoring their churches for forty or more years. Scottish preachers were known for long pastorates that covered a lifetime of ministry. Not often do we see that in America where we throw aside something old and long in nature. The late Don Tyler was pastor of Bethesda Baptist Church in Brownsburg, Indiana forty years and built a congregation from almost nothing to over 1600. Richard

Ahlgrim on the other hand, has been pastor of the Berean Baptist Church in Springfield, Illinois for more than forty years and still counting. Richard's church never exceeded many over 200 parishioners. Tyler was an aggressive evangelist; Ahlgrim took the route of building heaven into people before getting them into heaven. There's much to say to both approaches of reaching people with the Gospel. I dare say, Ahlgrim didn't have the fall out of professing Christians who didn't understand the issues involved in following Jesus. Both were commendable leaders in their own right. I learned a lot from both men. They taught me that good things take time.

Self Denial

Reading: Ephesians 4:21-24

"Your beauty should not come from outward adornment, such as braided hair and the wearing of gold jewelry and fine clothes. Instead, it should be that of your inner self, the unfading beauty of a gentle and quiet spirit, which is of great worth in God's sight" (1 Peter 3:3,4 NIV).

"I don't think I'm tangible to myself. I mean, I think one thing today and I think another thing tomorrow. I change during the course of a day. I wake and I'm one person, and when I go to sleep I know for certain I'm somebody else. I don't know *who* I am most of the time. It doesn't even matter to me." (Bob Dylan)

The Apostle Paul addresses the issue self: "Do not lie to each other, since you have taken off your old self with its practices and have put on the new self, which is being renewed in knowledge in the image of its Creator" (Colossians 3:9-11 NIV). "If we have been united with him like this in his death, we will certainly also be united with him in his resurrection. For we know that our old self was crucified with him so that the body of sin might be done away with, that we should no longer be slaves to sin, because anyone who has died has been freed from sin" (Romans 6:5-7 NIV).

Many are the Christians, who like Bob Dylan; don't know who they are most of the time. In a sense Howard Kaplan addresses the reason: The essential qualities distinguishing one person from another; individuality: *"He would walk a little first along the southern walls, shed his European self, fully enter this world"* Too many of us have not fully entered the world of the "New self," characterized as being crucified with Christ.

My friend, Derald Kruse, an attorney, epitomizes self-denial like no one else I know. "In effect, may we not say, the Lord's precept comes to this - the real displacement of self from the throne of life in its purposes and hopes, and the real enthronement of Another, comes to unqualified self-surrender. I attempt no refinements. We all practically understand what we mean when we speak about self and its surrender, and the enthronement of Jesus Christ. We mean that whereas yesterday our aims, many of them, some of them, one of them, terminated in our self today, so far as we know, they all terminate in our Lord. Yesterday, perhaps in some highly refined mode, perhaps in some mode not refined, we lived at least a part of our life to self; now, in full purpose, we live the whole of our life to Him who died for us and rose again. Yesterday it was very pleasant, as a good thing in itself, if some action, some influence going out from us, brought back praise, spoken or not spoken, to ourselves; now such a feeling is recognized as sin, if the pleasure terminates short of a distinct and honest reference to our Lord in us. (*Thoughts on Christian Sanctity* by H. C. G. Moule)

Imitator

Reading: Ephesians 5

"For you yourselves know how you ought to follow our example. We were not idle when we were with you, nor did we eat anyone's food without paying for it. On the contrary, we worked night and day, laboring and toiling so that we would not be a burden to any of you" (2 Thessalonians 3:7,8 NIV).

James Baldwin wrote: "Children have never been very good at listening to their elders, but they have never failed to imitate them." "Imitation, if it is not forgery, is a fine thing. It stems from a generous impulse, and a realistic sense of what can and cannot be done." James Fenton We use the word mime to imitate someone's behavior. As Christians we are to imitate the Lord.

"When we went to Germany as missionaries, our daughter was only eighteen months old. She never had a lesson in German, yet she learned to speak without an American accent. The reason was that she simply mimed the German speech forms." Dr. Merrill Tenney taught New Testament with distinction at the Graduate School of Wheaton College. Incidentally he also taught us many important principles of ministry. One was the value of a good example. He put it this way: `The best advertisement for your church is not a large bulletin board, but rather the example that is set when the town drunk becomes a Christian and lives a godly life." Wayne A. Detzler.

Do others regard you with such respect that they copy your lifestyle of godly living?

Preaching

Reading: Acts 17

"...I see that in every way you are very religious. For as I walked around and looked carefully at your objects of worship, I even found an altar with this inscription: TO AN UNKNOWN GOD. Now what you worship as something unknown I am going to proclaim to you. The God who made the world and everything in it is the Lord of heaven and earth and does not live in temples built by hands. And he is not served by human hands, as if he needed anything, because he himself gives all men life and breath and everything else" (Acts 17:22-25 NIV).

Many a preacher wished he could preach like the Apostle Paul. Paul's preaching could fit any audience. For example, Paul's preaching emphasized that God is not the one made, but the maker; that God made the universe; that God has made man so that he instinctively longs for God; that the days of groping and ignorance are past; that the day of judgment is coming; that the pre-eminence of Christ is the Resurrection.

"It is no unknown God but a risen Christ with whom we have to deal."[29] William. Barclay.

Now that's preaching. The kind we need in every pulpit in the world. The gospel message is for everyone in every place, in every situation to meet every need.

Pessimist or Optimist?

Reading: 2 Timothy 1

"For God has not given us a spirit of fear, but of power and of love and of a sound mind" (2 Timothy 1:7 NKJV).

"And the special gift of ministry you received when I laid hands on you and prayed—keep that ablaze! God doesn't want us to be shy with his gifts, but bold and loving and sensible." (2 Timothy 1:6 The Message).

My friend and well known author Dennis Hensley, of more than 30 books who is writer in residence at Taylor University, told me this story: "When I was 19 and in junior college, I took a course in philosophy. My prof happened also to be a rabbi. He went down the first row and handed each student a glass filled to the middle with water. He asked, 'Is it half empty or half full in your opinion? Are you a pessimist or an optimist?' Some students answered one way, some the other, and explained why. When he got to me he asked, 'Pessimist or optimist?' I upended the glass, drank the water, handed him back the empty glass and responded, 'Opportunist.' (He gave me an A and didn't stop laughing about that for days.)

"For our midterm exam, he gave us one question: 'Prove to me that this chair does not exist philosophically.' I wrote down on my paper, '*What* chair?' I turned in the paper and left the room. He gave me a B+ and told me later that he laughed for a week about that."

We have a gospel of power. Power to live the life God wants us to live; power to rise above our circumstances and power to conquer self. Realize your opportunities and trust God for the power to be a testimony for Him with love and common sense.

Ordinariness

Reading: Acts 4

"When they saw the courage of Peter and John and realized that they were unschooled, ordinary men, they were astonished

and they took note that these men had been with Jesus" (Acts 4:13 NIV).

I like ordinary people. It would have been fun to sit on the bank of the Sea of Galilee and listen to Peter and John spin tales of their fishing exploits. Courageous, but ordinary men. They are described as men who had been with Jesus. What a life! But, "even at the best of times," Oswald Chambers once said, "it does require the supernatural grace of God to live twenty-four hours of every day as a saint. We need grace daily to be exceptional in the ordinary things of life, and holy on the ordinary streets, among ordinary people."

I would liked to have eavesdropped in on a conversation between Peter and John while they described the daily rigors of living a consistent life for the Lord. I spent my entire ministry with people of no exceptional ability, degree, or quality; average. Oh, I know many of them were well off financially, others were highly educated and many were gifted, but it all came to being ordinary if God was in it.

"Average is a quality we must put up with. Men march toward civilization in column formation, and by the time the van has learned to admire the masters the rear is drawing reluctantly away from the totem pole." Frank Moore Colby.

Ralph Waldo Emerson wrote: "The mark of the man of the world is absence of pretension. He does not make a speech; he takes a low business-tone, avoids all brag, is nobody, dresses plainly, promises not at all, performs much, speaks in monosyllables, hugs his fact. He calls his employment by its lowest name, and so takes from evil tongues their sharpest weapon. His conversation clings to the weather and the news, yet he allows himself to be surprised into thought, and the unlocking of his learning and philosophy."

Like I say: I like ordinary people for I too, am ordinary.

Storms

Reading: Psalm 107

"Then they cried out to the LORD in their trouble, and he brought them out of their distress. He stilled the storm to a whisper; the waves of the sea were hushed. They were glad when it grew calm, and he guided them to their desired haven. Let them give thanks to the LORD for his unfailing love and his wonderful deeds for men" (Psalm 107:28-31 NIV).

I have lived in the mid-west where storms are frequent happenings. Believe me a thunderstorm is not something you want to be caught in. "The weapons of humankind may cause us to tremble, but what can compare with the awesome might of storms? It wasn't Japanese naval power, but nature, that nearly torpedoed the career of Admiral William `Bull' Halsey. The American admiral regularly outfought and outmaneuvered his Imperial enemies, but two typhoons sank several of his ships late in the war, sending nearly 1,000 sailors to a watery grave.

Sometimes one storm begets another. In a 24-hour period between April 3 and 4, 1974, one thunderstorm gave birth to 148 tornadoes in 13 states—with 15 twisters on the ground simultaneously. Tornado winds have been clocked at 138 mph." [30](from *How Majestic Is Your Name*)

Avoid friends who create a relational storm when you are together. Rather than marry a storm, cut your throat. If you are already married to a storm, climb up on the roof. Better to live on a corner of the roof than share a house with a quarrelsome wife. (Proverbs 21:9-10 NIV). Some wives need to climb on to the roof top to endure a storm.

"Then the LORD answered Job out of the storm. He said: 'Who is this that darkens my counsel with words without knowledge? Brace yourself like a man; I will question you, and you shall answer me'". (Job 38:1-3 NIV) The next time you are in a storm and I hope you are not ever there, don't overlook the lesson God may have for you.

To Sum It All Up

Reading: Acts 22

"Then he said: 'The God of our fathers has chosen you to know his will and to see the Righteous One and to hear words from his mouth. You will be his witness to all men of what you have seen and heard. And now what are you waiting for? Get up, be baptized and wash your sins away, calling on his name'" (Acts 22:14-16 NIV).

This is the summary of the Christian life: to know the will of God; and to hear His voice. As Christians we are ever listening for the voice of God above the voices of the world to tell us where to go and what to do. It doesn't take a rocket scientist to understand the simple truths of the Gospel. The problem comes when we add something which God never intended for us to understand. That leads to a rabbit trail of misunderstanding and confusion. Simply believe the gospel and obey the words of God. Let Him lead. Anyone can call on the name of the Lord if they are so minded.

"For there is no difference between Jew and Gentile—the same Lord is Lord of all and richly blesses all who call on him for 'everyone who calls on the name of the Lord will be saved'" (Romans 10:12,13 NIV).

Chasing the Wind

Reading: Ecclesiastes 2

"So I hated life, because the work that is done under the sun was grievous to me. All of it is meaningless, a chasing after the wind" (Ecclesiastes 2:17 NIV).

I am constantly surprised when I hear someone say they hate their work and find it meaningless. I am told that half the public in the work place are not pursuing work in the field for which they were equipped. On the other hand, I know of lot of people who not only love their work and find it meaningful, but insist they would work for nothing. Some do; others exaggerate.

James Russell Lowell comments about this: "Every man feels instinctively that all the beautiful sentiments in the world weigh less than a single lovely action".

Solomon wrote: "From the fruit of his lips a man is filled with good things as surely as the work of his hands rewards him." "All hard work brings a profit, but mere talk leads only to poverty." "One who is slack in his work is brother to one who destroys"." Do you see a man skilled in his work? He will serve before kings; he will not serve before obscure men". (Proverbs 12:14; 14:23; 18:9; 22:29).

Why is hard work important? James speaks to the issue: "Perseverance must finish its work so that you may be mature and complete, not lacking anything" (James 1:4 NIV).

Sun

Reading: Isaiah 45

"He speaks to the sun and it does not shine; he seals off the light of the stars" (Job 9:7 NIV).

How big is the sun? Our sun has the volume of 1.3 million miles times that of the earth! 99:8 percent of the mass of the solar system is taken up by the sun. It looks small because the earth is in orbit at a distance of nearly 93 million miles away. All life on earth is made possible by the light of the sun. When we burn wood or coal we are actually releasing stored energy from the sun. The sun plays an important part in man's efforts to keep track of time. The length of a day depends on the time the sun takes to return to a particular place in the sky as the earth rotates.

"So that from the rising of the sun to the place of its setting men may know there is none besides me. I am the LORD, and there is no other. I form the light and create darkness, I bring prosperity and create disaster; I, the LORD, do all these things" (Isaiah 45:6-7 NIV).

"I am God, the only God there is. Besides me there are no real gods. I'm the one who armed you for this work, though you don't even know me, So that everyone, from east to west will know that I have no god-rivals. I am God, the only God there is. I form light and create darkness; I make harmonies and create discords. I, God, do all these things" (Isaiah 45:5-7 The Message).

What is it that you don't get? How great is our God!

Sea Monsters

Reading: Psalm 104

"Praise the LORD from the earth, you great sea creatures and all ocean depths..." (Psalm 148:7 NIV)

In Moby Dick the albino sperm whale was the villain. The male sperm whale can grow to a length of 62 feet and can dive to depths of 3,720 feet. More frightful perhaps is the great white shark that can grow up to 40 feet long and feeds on seals and sea turtles. These sharks can swallow objects half their size. The Carcharodon megalodon shark grew up to 990 feet in length. Talk about a monster![31] (from *How Majestic is Thy Name*).

In the book of Job God speaks of the sea monster, the leviathan :"If you lay a hand on him, you will remember the struggle and never do it again. Any hope of subduing him is false; the mere sight of him is overpowering. No one is fierce enough to rouse him. Who then is able to stand against me?" (Job 41:8-10 NIV).

Jonah learned it is better to obey God than to tangle with a sea monster. A lesson most mankind has not learned. Jonah was inside the great fish for three days and three nights. He prayed to the Lord; his prayer ending with, "Salvation comes from the Lord." Upon the Lord's command, the fish vomited Jonah onto dry ground! God was in control of even the sea monsters.

Slack Bows

Reading: Psalm 78

"Like their fathers they were disloyal and faithless, as unreliable as a faulty bow" (Psalm 78:57 NIV).

"Faulty bow" means a slack bow. Have you ever, as a kid, had a five and dime model bow and arrow? You are enthused about using it. Then after a few times, you discover the arrows fall about five feet short of your intended target? It could well be because of a slack bow. That was Israel's problem. They didn't have a five and dime model bow; oh no, they had the sturdy model worthy of the power of God. They had all the pieces, but because of slackness it was ineffective. A slack bow has no purpose and gives no pleasure. So, one casts aside the bow. There is no reason for the Christian to work with a slack bow for as Paul wrote: "Greater is he that is in you than he that is in the world." We dare not attempt to face the world with a slack bow for "We wrestle not against flesh and blood, but against principalities, against powers, against the rulers of the darkness of this world, against spiritual wickedness in high places" (Ephesians 6:11, 12).

And God's provision is with us presently. "Greater is He." I have everything I need – when I need it. I am armed. We have all the capability for victory. We don't need to face the world with a slack bow.

Immortality of Influence

Reading: Acts 1: 1-5

"He gives strength to the weary and increases the power of the weak. Even youths grow tired and weary, and young men stumble and fall; but those who hope in the LORD will renew their strength. They will soar on wings like eagles; they will run and not grow weary, they will walk and not be faint" (Isaiah 40:29-31 NIV).

Some people have such influence on the world their influence has a certain immortality. This was true of the Apostles and others singled out by God in the Bible. An immortality of influence prevailed in the early church. How did they have such an impact on the world? It was through the empowerment of the Holy Spirit.

"We often call the Holy Spirit the Comforter. In Wycliff's era comforter had a different meaning. From the word *fortis,* which means brave, the Comforter is the one who fills us with courage and strength."[32] (William Barclay)

To learn this we must be still. "We must wait upon the Lord who shall renew our strength." This means we must practice passiveness. Amidst all the striving we must have time to wait on God and to receive the courage and strength.

What Matters Most

Hebrews 3

"As has just been said: 'Today, if you hear his voice, do not harden your hearts as you did in the rebellion.'" (Hebrews 3:15 NIV).

It is not what matters tomorrow for no man knows what a day will bring; however, what matters most focuses on today and if there should be a tomorrow, we will take up the same strategy for living. "The things that matter most must never be at the mercy of things that matters least. If you don't change your direction, you'll end up where you're heading." Goethe

My health in the future is important to me; what counts just now is what it is today and how I can best deal with it. As Walter Matthau observed in response to a heart attack: "My doctor gave me six months to live, but when I couldn't pay the bill he gave me six months more."

What is to be gained? Jesus said, "What good is it for a man to gain the whole world, but forfeit his own soul." It never hurts to examine what direction we are headed and make necessary corrections that fall in line with what matters most. "This made the Jews ask, 'Will he kill himself? Is that why he says, 'Where I go, you cannot come'? But he continued, 'You are from below; I am from above. You are of this world; I am not of this world. I told you that you would die in your sins; if you do not believe that I am the one I claim to be, you will indeed die in your sins'" (John 8:22-24 NIV).

Seed

Reading: Genesis 1

"For you have been born again, not of perishable seed, but of imperishable, through the living and enduring word of God." (1 Peter 1:23 NIV).

Jeanette, a nurse by profession, also teaches a primary Sunday School class of children. She is most creative. One year she taught her students something about gardening. With varying tomato seeds the class grew a whole lot of tomato plants and sold them to the folks in the Perrydale Church. It was a huge success. All the proceeds went to a missionary orphan home in a third world country. The children were enthused about their gardening skills and learned a lot of lessons about creation and growth.

"Sow your seed in the morning, and at evening let not your hands be idle, for you do not know which will succeed, whether this or that, or whether both will do equally well" (Ecclesiastes 11:6-7 NIV). "He who goes out weeping, carrying seed to sow, will return with songs of joy, carrying sheaves with him" (Psalm 126:6 NIV).

"As he was scattering the seed, some fell along the path, and the birds came and ate it up. Some fell on rocky places, where it did not have much soil. It sprang up quickly, because the soil was shallow. But when the sun came up, the plants were scorched, and they withered because they had no root. Other seed fell among thorns, which grew up and choked the plants. Still other seed fell on good soil, where it produced a crop-a hundred, sixty or thirty times what was sown. He who has ears, let him hear" (Matthew 13:4-9 NIV). "It is like a mustard seed, which is the smallest seed you plant in the ground. Yet when planted, it grows and becomes the largest of all garden plants, with such big branches that the birds of the air can perch in its shade".(Mark 4:31-32 NIV). "He replied, 'Because you have so little faith. I tell you the truth, if you have faith as small as a mustard seed, you can say to this mountain, 'Move from here to there' and it will move. Nothing will be impossible for you'" (Matthew 17:20 NIV).

In Search of Explanations

Reading: Job 40

"Brace yourself like man; I will question you, and you shall answer me" (Job 40:7 NIV).

I remember when I was a child and my folks demanded something of me. It was a question in the back of my mind: "Why? Give me an explanation!" Then I became a parent and often heard from my own children: "Why? Give an explanation." The human spirit wants to know why for everything.

Job wanted to know about suffering. He demanded: "Why?" At some point God, rather than give Job an answer, replied: "Do you presume to tell me what I'm doing wrong? Are you calling me a sinner so you can be a saint?" (Job 40:8 The Message).

No, unlike God, my parents exploded, as did I when my turn came to raise a family. The fact that our children know more than we did at that age, is not resulting in much good. It is not producing better children nor better parents. Contemporary child rearing is in trouble in our culture. It is correct and desirable to tell a child to "get on with it; you don't need to know the why for everything? Hear?"

Whatever It Takes

Reading: I Corinthians 15

"Therefore, my dear brothers, stand firm. Let nothing move you. Always give yourselves fully to the work of the Lord, because you know that your labor in the Lord is not in vain" (1 Corinthians 15:58 NIV).

Royal and Edsel Lindquist bought a worn out ambulance in 1953, threw their instruments in the coffin chamber and cris-crossed America and Europe forty years in itinerant evangelism preaching the Gospel. Royal thought it too flamboyant to go by the name, the Royal and Edsel Ministry Team, so he dropped the Royal and used "Lin" for his name. Edsel was red headed. I suppose if my mother hung the moniker of Edsel around my neck, I'd grow red hair too. The only other Edsel I am familiar with is one of the Ford boys of automobile fame. He built an Edsel in the 1950s; a lemon. So Edsel conscripted the name "Red." Whatever it takes. Those boys sped through blazing heatstroke country of the Plains States during the summer and followed the snowplows of Wyoming in the winter in order to reach their next preaching appointment. God blessed them in a mighty way. Royal has since shoved off to heaven, and Red, who lives with his wife, Naomi, resides in Thief River Falls, Minnesota, where plenty of thieves still abound. You will find old Red without much hair these days, but still fire in his spirit as he serves in a little Swedish Church doing whatever it takes. The days of their kind of sacrifice is seldom seen anymore; they were the heroes of yesteryear who believed God would bless their little bit while they did whatever it takes.

Whoops

Reading: Genesis 1

"And God said, "Let there be light," and there was light. God saw that the light was good, and he separated the light from the darkness" (Genesis 1:3-4 NIV);
God called the dry ground 'land,' and the gathered waters he called 'seas.' And God saw that it was good." (Genesis 1:10-11 NIV*). "The land produced vegetation: plants bearing seed according to their kinds and trees bearing fruit with seed in it according to their kinds. And God saw that it was good"* (Genesis 1:12 NIV*). "He also made the stars. God set them in the expanse of the sky to give light on the earth, to govern the day and the night, and to separate light from darkness. And God saw that it was good"* (Genesis 1:16-18 NIV).

My friend Sharon sent an email of addresses for a breakfast meeting and announcing a change in someone's email address. It was wrong, not Sharon's doing, but her friend who gave the wrong information. So she corrected herself by starting with "Whoops!"

I have seen hundreds of new born babies in my time. Proud fathers would ask: "Isn't she beautiful?" Most often I left the hospital thinking, it's a baby all right: "Whoops! God missed that one when it came to handing out beauty." No problem with God for by the time the child has reached past adolescence; he or she is a remarkable thing of beauty. Well, in some cases the beauty that is from within.

Are we not thankful that when God created the Heavens and the earth, the sun, moon, stars, night and day that we don't have to say: "Whoops! God you surely missed it there?" Some people marry only looking for riches, not because they truly love their partner. It's tragic that often, after the fact, such a person reveals that it was a "Whoops" kind of arrangement. So the sincere partner ends up on the rooftop. Any one in business is faced with the "Whoops" consideration frequently. We had best give prayerful consideration and caution in our decisions lest we live a lifetime of "Whoops!"

Wisdom

Reading: Psalm 11

"A false balance is abomination to the Lord: but a just weight is his delight" (Proverbs 11:1.NAS).

"The fear of the LORD is the beginning of wisdom; a good understanding have all those who do his commandments. His praise endures forever" (Psalm 111:10 NAS).

There is enough swindling in the market place today that it makes it difficult to know who you can trust. Often it is only in hindsight that, after falling for a swindle, we say: "Well, I learned something; it won't happen again."

"For nothing can seem foul to those that win." William Shakespeare

That's just the point of our vulnerability, we set ourselves up to become a victim of a swindle again. For as O. Henry once wrote: "It was beautiful and simple as all truly great swindles are."

"Understanding of what is true, right, or lasting is insight: One cannot have wisdom without living life." (Dorothy McCall). Henry David Thoreau wrote: "Common sense; good judgment: `It is a characteristic of wisdom not to do desperate things'"

Job had God's wisdom when he said of the counsel of his friends: "Doubtless you are the people, and wisdom will die with you!" (Job 12:2 NIV)

We must be on guard to differentiate between the wisdom of this world and the wisdom of God. "Wisdom takes place in conditions that treat knowledge as information, as something to be used. If you want to teach wisdom, you find yourself going against the stream constantly. Educational organizations have no interest in how you live, or even if you do live. The primary ethical concerns of a school have to do with not stealing books from the library, not cheating on your exams, and not plagiarizing in your papers." Eugene Peterson

---

When the Tide Goes Out

Reading: Psalm 139

"O LORD, you have searched me and you know me. You know when I sit and when I rise; you perceive my thoughts from afar. You discern my going out and my lying down; you are familiar with all my ways. Before a word is on my tongue you know it completely, O LORD" (Psalm139:1-4 NIV).

"When the tide goes out you can tell who's naked." Warren Buffett, commenting on the Enron scandal.

We think we can hide what we are doing, and sometimes it appears to work in the real world. But we need to be reminded again and again that God knows our every move, and we should live in accordance to please him, not play the part of the hypocrite. As you read the Bible you see some characters who think they can fool God. They think that they can live in secret and nobody will know. Ananias and Sapphira sold some land and supposedly brought all the money to the apostles, but they had kept back some of it for themselves. Peter told them "...you have not lied to men but to God" (Acts 5:4)

There will come a day when the tide goes out in our lives, and if we are not found in Christ, we will find ourselves naked before a holy God.

Success Isn't Always in View

Reading: Acts 17

"When they heard about the resurrection of the dead, some of them sneered, but others said, 'We want to hear you again on this subject.' At that, Paul left the Council. A few men became followers of Paul and believed. Among them was Dionysius, a member of the Areopagus, also a woman named Damaris, and a number of others"(Acts 17:32-34 NIV).

Americans like to taste success and say: "We're on a roll!" The implication is that there is nothing that cannot be achieved. Upward and onward becomes our model. That is, until we hit the wall in the stock market and are stabbed wide awake to the reality that nothing goes straight up all the time.

Case in point. The Apostle Paul had less success in Athens than anywhere else. All the Athenians wanted was to hear themselves talk. They were not interested in conclusions. Some mocked Paul; some said: "We will hear about this again;" Some believed, accepting the terms of God. Wise men know that only fools will reject the offer of God. There was some good that came out of this: Dionysius the Areopagite and Damaris became Christians. The Gospel makes its appeal to all people regardless of class or condition. We are not always aware of the amount of success when we preach the Gospel, but it does succeed in breaking into the hearts of people and saving them.

Vision Statement

Reading: Haggai 1

"During the night Paul had a vision of a man of Macedonia standing and begging him, 'Come over to Macedonia and help us.' After Paul had seen the vision, we got ready at once to leave for Macedonia, concluding that God had called us to preach the gospel to them" (Acts 16:9-10 NIV).

Churchmen are taken up with mission statements these days. What the church needs is a vision statement. Case in point: Cyrus King of Persia believed he should rebuild the house of God. The Jews, living in captivity, had found prosperity, living in elaborate homes, and at the time were not interested in building the Lord's house. They tramped for months to Jerusalem. There they viewed the ruins, desolation, weeds, etc. They were faced with great difficulties from the outside. But herein is a message for the church today: their hearts were tested to the fullest. Haggai covers the same period. In verse 2, chapter 1, the people said: "The time has not yet come for the Lord's house to be built." The story of "The Lost Vision." They had a prepared heart, but failed because they lacked a faithful, steadfast spirit. They limited God. Haggai challenged them to "Give careful thought to your ways."

Many churches need to take two steps back to consider their vision and then move ahead.

The Will

Reading: Matthew 26

"I came down from heaven not to follow my own will but to accomplish the will of the One who sent me" (John 5:30 The Message).

Sometimes we say that we have a right to our own will. This is the view of the world and what they expect. Jesus saw it differently and expects us to see the same in our response to God: "not as I will, but as you will." There were no conditions that Jesus imposed on the Father. How can we give pleasure to God, the pleasure he seeks and deserves, if we insist on having our own way according to our own will? We can't. Hence, the mature Christian allows God to overrule reason and guide us in every area of our minds. That's how we live life out in terms of our humanity. It is only then that I do not limit God by my selfishness. In those circumstances where we insisted upon having our own will, we met with confusion, failure and disappointment.

As a young child knows no limit to his own will; it is the only reality to him. It is not that he wants at the outset to fight other wills, but that they simply do not exist for him. As mature Christians we must grow up and turn our will over to the Lord.

Face

Reading: Psalm 16

"See that you do not look down on one of these little ones. For I tell you that their angels in heaven always see the face of my Father in heaven" (Matthew 18:10 NIV).

"For God who said, 'Let light shine out of darkness,' made his light shine in our hearts to give us the light of the knowledge of the glory of God in the face of Christ" (2 Corinthians 4:6 NIV).

We look forward to seeing the face of Christ when we get to glory.

Alfred Lord Tennyson made famous the poem:

And may there be no sadness of farewell,
When I embark,
For tho' from out our bourne of Time and Place
The flood may bear me far,
I hope to see my Pilot face to face
When I have crossed the bar.

D. L. Moody said: "To see His star is good, but to see His face is better."

Carrie E. Beck wrote a powerful hymn:

Face to face with Christ my Savior,
Face to face – what will it be –
When with rapture I behold Him,
Jesus Christ who died for me?
Face to face I shall behold Him,
Far beyond the starry sky;
Face to face in all His glory,
I shall see Him by and by.

Experiencing Trials

Reading: 2 Timothy 4:1-8

"But you, keep your head in all situations, endure hardship, do the work of an evangelist, discharge all the duties of your ministry" (2 Timothy 4:5 NIV).

To a young pastor...

Glad to hear you are experiencing trials. God doesn't always send trials to young pastors, because they can't handle them. Welcome to the ministry. As you record your thoughts, emotions and responses in your journal — thoughts concerning both your peers and those whom you serve. Remember that being in the ministry is like the scaling of Mount Everest — exhilarating, exhausting and dangerous. Or as Benjamin Hicks wrote of those who preach: they find themselves either in a storm, heading into a storm or just coming out of a storm.

The way to compassion is through grieving, grieving of circumstances over which we have little or no control. Sometimes everything in life seems to be a trial with suffering the sole entree' on our plate. God either served it up to us or allowed it to be served. But how do we feed about what is set before us without being overwhelmed? And when we are overwhelmed to whom do we flee? The life of faith is the most penetrating of all callings.

Shall we feast only on that which appeals to our tastes? As children we found fries more appealing to our taste than other vegetables. We'd carefully hide peas under the rim of our plate, hoping Mother wouldn't notice, at least until after we'd gone out to play. Only later in life, did we realize that what we deposited under the rim of the plate — out of sight or so we thought — was more nutritious than what satisfied our tastes at the time. As Christians, trials are usually what we hide under the plate.

I pray that God may spare you from trials as much as possible. ...Live by faith as you embrace your trials. It was Fenelon who said: "Confidently trust in God even when you do not see what He is doing. Trust that God, with great compassion, gives you trials in proportion to the help that He wants to bring to you."

"He puts a smile on my face. He's my God" (Psalm 42 The Message).

Who Will Prepare the Way

Reading: Matthew 3:1-12

I will send my messenger ahead of you, who will prepare your way" (Mark 1:2 NIV).

Messengers are an interesting lot. Often unknown, seldom appreciated, apparently expendable, messengers frequently pay with their lives. Pheidippides ran twenty-five miles to carry news of an Athenian victory over the Persians on the plain of Marathon and gasped out his message, "Rejoice, we conquer." Then fell to the ground dead. (1972 Marathon, World Book Encyclopedia, pl5O), J

John the Baptist became well known and brought a great message - "Prepare the way for the Lord" - then faded into the background, was imprisoned and was beheaded at the request of the daughter of Herodias (Matthew 14:6-12). Others of God's messengers were "stoned; they were sawed in two; they were put to death by the sword. They went about in sheepskins and goatskins, destitute, persecuted and mistreated. These were all commended for their faith..." (Hebrews 11:37,39).

We are God's messengers to tell others about Jesus Christ, what He has done for us. Not an easy assignment. In moments of discouragement and self-doubt, moments when we want to toss in the towel, reflect on this: God goes ahead and prepares the way. "Consider him who endured such opposition from sinful men, so that you will not grow weary and lose heart" (Hebrews 12:3).

"And how can they preach unless they are sent? As it is written 'How beautiful are the feet of those who bring the glad news'" (Romans 10:15).

On Being Spiritually Alert

Reading: Matthew 16:26—17:14

"'This is My Son, marked by my love, focus of my delight. Listen to him'. When the disciples heard it, they fell flat on their faces, scared to death." (Matthew 17:5 The Message).

Every Christian benefits from great moments in life when God reaches his consciousness in unusual ways and through uncommon circumstances. He remembers previous times when God was working in his life. He comprehends that it is in remote places and solitary moments when God reveals his glory. Here, it was on a high mountain when Peter finds that listening is better than babbling about what he may do for Jesus. With open eyes he sees the glory of the Lord. Great moments are just moments when the Christian brings good opinion to the Lord. To fathom and love truth for itself, not just facts, is the Christian's goal.

"The truth of a thing, then, is the blossom of it, the thing it is made for, the topmost stone set on with rejoicing. Truth in a man's imagination is the power to recognize this truth of a thing. And wherever, in anything that God has made; is the glory of it, be it sky or flower or human face, we see the glory of God, there a true imagination in beholding a truth of God." (*Discovering the Character of God*, George MacDonald, Bethany House p. 66).

Redeeming the Time

Reading: Psalm 121

"Redeeming the time because the days are evil" (Ephesians 5:16 KJV).

Even though in Indiana we don't turn our clocks forward in the spring or backward in the fall of the year, we're conscious of the practice in the rest of the country. Seems like we should be doing something; at least for those of us who have lived in various other time zones nationally. I was reminded of a time change one weekend when Davina and I flew to California to see our son Peter, who flew in from London, England. We enjoyed our brief time together, even though our internal clock was struggling to stay awake during normal waking hours. Peter loses a day traveling back to his distant home; we gain or lose a couple hours. As one gets older, he learns to sleep when he can and not to worry when be can't.

Reminds me of insomniacs like Jacob, who said to Laban, "I have been with you for twenty years now ... This was my situation: the heat consumed me in the day time and the cold at night and sleep fled from my eyes" (Genesis 31:38,40); like Ahasurerus who could not sleep on the night set aside to hang Mordecai (Esther 6: 1); like the wicked who "cannot sleep till they do evil; they are robbed of slumber till they make someone fall (Proverbs 4:16); like Nebuchadnezzar had dreams; his mind was troubled and he could not sleep, (Daniel 2:1); like King Darius, who stayed up all night while Daniel was in the lion's den (Daniel 6:18).

One of the most interesting analogies God uses to express his great care for believers, in a way has to do with time. "...He who watches over you will not slumber; indeed, he who watches over Israel will neither slumber nor sleep" (Psalm 121:3,4).

Beulah Land

Reading: Psalm 16

"Therefore my heart is glad, and my tongue rejoices; my body also will rest secure, because you will not abandon me to the grave, nor will you let your Holy One see decay. You have made known to me the path of life; you will fill me with joy in your presence, with eternal pleasure at your right hand" (Psalm 16:9-11 NIV).

John Bunyan an English preacher, wrote *The Pilgrim's Progress* in 1678. He was in jail at the time, for preaching without a license. The book is a religious allegory in which people and places represent vices and virtues. Christian, the hero, sets out from the City of Destruction to go to the Celestial City (heaven) or Buelah land.

Like the Psalmist and John Bunyan, I, too, have a need for assurance of heaven and my home in the presence of God. In Christ we can have that steadfast hope and longing for our eternal home.

I love the lyrics to this song about Beulah Land:-

I'm kind of homesick for that country
Where I've never been before;
No sacrifice will there be spoken
Where time won't matter anymore.
I call it Beulah Land; I'm longing for you
and some day on thee I'll stand
There my home shall be eternal
Beulah Land, sweet Beulah Land.

"Delete the thought of heaven from man's lexicon and he is soon reduced to a one-dimensional environment, living without any invisible means of support." Paul Minear

---

Fire

Reading: Psalm 50

"Then Elijah said to them, "I am the only one of the LORD's prophets left, but Baal has four hundred and fifty prophets. Get two bulls for us. Let them choose one for themselves, and let them cut it into pieces and put it on the wood but not set fire to it. I will prepare the other bull and put it on the wood but not set fire to it. Then you call on the name of your god, and I will call on the name of the LORD. The god who answers by fire-he is God." (1 Kings 18:22-24 NIV).

The friction match was invented by John Walker, an English chemist. So we could then contain fire; or could we? "Lightning sparks some 7,500 forest fires in the United States every year, about twenty fires a day."[33] (from *How Majestic is Thy Name*). 4,000 Americans die each year because of fire. Yet how we need fire to keep our ecosystems in balance. Forests and grasslands are needed in order to provide reforestation.

We were burned out of our first church and home in 1952. Fortunately, we managed to escape just ahead of the flames. I remember it well, as a snowy sub zero Ohio night. I couldn't find my trousers and I didn't want to go appear before a curious crowd of people sans my clothes. Ditch the pride; I left in a hurry.

"But fire came down from heaven and devoured them. And the devil, which deceived them, was thrown into the lake of burning sulfur, where the beast and the false prophet had been thrown. They will be tormented day and night for ever and ever" (Revelation 20:9-10 NIV). "Then death and Hades were thrown into the lake of fire. The lake of fire is the second death. If anyone's name was not found written in the book of life, he was thrown into the lake of fire" (Revelation 20:14-15 NIV).

It is not popular to hear sermons on hell; we are too interested in living forever and enjoying our 401Ks, not realizing that all this is but a mistaken notion of our longevity and destiny. Read the Gospels and see that God didn't send His Son to die on the cross as a do-gooder. What is at stake are the souls of those whom God has created; fallen souls who need a Savior, lest they be cast into everlasting hell. Check it out.

Earth

Reading: Job 26

"But it is God whose power made the earth, Whose wisdom gave shape to the world, who crafted the cosmos" (Jeremiah 10:12 The Message).

"Speeding around the sun at 18.5 miles per second, the earth completes one orbit every 365 days, rotating on its axis every 23 hours, 56 minutes and 4 seconds.[34] (from *How Majestic is Thy Name*).

No wonder the Psalmist exclaims, "How awesome is the Lord Most High, the great King over all the earth" (Psalm 47:2).

"One generation passeth away, and another generation cometh: but the earth abideth for ever. The sun also ariseth, and the sun goeth down, and hasteth to the place where he arose" (Ecclesiastes 1:4,5. Hebrew Bible) (Ernest Hemingway's book title *The Sun Also Rises* (1926) comes from this passage).

"After one look at this planet any visitor from outer space would say "I WANT TO SEE THE MANAGER." (William Burroughs)

My first consciousness of earth as I remember was to eat a spoonful of dirt. Everybody needs a little dirt in their diet. It's good for the digestion. God "suspends the earth over nothing" (Job 26:7). What a pleasure it is to enjoy the earth which God gave to us. But there's a new heaven and earth coming which is far better!

Bones

Reading: Galatians 6:1-10

"Live creatively, friends. if someone falls into sin, forgivingly restore him saving your critical comments for yourself" (Galatians 6:1 The Message).

We envy children their energy and imagination. One summer five of our grandchildren spent a week at a ranch in western Washington. Cowboy country. Aunt Lori (daughter) and Uncle Timm, entertained the kids. Each cowpoke did daily chores, but not without complaint. Afterward, they explored and romped the fields learning about horses, mules, cows and dogs. Spontaneous combustion! In order not to forget the memories, the kids packed some large bags with bones for the trip home, each with mementos of the week. Bones. Animal bones. Lots of bones!

The mothers, Brenda and Colleen (our daughters) arrived a week later to rescue their sister Lori. They stuffed the van with personal luggage and lots of bones for the trip home. Imagine driving up behind their van with those cowpokes looking out among the bones. They were important bones. How could there be anything better than stashing a cow bone under the bed? It could be protection should a burglar break in to rob them. An interesting "Show and Tell" in school.

Bones are important to us all. Eve was fashioned beginning with a bone taken from Adam (Genesis 2:21,22);

Samson slew a thousand men with the jawbone of a donkey (Judges 15:15); A dead man revived when he touched the bones of Elisha (2 Kings 13:20,21); Ezekiel saw a valley of dry bones in a vision (Ezekiel 17:1-14).

Bones were important to God also. His own son became human with a body of flesh and bones. His desire was that bones would not be broken when we consider the information offered in John 19:33,36: "But when they came to Jesus and found that he was already dead, they did not break his legs ... These things happened so that the Scripture would be fulfilled."

Bones are important to us in the spiritual realm. Paul implies that mended bones concern the domain of love among believers. Brothers, if someone is caught in a sin, you who are spiritual should restore him gently" (Galatians 6:1). The verb "restore" is a picture of a surgeon setting a broken bone. Bones are important.

The Driver's Seat

Reading: Mark 8:29-9:7

"Anyone who intends to come with me has to let me lead. You're not in the driver's seat. I am" (Mark 8:34 The Message).

Americans love their automobiles; we have so many of them. Sixty years ago we built homes without garages, or if there was a garage, it was but one. After World War II homebuilders preferred homes with two car garages, but current new construction often includes garage space for three cars. Despite how many cars we own, we generally prefer the driver's seat; we like to be in control. The disciples of Jesus liked being in control also, though they had no automobiles.

An automobile is not the point, but control is. Jesus told His disciples He needed to go to Jerusalem. He was facing death, but would rise again. Peter protested: "Impossible!"

Brushing Peter aside, Jesus told disciples that when it came to His life, they were not in control. They were not in the driver's seat, neither were they in control of their own lives. For the disciples, the driver's seat belonged to Jesus. He was in control.

When Jesus is in the driver's seat of our lives, destination is assured, not by self-determination, but by the wisdom and power of the God who is leading us. Safe arrival is assured when the Lord is in control and we will arrive on time. The route of choice belongs to the Lord. True, we may not arrive at our destination in the time expected, but God's timing is perfect. Unless we agree before hand, drivers follow a route of their choice, not the passengers. We, like the disciples, resist letting God in the driver's seat because we, like Peter, think we know better. We are comfortable with power in our control. As for yourself, think of times when you have jumped into the driver's seat ahead of the Lord; has it not invariably led to disappointment, confusion and sometimes, disaster? When you've yielded the driver's seat to the Lord, have you not always arrived at the right place and on time?

Place Your Life Before God

Reading: Romans 12

"Offer your bodies as living sacrifices, holy and pleasing to God—this is your spiritual act of worship" (Romans 12:1 NIV).

Take your everyday, ordinary life – your sleeping, eating, going-to-work, and walking around life – and place it before God as an offering. Embracing what God does for you is the best thing you can do for him. Don't become so well-adjusted to your culture that you fit into it without even thinking. Instead, fix your attention to God. You'll be changed from the inside out. Readily recognize what He wants from you and quickly respond to it. Unlike the culture around you, always dragging you down to its level of immaturity, God brings the best out of you and develops well-formed maturity in you.

If you preach, just preach God's Message, nothing else: if you help, just help, don't take over; if you teach, stick to your teaching: if you give encouraging guidance, be careful that you don't get bossy; if you're put in charge, don't manipulate; if you're called to give aid to people in distress, keep your eyes open and be quick to respond; if you work with the disadvantaged, don't let yourself become irritated with them or depressed by them. Keep a smile on your face.

"Love must be sincere..." (Romans 12:19) Love from the center of who you are; don't fake it. Run for dear life from evil; hold on for dear life to good. Be good friends to all around you. Love knowledge and fear the Lord.

Of Frozen Pipes and Earmuffs

Reading: 1 Peter 1:3-16

"As obedient children, do not conform to the evil desires you had when you lived in ignorance. But just as he who called you is holy, so be holy in all you do; for it is written: 'Be holy, because I am holy'" (1 Peter 1:14-16 NIV).

It's a cold winter night, wind chill minus 53 degrees. Public service announcements advise, no school tomorrow. Weather men advise: wrap your water meters; if they freeze it costs a hundred dollars for repair. The phone rings about ten o'clock in the evening. It's the neighbor on the line: "Have you wrapped your water meter?" I said, "I don't know what a meter looks like, but let's brave the cold and find out." We found the meters attached to the side of our homes, and at the risk of freezing ourselves, we slapped earmuffs on them and returned to the fireplace inside. A few days later while replacing a broken sump pump in the basement, I tripped over a device alongside the pump. What was that? It read: WATER METER, with numbers registering water flow. So, that's the water meter, safe, secure, warm! No doubt the meter reader chuckled as he came upon the little electronic boxes outside our homes, telling him how much water we'd consumed that month. Why, he could have died laughing about meters wearing pink ear-muffs. O well, many are cold; few are frozen!

There is no advantage to ignorance—whether it's water meters, or living the Christian life. Ignorance is not only, not bliss (blessed), but is the wrong road. That's what the Apostle Peter is talking about when he said, "Don't lazily slip back into those old grooves of evil, doing just what you feel like doing. You didn't know better then you do now. As obedient children, let yourselves be pulled into a way of life shaped by God's life, a life energetic and blazing with holiness. God said, 'I am holy; you be holy'" (1 Peter 1:14-16 The Message).

Wiped Out to a Mere Echo

Reading: Acts 18:1-10

"But Paul's efforts with the Jews weren't a total loss, for Crispus, the meeting-place president, put his trust in the master. His entire family believed with him" (Acts 18:7 The Message).

Rivalries are a reality in the classroom, the workplace and on the athletic field; they produce winners and losers. Winners take home trophies; losers become mere echoes of what might have been. Competition teaches us good lessons about life, win or lose. One of the best lessons learned in a competitive game is to get whipped by an opponent. Wiped out!

Cynthia Ozick writes a humorous story about Mr. Emerson's college class in Freshman Composition. Cynthia and Chester, a friend, wrote – were intended to write – as rivals as yoked competitors under the whip (Emerson's) "Got you that time, didn't she? Made you look small, didn't she?" he chortled at Chester. And, the following week, to me: "Males beat females, it's in the nature of things. He's got the stuff, the genuine shout. He's wiped you out to an echo, Miss, believe me." (The story of Cynthia Ozick's class in freshman composition appeared first in *The New Yorker* and is cited from *The Best American Essays*, 1993, Joseph Epstein, Editor. P223.)

Often we get wiped out, reduced to an echo in a given situation: then something unexpected happens, revealing what looked like a loss, is actually a gain. It happened to Paul; it happens to us.

I have friends who bought a small spread in the country and named it: TOTAL LOSS FARM; But it was nothing of the like. It was simply their way of admitting they knew little about gardening; but were willing to tend it as best they could, and make a home, a happy dwelling place for their retirement years. The name TOTAL LOSS was like a self-fulfilling prophecy. Sometimes we fail, but we're not necessarily failures.

Of Doubt and Disobedience

Reading: Jude 17-25

"Jumping out of the boat, Peter walked on the water to Jesus. But when he looked at the waves churning beneath his feet, he lost his nerve and started to sink. He cried, 'Master save me!' Jesus didn't hesitate. He reached down and grabbed his hand. Then he said, 'Faint-heart, what got into you?'" (Matthew 14:29-31 The Message).

"Be merciful to those who doubt…" (Jude 22 NIV).

"Many times he delivered them, but they were bent on rebellion and they wasted away in their sin" (Psalm 106:43 NIV).

It is humbling to experience doubt, especially after spending fifty years walking with the Lord. But sometimes it is necessary for the very reason that we need humility. There are times when the devil uses doubt to crowd us; at other times the Lord uses doubt to our benefit. He stirs us to doubt to appreciate faith. Jesus said, "The truth shall make you free." Free for what reason? To live the truth in obedience to God and His Word. To doubt is not necessarily wrong; Thomas doubted Jesus and from it issued a tremendous witness later when Thomas said, "My Lord and My God." Jesus turns doubters to immediate action. And He is gentle in dealing with us in our doubts. Nicodemus doubted, but Jesus was patient with him; John the Baptist doubted, but Jesus praised him as a great man; Thomas doubted, but he learned about the sensitivity of Jesus.

Best we be forewarned against a rebellious heart, than a doubting one. Kierkegaard once said, "People try to persuade us that the objections against Christianity spring from doubt. This is a complete misunderstanding. The objections against Christianity spring from insubordination, the dislike of obedience, rebellion against all authority. As a result people have hitherto been beating the air in their struggle against objections, because they have fought intellectually with doubt instead of fighting morally with rebellion."[35]

Quickly As a Dream

Reading Psalm 90

"We glide along the tides of time as swiftly as a racing driver, and vanish as quickly as a dream" (Psalm 90:5 The Message).

In his novel, *The Second Coming*, Walker Perky posed the question, "Is it possible for people to miss their lives in the same way one misses a plane?" The answer is yes, if all we know is schedules. Perky describes such a life: "Not once in his entire life had he allowed himself to come to rest in the quiet corner of himself but had forever cast himself forward from some dark past he could not remember to a future which did not exist. Not once had he been present for his life. So his life had passed like a dream." (Quoted from *Reversed Thunder*, by Eugene H. Peterson. P192)

We may not enjoy our present state. Either God seldom measures up to our hopes for ministry – so it seems; or joy escapes because we fail to achieve self-imposed goals; or we suffer in unanticipated ways; or we despair of friends; or we are unable to handle success at any level. We just can't enjoy the present condition. Therefore we live under a clout of resignation, hoping for a better tomorrow. All of us succumb to this state at times.

Make the best of each day looking for those things for which we can be thankful and for what we can enjoy, knowing that life can quickly pass us by as a dream. Why not spend a few minutes writing on paper now or discuss with a friend this tendency not to relish the present. Complete this sentence, I am thankful today for the present because _______________

Humming the Tune

Reading: 2 Timothy 2:1-13

"So, my son, throw yourself into this work for Christ. Pass on what you have heard from me –the whole congregation saying Amen! – to reliable leaders who are competent to teach others." (2 Timothy 2:1,2 The Message).

Amid the usual excitement of Christmas, Aaron, at age eight, began playing on the piano an old familiar melody, "Up on the Rooftop." Aunts, uncles, siblings, cousins, grandma and grandpa were quieted down and listened to the music. Uncle Pete then slipped in alongside Aaron and began playing the accompanying music to go along with Aaron's song. They played the tune repeatedly, much to the delight of everyone there. Peter then suggested to Aaron: "Let's write our own song." Aaron responded enthusiastically to the idea, but wondered: "How do we write a song?"

Peter said, "Aaron, first hum a short tune, any tune." Aaron began playing with keys on the piano, but Peter persuaded him to hum a simple tune of his own, and then they would find the proper keys on the piano to play. In minutes Aaron was playing his tune with his Uncle Peter playing the accompanying part. Then they added two variations to the original tune, so they could go from one section to another without stopping. Later that day, I noticed Aaron sitting on the piano bench with his younger brother, Michael, and overheard Aaron say, "Michael, before you start playing, you've got to hum the tune."

Think before you practice. Thoughts from our head and our heart spill over into actions. Think first of pleasant things which will result in kind deeds.

"Finally, brethren, whatever is true, whatever is honorable, whatever is right, whatever is pure, whatever is lovely, whatever is of good repute, if there is any excellence and if anything worthy of praise, let your mind dwell on these things. The things you have learned and received and heard and seen in me, practice these things, and the God of peace shall be with you" (Philippians 4:8,9 NAS).

Bad-mouthing Others

Reading: James 4:1-12

"Don't bad-mouth each other, friends. It's God's Word, his Message, his Royal Rule, that takes a beating in that kind of talk. You're supposed to be honoring the Message, not writing graffiti all over it. God is in charge of deciding human destiny. Who do you think you are to meddle in the destiny of others?" (James 4:11,12 The Message).

Judging others is a dangerous practice; but most of us do it anyway, sometimes out of habit. Is there ever a right place or reason for judging someone else? It depends on whose ox is gored. When we're recipients of judgment from others, we thrash in pain, crying foul. On the other hand, when we're judging someone else, we pass it off – as easily as it is to say, "He deserves his lot in life, it couldn't happen to a better guy, he made the bed, let him lie in it." Judging seldom does more than fling others on the rocks of hopelessness, anger and despair; it doesn't heal.

Best that we pray for others, rather than judge them. Let God judge. When Jesus judges, when He cries, "Woe to you," He invites us to the Father's house. God is always seeking to bless, to restore, to bring us home. Jesus comes to us, not with his fist doubled up to beat on us. He comes to assure us that we are blessed and that He is in our midst to help, to rescue. He comes as the Savior.

Better yet, that we confine judgment to our own lives. Isn't that what the Apostle Paul was calling the Corinthian Church to do? We confess our sins, not some one else's. "Anyone who eats the bread or drinks the cup of the Master irreverently is like part of the crowd that jeered and spit on him at his death. Is that the kind of 'remembrance' you want to be part of: Examine your motives, test your heart, come to his meal in holy awe" (1 Corinthians 11 The Message).

Tom Younger

(Thoughts on judging from *Life Can Begin Again, Journey Without Luggage* by Helmut Thielicke)

The Kentucky Cycle

Reading: Ephesians 4:17-32

"Get rid of all bitterness, rage and anger, brawling and slander, along with every form of malice. Be kind and compassionate to one another, forgiving each other, just as in Christ God forgave you" (Ephesians 4:31.32 NIV).

An interesting story appeared in the November 1, 1993, issue of the New Yorker magazine, a portion of which I quote. It is about what the author describes as the Kentucky Cycle. The reference to Kentucky is not to disparage Kentuckians, but it illustrates an important truth for all of us. "Schenkkan told me he is fascinated by the importance we give to family legacies, and by the way things get handed down. Our family sagas continue to play themselves out in ways we're completely unaware of but that are still very potent. He believes that this is a strong force in The Kentucky Cycle."

"My wife (Schenkkan's) tells a wonderful story about a friend of hers who used to cut a pot roast in a really idiosyncratic way. Mary Anne said, 'Why do you do that?' And she said, 'I don't know. That's how my mother used to – I'll ask her.' She asked her mother, and her mother said, 'That's how your grandmother taught me.' The mamaw was alive, and they said, 'Mamaw, why did you do this?' And she said, 'We only had one pan, and it was a small pan. It was the only way you could get a pot roast in the oven.'

"Schenkklan goes straight from this humorous story to a serious commentary on it. 'How often are we, as emotional beings trimming our emotional psychic selves to fit a context that was true three or four generations back, that have no relevance today! We're still acting out those old feuds, those old arguments, those old issues.'"

Are you harboring bitterness in your soul against someone? Hear Eugene Peterson's paraphrase of our Ephesians' text: "Make a clean break with all cutting, backbiting, profane talk. Be gentle with one another, sensitive. Forgive one another as quickly and thoroughly as God in Christ forgave you" (The Message).

Don't continue to harbor bitterness because it has been a habit, or because you emulate the harsh feelings of another person.

O Lord, expunge any vicious cycle of bitterness I carry toward others.

Of Milkshakes and Love

Reading: Luke 18:35-Luke 19:11

"Zacchaeus, hurry down. Today is my day to be a guest in your home"(Luke 19:5 The Message).

I stood quietly by the casket that day, while a family was paying its last respect to a deceased Dad and Grandfather, Elijah Krick. Amid the tears in this final farewell on earth, Jeff, the grandson, stepped up to the casket, slipped a dollar into his Grandpa's coat pocket and said, "The last one's on me, Grandpa." The display provided the family with a moment of relief, no small amount of love and a closure. The family stood locked together in an embrace, mingled with tears. They broke into spontaneous, but subdued, laughter. Sensing that I was unaware of the meaning of his gesture with the dollar bill, Jeff told me about a favorite memory as a boy: those days when Grandpa Krick would pick him up after school, drive him to McDonald's where they drank milkshakes. Jeff is in his twenties. Someday he also is likely to be a grandfather. I can see it now; when Jeff's a grandfather he will no doubt find a way to take his grandchildren for milkshakes and tell them about their great-grandfather. What a loving and gentle man he was.

It's interesting, asking people what they remember about their deceased loved ones. One could imagine that memories would center on big events, and sometimes they do; like the trip you took together to Europe in prior years. There is nothing wrong with generous acts of a gratuity to loved ones; however, very often, memories center upon little things: a smile, a forgiving moment, a gentle reprimand, or just a chocolate shake. Little things like milkshakes reveal lasting love long after the shakes are gone.

When Jesus was passing through Jericho, He looked up into a tree and saw Zacchaeus, called to him, "Zacchaeus, hurry down. Today is my day to be a guest in your home." I'm sure Zacchaeus remembered more than a casual social engagement. Behind the look of Jesus, there was eternal love.

More Fit of Mind

Reading: Mark 8:27-38

"It is necessary that the Son of Man proceed to an ordeal of suffering, be tried and found guilty by the elders, high priests, and religion scholars, be killed, and after three days rise again. He said this simply and clearly so they couldn't miss it" (Mark 8:31 The Message).

There are times when God deals with us simply and conclusively, but we're unable to digest what's going on or what its intention is for us. We're just not in the frame of mind to accept more than the fact of the adventure. I observed this one night in my wood carver's group. There were six of us, one woman and five men. We carve birds, ducks, and sculptures.

Gene, who was present one evening, didn't pick up a knife or tool to carve the whole night. He was there only in body. I asked if he were all right. He said, yes, that he'd get to carving before the evening was over. But he never did. As we were cleaning up, ready to go home, Gene, said to me, "I just wasn't capable of carving tonight; my aunt died this afternoon. It kind of shakes you up."

I think that's what occurred with the disciples when Jesus first announced he would be killed, but rise again. They could scarcely react any more than my friend, Gene, when they heard the pronouncement of the cross. The mystery and interpretation would have to come later, when the disciples were in a more capable frame of mind. The disciples had to consider later, the implications of Christ's death. And also how that they expected to bear a cross, if they intended to follow him. "If any man will come after me, let him deny himself, and take up his cross, and follow me."

Now concerning Gene, I'll have an opportunity to ask him about the significance of death. Something we all have to think about and decide whether we intend to follow Jesus.

The Ministry of Interruption

Reading: Acts 26:19-32

"That was too much for Festus. He interrupted with a shout: 'Paul, you're crazy! You've read too many books, spent too much time staring off into space! Get a grip on yourself, get back in the real world!' But Paul stood his ground" (Acts 26:24 The Message).

Interruptions are a part of life; they go with the territory. We all get them; they come in all sizes and colors, sometimes in avalanche quantities. Two pastors, a young man and an older veteran were comparing notes about their respective ministries. The young man commiserated that unexpected intrusions during his normal ministry, often prevented ministry to others. The veteran pastor graciously pointed out to the young fellow: "I think those interruptions are our ministry."

Not all encroachments upon our time, come from people; often they come from some mechanical failure. Like the time the fan on the furnace yelped like a wounded helicopter, the propeller imploded on the sump pump, the water pipe froze at the juncture where the pipe ran outside the home. All this occurred in the same day, the day I was called to a funeral fifty miles away, the burial sight twelve miles further, with the temperature shivering at a minus 53 degrees wind chill. Interruptions are a part of life; we all get them. They come in all sizes and colors, sometimes in avalanche quantities.

Interruptions are experienced in one of three ways. Some come by means of the night; it is then in the morning we face a new day. Other breaks in routine come from suffering; suffering has a way of slowing us down. Then there is the grave. However, in death interruptions cease; there is no night in heaven, no suffering. What is important is how we view and then respond to interruptions. That's the secret to ministering to others; by asking God for wisdom to receive interruptions as coming from Him. We receive a new look at both interruptions and interrupters. The next time someone breaks into your routine, smile, breath a prayer of thanks to God for the intrusion, listen and look for a positive way to minister to the one interrupting you.

Our text has Paul in prison. By this interruption, God gave Paul the benefit of the value of time, checked the forces of evil, gave him the joy of a fresh beginning, and showed him that God's plans were largely of more importance than Paul's.

Morrison puts interruptions in perspective. "The more earnestly we take our life, and feel that it is a race and not a sauntering, the more we fret and sometimes nobly fret, at the insistence upon interruption." By recognizing unexpected intrusions as divine interruptions, we can cut back on stress. Perhaps we can cut back on our blood pressure pills also!

Rain

Reading: Genesis 7

Seven days from now I will send rain on the earth for forty days and forty nights; and I will wipe from the face of the earth every living creature I have made. And Noah did all that the LORD commanded him" (Genesis 7:4-5).

"You don't know enough to come out of the rain!" How many of us have been accused of this aberration over the years? Yet, there is something about a walk in the rain that quiets the soul, nourishes the senses, (Kodak). The indictment of me coming from my Mother still brings a smile: "You don't know enough to come in out of the rain." Here I am living in a wonderful state where rain is in abundance. Did you know it takes ten days flight for rain to fall from the sky to the earth; that Oregon can grow great lettuce for it takes six gallons of rainwater for a single serving; that a glass of milk just eight ounces of the white stuff takes 49 gallons of rainwater; that the steak I ate last night for dinner only took 2,600 gallons more?[36] (from *How Majestic is Thy Name*).

You may think you'd not enjoy living in Oregon in the wintertime. Let me tell you we see all the snow we want in the four mountain tops surrounding the Salem area; we mow our green lush lawns all through the winter; we enjoy many of our flowers in wintertime as well; we have clean air, a phenomenon not available in most urban areas. Yes, we are blessed. There is nothing like a fresh drink of Oregon water!

"He will be like rain falling on a mown field, like showers watering the earth. In his days the righteous will flourish; prosperity will abound till the moon is no more" (Psalm 72:6-7 NIV).

Flowers

Reading: Matthew 6:28-30

"We spring up like wildflowers in the desert and then wilt, transient as the shadow of a cloud" (Job 14:2 The Message).

"Flowers," wrote Ralph Waldo Emerson, "are a proud assertion that a ray of beauty out values all the utilities of the world." My greatest memory of the beauty of flora and fauna takes me back to 1975 when my wife and I visited New Zealand and stood on top of Mount Cook. The rays of the sun danced on a vast field of wildflowers of all colors and different hues. Most spectacular were the many varieties of mountain buttercup (Ranunculus) and daisy (Celmisia). The Mount Cook Lily, Ranunculus lyallii is the largest buttercup in the world.

New Zealand reminded me a lot of Western Oregon. Many transplants from other parts of the country migrate to Oregon and are elated at how much their ability to grow and tend flowers. We are blessed with beauty year round. This is God's way of reminding us not to fret about our circumstances but to put our faith in Him.

"The grass withers and the flowers fall, because the breath of the LORD blows on them. Surely the people are grass. The grass withers and the flowers fall, but the word of our God stands forever" (Isaiah 40:7-8 NIV).

Correction All Around

Reading: Proverbs 15:16-32

"He who ignores discipline despises himself, but whoever heeds correction gains understanding" (Proverbs 15:32 NIV).

"The rod of correction imparts wisdom, but a child left to himself disgraces his mother" (Proverbs 29:15)

One day a pre-schooler threw a fit of rebellion, called his teacher a name in language inappropriate for any adult use, not to say, a child. The teacher admonished the kid without success, upon which she marched him kicking and screaming all the way to the principal's office. The boy continued his snit. At that point a policy has to be invoked by the principal, to phone the parent and recommend a supervised spanking. If permission to spank is granted, the disobedience is addressed by applying appropriate measures, teaching the child this behavior is unacceptable. Discipline was administered in this case, at the level of the child's posterior. The mother of the boy gave permission, noting her son hadn't heard the last of it; she would confront his ill-gotten behavior when he returned home.

While there may not be simple solutions to handling disobedient children, we applaud educators and parents who work together as in the instance cited. Parents who challenge outbursts of rebellion in children are less likely to face the same objectionable behavior when the child becomes a teenager. If, as teens, there is still need for correction – and it is quite likely – the child has learned there is precedent for the correction. The child knows his parents care enough to face him with tough love.

The rest of the story is that there were two pre-school boys with the same last name; a detail the principal had not noticed before he called the mother. Yes, he phoned wrong mother. Imagine the explaining her son, as innocent as the whitest lily on the pond, did to assure his mother he was not the guilty boy after he got spanked. By evening all apologies issued to the guilty and the innocent, resulted in good will from all parties. The next day, both little guys showed up for class; one with a cherubic look of relief and one with a cherubic look of respect for his teacher.

God doesn't make mistakes about who needs correction. Sometimes we do, and when we do, we must admit it. Better that we risk mistakes, than ignore the need for discipline.

Seizing the Moment

Reading: 17:1-12

"Jesus took Peter and the brothers, James and John, and led them up a high mountain. His appearance changed from the inside out, right before their eyes. Sunlight poured from his face. His clothes were filled with light. Then they realized that Moses and Elijah were also there in deep conversation with him. Peter broke in, 'Master, this is a great moment! What would you think if I built three memorials here on the mountain – one for you, one for Moses, one for Elijah?'" (Matthew 17:1-4 The Message).

The great moment when Peter saw the glory of Christ is nearly lost to Peter because he began talking when he should have been listening. I have no idea how many great moments with God I may have lost in life – for the same reason – quick to talk, slow to listen. What of the great moment in Paul's life on the Damascus road? Had Paul spent three years talking about it, rather than three years on the backside of the desert, which he did, listening to God, would he have been stronger? Do you think Paul's calling from God could have withstood the fierce onslaught from the enemies of the Gospel of Christ? What of the great moment in Joseph's life, sold into slavery at the hands of his brothers? Would Joseph understand the necessity of forgiving his brothers, had he not been listening to God? How about the great moment in Mary's life, while she was bearing the child Jesus, the Messiah? Babbling among friends in town of this incredible event seemed the natural thing to do. Mary chose to listen instead, to ponder the ways of God with her life.

Think of the great moments in your life. Those moments of joy, like taking a life partner, birth of a baby, a job promotion. How about those moments of confusion and disappointment, which come unexpectedly? What will you do upon hearing your doctor say, "I think you have an option to surgery. Chemotherapy." If the doctor's advice were good news, will you respond with thanks for the joy of the good news? Hearing the bad news, do you think you will respond with anger, shaking your fist at God, searching for words to say, rather than listening to God? Great moments need not be lost to us. In our Bible reading today, the disciples did capture the great moment recognizing and proclaiming Jesus as the Messiah.

Great moments are often lost to us; sometimes because of fear and sometimes because of our babbling. There is no guarantee of power. How we need to listen to the words of the Lord. Where would we be, if it were not for the patience of God?

We should try to wake up each day with a prayer on our heart: "Lord, help me see your glory as my day unfolds before you. Teach me to listen patiently and learn the lessons in my journey that will enable me to grow in your likeness."

Working to Give

Reading: Matthew 6:19-34

"Do not store up for yourselves treasures on earth, where moth and rust destroy, and where thieves break in and steal. But store up for yourselves treasures in heaven, where moth and rust do not break in and steal. For where your treasure is, there your heart will be also" (Matthew 6:19-21 NIV).

One Sunday while talking about giving, I mentioned a news article about a friend, James E. Kelley, who gave the Washington House a gift of $500,000. The Washington House treats people for substance abuse. Later, a man in our congregation asked, “Do you happen to have Kelley's address?” Then he handed me an encouraging card, asking if I'd send it to Kelley. It read: “My pastor said you made a donation to Washington House in Fort Wayne. Washington House made a big difference in my life, where I was treated for alcohol abuse in October 1986. They have a great program for alcohol and drug abuse and through their programs and Jesus Christ, I have been free from alcohol for seven years. Thank you your concern for others in giving. I am one in appreciation.” Signed: David Rollins. November 1993

I phoned Kelley, read the card to him and thanked him for being an example of one who exercised the gift of giving. He told me he would soon be 76. “The only reason I keep working at this age – I don't need money – is just for the joy of giving it to help others.”

“You'll not likely go wrong here if you keep remembering that our Master said, ‘You're far happier giving than getting’” (Acts 20:35 The Message).

O For a Grateful Spirit

Reading: Colossians 2:6-23

“Give thanks in all circumstances for this is God's will for you” (1 Thessalonians 5:18 NIV).

I first became aware of the importance of a grateful spirit from my mother. As a lad we had a few relatives who, without children and of great income, remembered us on holidays with gifts. They varied from clothes to subscriptions to the *Reader's*

Digest and the *National Geographic*. Frequently a check was tucked in the note. But the gift my sister and I prized most was the box of a hundred suckers with safety sticks. My uncle invented the sticks and manufactured candy. We'd receive two boxes of suckers during the course of a year.

Mother insisted we write thank you notes for the gifts before we were allowed to eat the suckers, read the magazines, wear the clothes or cash the checks. At times we phoned our thanks. Mom not only made us aware of the need to acknowledge a gift, but also that a thankful spirit was a practice to be cultivated. Although we are no longer children, sis and I learned that an appreciative spirit is an important characteristic to cultivate.

We live in a society possessed by a huge amount of ingratitude. And that has always been true with every generation. Nine of ten lepers whom Jesus healed, offered no thanks. In 1848 Russia helped Austria defeat a Hungarian uprising. Austria's Prince Schwarzenberg, when asked what Austria owed Russia for their help replied, "Austria will astound the world with the magnitude of her ingratitude." Another example of a thankless spirit occurred in 1966. Charles de Gaulle treated American troops with utter disdain. Not long before Allied troops had liberated France from Hitler's domination. The fact of France's partnership with Allied nations in NATO notwithstanding – de Gaulle told American troops to get out of France. "Do you want us to move American cemeteries out of France as well?" asked Secretary of State Dean Rusk. His was a tone of bitter hurt. Hurt is how liberators leave; which is why they must never go ashore in search of thanks. The Apostle Paul charged mankind in general of ingrates when he wrote, "For although they knew God, they neither glorified him as God nor gave thanks to him, but their thinking became futile and their foolish hearts were darkened" (Romans 1:21).

Tom Younger

Living Out Thanksgiving

Reading: Exodus 13:1-10

"My counsel for you is simple and straightforward: just go ahead with what you've been given. You received Christ Jesus, the Master, now live him. You're deeply rooted in him. You're well constructed upon him. You know your way around the faith. Now do what you've been taught. School's out; quit studying the subject and start living it! And let your living spill over into thanksgiving" (Colossians 2:6,7 The Message).

Walking in the Light as Christians means among other things, to let our lives spill over with thanksgiving. Surely, we have a lot to be thankful for. Israel was encouraged to "Remember this day, which you came out from Egypt, out of the house of bondage" (Exodus 13:3). It might help us, before we get all bothered with searching out how to use spiritual gifts, how to share Christ with others or how to teach a class, to check our appreciation for who we are in Christ.

Now of what benefit is a grateful spirit? I suggest several benefits, leaving it to you to expand the list. Gratitude empowers us to do all to the glory of God. (1 Corinthians 10:31). It enables us to throw ourselves wholeheartedly into life, like Hezekiah, who "in every work that he began in the service of the house of God, and in the law, and in the commandments to seek his God. He did it with all his heart and prospered" (2 Chronicles 31:21). Thanksgiving puts in us a fresh heart, invigorates our work, enlivens our speech, and opens doors of service, setting the stage for developing new friendships.

For instance, friends of mine prayed one evening before they began eating at Richards Restaurant. They were unaware of being observed by Burt and Bobbie Derusha who were occupying a nearby table. The Derushas, bone tired from moving that day, introduced themselves to Judy and John, my friends. "Where do you folks go to church?" asked Burt. "We are the Derushas and have just moved to town and are in need of a church home. We appreciated your taking time to give thanks for your meal and thought we would like to attend church with you on Sunday." Bobbie and Burt joined Judy and John in church that very week-end. The Derushas determined that day that they had found a good church home, thanks to their new friends, John and Judy. It all started with the expression of a grateful spirit.

Try living one entire day in utter thanksgiving. Balance every complaint with five gratitudes, every criticism with five compliments. The time will come when we find ourselves saying, "Not 'please,' but 'thank you," as Annie Dillard notes in the *Pilgrim At Tinker Creek*.

A Father's Legacy

Reading: Hebrews 11:1-10

"A good man leaves an inheritance to his children's children..." (Proverbs 13:22 NAS).

Being a father ranks high on the list of privileges for which I am thankful. Having fathered five children myself, I am blessed each day. As years pass fathers move with their children through eras symbolized by diaper bags, kindergartens, reading and studying, Sunday school, church, conversion and baptism, little league, 4-H, debate club, dissecting frogs, dating, driving for the first time, reporting auto wrecks he or she became involved in, disappointments, failures, colleges, freedom from parents supervision, serious courtship, marriage, grandchildren, switching roles with parents as they care for them in old age, preparing for the day when children will become as parents to us, and finally death when we are stored in the memories of one or two generations.

Many a spiritual legacy is created in the action packed life of a father. I'm sure you and I want to establish a spiritual legacy for our children assuring them the 'mercy' and 'righteousness' of the Lord for a long time to come. That was the promise to Caleb: "Surely the land on which your foot has trodden shall be an inheritance to you and to your children forever, because you have followed the Lord [your] God fully" (Joshua 14:9). As fathers we have the responsibility to be God-fearing, keeping His covenant, obeying his commands, and living God-honoring lives.

Few of us know of our spiritual heritage beyond a generation ago. But I learned from Tom Zook while he was doing some finish work in our basement room, that in 1741 an eighth generation grandfather Zook, who was a Christian [Anabaptist], served prison time in Europe, because he refused to let his children be baptized by the state church. He was released from prison on the condition he leave his country. He came to America and now a quarter-century later our friend, Tom Zook, is enjoying the spiritual legacy of seeing his own daughters [Ann Zook Schherk and Susan Zook Morris] and his grandchildren walk with the Lord in the shadow of a godly man who in reality is unknown to us, except for the fact that his name is recorded in the Book of Life in heaven, in Foxes Book of Martyrs and the genealogical record under the name 'Zook'. Like that of Abel, he "being dead yet speaketh" (Hebrews 11:4 KJV).

Pleasing God

Reading: Genesis 6:9-22

"Noah was a righteous man, blameless among the people of his time, and he walked with God...So God said to Noah...'Make yourself an ark of cypress wood,'...Noah did everything just as God commanded him" (Genesis 6:9,13,14, 22 NIV).

As Christians we make many decisions each day in our walk with God, some of which in retrospect, are not among our better ones. However, we never regret those decisions clearly aimed at pleasing God. There is no satisfaction to compare with obeying Him. Consider those in the Bible whose commitment was to follow the Lord.

"The Lord had said to Abram, 'Leave your country, your people and your Father's household and go to the land I will show you'...So Abram left, as the Lord had told him" (Genesis 12:1,4).

"Now the Lord had said to Moses in Midian, 'Go back to Egypt, for all the men who wanted to kill you are dead.' So Moses took his wife and sons, put them on a donkey and started back to Egypt. And he took the staff of God in his hand" (Exodus 4:19,20).

[Joshua commanded] "Choose for yourselves this day whom you will serve, whether the gods your forefathers worshipped beyond the River, or the gods of the Amorites, in whose land you are living. But as for me and my household, we will serve the Lord.' Then the people answered, 'Far be it from us to forsake the Lord to serve other gods! We will serve the Lord" (Joshua 24:15,16,20).

"When the king heard the words of the Book of the Law, he tore his robes...And renewed the covenant in the presence of the Lord –to follow the Lord and keep his commands, regulations and decrees with all his heart and his soul." (2 Kings 22:11,23:3).

At the end of that time, I, Nebuchadnezzar, raised my eyes toward heaven, and my sanity was restored. Then I praised the Most High: I honored and glorified him who lives forever. His dominion is an eternal dominion...At the same time my sanity was restored...Now I, Nebuchadnezzar, praise and exalt and glorify the King of heaven" (Daniel 4:34,37).

"As Jesus was walking beside the Sea of Galilee, he saw two brothers, Simon called Peter and his brother Andrew. They were casting a net into the Lake, for they were fishermen. 'Come, follow me,' Jesus said, 'and I will make you fishers of men.' At once they left their nets and followed him" (Matthew 4:18-20).

"The jailer called for lights, rushed in and fell trembling before Paul and Silas...He asked, 'Sirs, what must I do to be saved?'...The jailer brought them into his house and set a meal before them, he was filled with joy because he had come to believe in God – he and his whole family" (Acts 16:31,34).

A Beggar Attitude

Reading: Philippians 4:10-23

"Now faith is the assurance of things hoped for, the conviction of things not seen" (Hebrews 11:1 NIV).

Dr. Gresham Machen, professor of apologetics at Westminster Seminar, used to say, "The beggar attitude." God is in the business of making beggars out of all His disciples. The natural man bristles at this. He wants to be self-sufficient, capable, wanting nothing. According to the world's standard, the church at Laodicea had arrived. It was rich, increased with goods, and need of nothing (Revelation 3:17). Yet Jesus said it was the worst of all His churches, fit to be thrown out.

I love to be self-sufficient! I loathe depending upon someone else! Yet God continually whisks away my resources until I crawl like a beggar to His door and ask for help. This is because I stubbornly refuse to be like a beggar in spirit. The Bible is full of beggar-spirited people: Abel, the Syrophoenician women, the publican and others. They received the blessing while the self-sufficient ones went away empty. Jesus said I must become as a child. Is there ever a greater beggar than a child? Beggary is a child's nature and never a blush about it. This is the way God wants us to be. It is when I beg that God is able to put His (not my) resources into my hands and after all; nothing works like God's power.

The spiritual beggar has a keen eye of faith, a proper system of values and a successful method of prayer. He knows that when all the niceties are strained out of his coming to God, the whole matter boils down to "his need and God's supply." That is why beggars are direct, simple, and expectant. What a beggar George Mueller, that great man of prayer, was. Lord, may heaven's doors be open toward me like it was toward Mueller!

The Way Back Is the Way Out

Reading: Genesis 13:1-18

"Abram went up from Egypt to the Negev...where he had first built an altar. There Abram called on the name of the Lord" (Genesis 131,4 NIV).

When Henry Grady, the gifted editor and orator of Atlanta, was at the peak of his career he suddenly realized that he had been neglecting the things of God. With all his popularity he felt emptiness and a deep dissatisfaction. The armor of his soul had rusted through neglect of prayer and worship. As a boy he had professed faith in Jesus Christ and allegiance to him; but devotional habits had been buried under the interest and concerns of his professional life.

One night in the midst of his greatest popularity, when he concluded one of his great speeches, he contacted a few of his closest associates and said, I am leaving the city for a little while. I am going to see Mother in her little home. I have something I want to tell her. He took a back road to his mother's cottage, and when he greeted her he said, "All this fame, all this notoriety, all the applause does not satisfy my heart. I once thought that I was a Christian; but if I was, I have strayed far away from God. Now, Mother, I want to ask you if I may kneel at your knees like I did years ago and offer a simple prayer. Then when I get in bed, will you tuck the covers around me like you used to do when I was a little boy? Will you bend over me and pray for me as you used to do that God may teach me and help me and guide me?" Of course she would. What Christian mother would not feel a deep joy in her heart when such a request was made.

Henry Grady knelt at his mother's knee and offered a simple prayer. Then when he was ready for bed his mother came and tucked him in. She bent over him and with tears flowing down her cheeks she prayed for her son and committed him once more to the Savior. She kissed him and left the room. Very early the next morning he came to his mother's room and said, "Mother I was a little child last night. I felt drawn to Jesus, and he spoke to my poor, wandering heart." And as he spoke there was a light on his face like the brightness of the dawning day. (The story of Henry Grady as told by John Reed Miller in *My Turn*)

Whatever has complicated or cluttered up your life, there can be forgiveness and newness of life for you at the old altar. You may have neglected that altar a long, long time. Your activities, your business or interests may have crowded out the things of God. The way back is for you the way out.

You can find the same blessing from the Lord, the same relief and release, a new joy and peace if you pray.

"Out of my shameful failure and loss,
Jesus, I come to thee.
Out of unrest and arrogant pride
Into thy blessed will to abide,
Jesus, I come to thee."

Singing From the Heart

Reading: 1 Timothy 1:1-11

"The goal of this command is love which comes from a pure heart and a good conscience and a sincere faith" (1 Timothy 1:5 NIV).

Last week Luciano Pavarotti taught a class to 14 opera students in Staccato Italian. For three hours Pavarotti dispensed criticism with Old World charm. As he sat behind a table to one side of the stage, the students who were working on master's degrees in voice, filed past him with nervous smiles and launched into their arias. Some voices fell flat, while others complained or pounded like a tired heart. Pavarotti insisted they not waver from the text: the human passion and conflict that is opera. He sprinkled his comments with Italian. "It sounds like sofecha; give it heart," he said, using the Italian word for theory. As the arias wafted through the auditorium and spilled onto 65th Street (NY), Pavarotti added, "It is a beautiful thing to see in a young singer, with everything coming from the heart."

The major meaning of the heart in the New Testament is figurative: the center of life, feeling, and even spiritual response. We are to forgive one another from our hearts "This is how my Heavenly Father will treat each of you unless you forgive your brother from your heart" (Matthew 18:35 NIV). When we obey God, we should do so wholeheartedly, from the bottom of our hearts. "But God be thanked, that though you used to be slaves to sin, you wholeheartedly obeyed the form of teaching to which you were entrusted" (Romans 6:17 NIV).

The New Testament refers to the heart from which pours our emotions, reasoning, spiritual instincts, and God-consciousness. An anonymous Christian once said, "Hardening of the heart ages more people than hardening of the arteries."

Pavarotti urged his students to sing not from theory, but with heart. Likewise, we are required as Christians to live lives in tune with the heartbeat of God.

The Right Choice

Reading: Exodus 2:11-25

"Moses...went out to his brethren, and looked on their burdens... So he looked this way and that way and when he saw there was no one around, he struck down the Egyptian and hid him in the sand" (Exodus, 2:11, 12 NAS).

When Moses looked at his burdened brethren, he contemplated their lot with sympathy. It was then that "He chose to be mistreated along with the people of God rather than to enjoy the pleasures of sin for a short time. He regarded disgrace for the sake of Christ as of greater value than the treasures of Egypt, because he was looking ahead to his reward. This look upon his brethren caused him to cast his lot with them. A noble look.

But then when he "looked this way and that way" before taking a man's life, he failed to discern God's timing for Israel's deliverance. He fell short in his own readiness for the task; He neglected to assess his brethren's readiness for the move. He misread the means of deliverance; it was to be by the staff not the sword; by the meekness, not the wrath of Moses. He thought that his own people would realize that God was using him to rescue them, but they did not. (Acts 7:25 NIV). Moses' zeal for the welfare of his people caused him to run ahead of God. His timing for the release of Israel impelled him to the crime of murder. For which he could not be excused.

From this incident in Moses' life we can learn a lot. Good intentions are not enough. When leading people we can't assume they understand. When we lead and people do not follow, there may be a good reason. When we have to look this way and that way to see if anyone is observing our actions, we can be pretty sure that what we are contemplating doing is doubtful and wrong in God's sight..

Why We Honor God's Name

Reading: 1 Corinthians 10: 23-11:1

"So whether you eat or drink or whatever you do, do it all for the glory of God. Do not cause anyone to stumble whether Jews, Greeks, or the church of God" (1 Corinthians 10:31,32 NIV).

We honor God's name because of all that He has done for us:

Forgiveness of sins: For His name's sake, the Lord forgives our sins. "I write to you, dear children, because your sins have been forgiven on account of his name" (1 John 2:12).

Guidance: "He guides me in paths of righteousness for his name's sake". "Since you are my rock and my fortress, for the sake of your name lead and guide me" (Psalm 23:3, 31:3).

Deals with us: "But you, O Sovereign Lord, deal well with me for your name's sake; out of the goodness of your love, deliver me" (Psalm 109:21).

Revives us: "For your name's sake, O Lord, preserve my life; in your righteousness, bring me out of trouble" (Psalm 143:11).

Service: For His name's sake we ought to serve Him. "Dear friend, you are faithful in what you are doing for the brothers, even though they are strangers to you. They have told the church about your love. You will do well to send them on their way in a manner worthy of God. It was for the sake of the Name that they went out, receiving no help from the pagans" (3 John 5-7 NIV).. "You have preserved and have endured hardships for my name, and have not grown weary", (Revelation 2:3 NIV).

Sacrifice: "And everyone who has left houses or brothers or sisters or father or mother or children or fields for my sake will receive a hundred times as much and will inherit eternal life" (Matthew 19:29 NIV).

Willing to suffer reproach: "All men will hate you because of me, but he who stands firm to the end will be saved". "Then you will be handed over to be persecuted and put to death, and you will be hated by all nations because of me" (Matthew 10:22,24:9).

A Life Well Ordered

Reading: Matthew 26:17-30

"While they were eating, Jesus took bread, gave thanks and broke it, and gave it to his disciples, saying. 'Take and eat; this is my body.' Then he took the cup, gave thanks and offered it to them saying, 'Drink from it, all of you. This is my blood of the covenant, which is poured out for many for the forgiveness of sins.'" (Matthew 26:26,27 NIV).

A.B. Bruce wrote, "Jesus intimates that the new covenant concerns the many, not the few – not Israel alone, but all nations; it is a gospel which He bequeaths to sinners of mankind." (A.B. Bruce, *The Training of the Twelve* p 361) Bruce contends that the cross was well ordered. It connects the blessing of pardon with the sacrificial death of Him through whom it comes to us. It provides that sin shall not be pardoned till it has been adequately atoned for by the sacrifice of the sinner's Friend. It is just and right that without the shedding of the Righteous One's blood there should be no remission for the unrighteous. It serves well the interest of divine love, as it gives love a worthy career and it is admirably adapted to the elevation of a fallen, degraded race; out of a state of corruption into a state of holiness.

Well ordered; just as Christ's death on the cross was well ordered, so our lives lived in submission to Christ are well ordered. As Paul Rees point out, "The highest forms of self-expression are to be found not in the lotus gardens of self-gratification but in the gymnasium of self-renunciation." Since we live in a society of self-aggrandizement – thirst for power, wealth, position and reputation equates with success, submission to Christ is likened to weak character. It's not fashionable to address the theme of self-renunciation. Neither is it trendy to practice it. But by not doing so, we simply repeat mistakes other Christian societies have made, such as Denmark, where Soren Kierkegaard pointed out that we ought not to forget self-denial.

Faith

Reading: Romans 4:1-8

"Now when a man works, his wages are not credited to him as a gift, but as an obligation. However, to the man who does not work but trusts God who justifies the wicked, his faith is credited as righteousness" (Romans 4:4,5 NIV).

Few subjects are more important for us to understand than that of faith.

1. Born into eternal life through faith
2. Declared righteous before God by faith.
3. Forgiven by faith.
4. Healed by faith.
5. Understand the mysteries of creation by faith.
6. Learn God's word by faith.
7. Overcome the world by faith.
8. Walk by faith, not by sight.
9. Enter God's rest by faith.
10. Controlled and empowered by the Holy Spirit by faith.

11. Can only please God by faith.
12. Everything we seek to do for God that is not from the source of faith is sin.

Faith is the source of our strength, our provision, courage, guidance, victory over the world system, the flesh and the devil.

Faith is the only thing that can sustain us in the trials and persecutions predicted for the last days.

"But without faith it is impossible to please God, because anyone who comes to him must believe that he exists and that he rewards those who earnestly seek him" (Hebrews 11:6 NIV).

Joy a Hundred Times Over

Reading: Matthew 19: 16-30

"...anyone who sacrifices home, family, fields – whatever— because of me will get it all back a hundred times over..." (Matthew 19:29,30 The Message).

God called Everett Haines into the ministry in 1952. He worked by day as a carpenter and studied by night for the ministry he was about to enter. Upon his appointment to a Methodist Church in Wolf Lake, Haines moved his wife and daughters – Martha and Nancy (and a sister yet to be born) – into the parsonage. Several years later, God sent Haines to serve five churches at once, in LaGrange County. From there he served two churches in Waterloo; moved on to Huntington (Noblesville) and finished his pastoral career in Wolcottville (Woodruff Grove), all in Indiana. He continued preaching Sundays, pinch hitting for pastors who were ill or away on vacation and retired after 27 years of ministry.

Martha and Nancy had good times growing up as "Preacher's Kids", cutting away brush to get into the parsonage, evicting tenants in the parsonage (eighteen incumbent rats) before moving in; paying out more for D-Con to rid the rats than milk to feed the kids; using corn cobs to plug entry points of unwanted critters; crying together as a family; learning of parish family squabbles by listening through the heat ducts as people vented pent-up frustrations to Dad downstairs; observing times when political opinions called for Republicans to sit on one side of the church, Democrats on the opposite side; witnessing Dad – often too exhausted to preach – laboring on, committing intense loyalty to God, who honored him with the high calling of preaching the Gospel of Jesus Christ. Haines never preached before large congregations, sometimes as few as fifty people were present. Yet, he was faithful. He did like Mary, when she poured out precious perfume upon the body of Jesus. He did what he could, when he could.

In retrospect, Dad still reminds his family and friends of Jesus' words: "anyone who sacrifices home, family, fields – whatever – because of me will get it all back a hundred times over, not to mention the considerable bonus of eternal life. This is the Great Reversal: many of the first ending up last, and the last first" (Matthew 19:19,30 The Message).

Nothing Is Coincidence

Reading: Romans 8:18-27

"...waiting does not diminish us, any more than waiting diminishes a pregnant mother. We are enlarged by waiting" (Romans 8:22,23 The Message).

One evening I slipped over to the Mount Diablo Medical Center in Concord, California to pray with my friend and colleague, Carrel Aagard. He had been scheduled to undergo a heart catheterization, but it was postponed because of a staphylococcus infection. The wait was on. I dearly loved this man; a veteran missionary of more than 30 years, an encourager like none I had ever seen; unrelenting in his compassion to see others come to Christ. We prayed together and I promised to return on the morning of the scheduled heart catheter procedure. I gave Carrel a copy of Ulrich Schaffer's *Greater Than Our Hearts* – his prayers and reflections. Two days later I walked into Carrel's room to pray with him, but he wasn't there. The medical team had taken him early. Spotting Ulrich's prayers and meditations on the table beside Carrel's bed, I sat reading it. I noticed that alongside two of Schaffer's poems, Carrel had made a notation. One poem was titled: *Nothing is Coincidence.* Mt D. M. C. (Mount Diablo Medical Center) 7/22/85, apparently Carrel had come to terms with the frustration of postponing the rescheduling a procedure because of a staff infection. The poem read;

> I don't believe in coincidence anymore
> Because I know
> That which seems coincidental
> Is exactly the plan
> God is pursuing for my life
> With loving certainty.
>
> Above all coincidences
> I see the palms of hands
> Into which is written my name;
> Ulrich Schaffer
> You belong to me
> Stay with me,
> I love you.
> (Mt. D,M.C. 7/22/85)

The other notation was alongside the poem *Confusions.* In Carrell's handwriting on the morning before surgery was the notation: 7/24/85 "Heart Cath." The poem read:

> Show me where I am imagining things
> Show me where my feelings are sentimental,
> Superficial and dishonest,

Where I feel sorry for myself,
Where I pretend to be in pain.
And teach me to experience
The joy in suffering,
The faith in danger,
And a yearning for your testing.

After reading a few minutes, a nurse entered the room and asked, "Are you Carrel's pastor?" I affirmed it was so. She requested I go with her into the surgery room. Carrel needed me; he was struggling. We entered the room and found Carrel, dead. There were the two physicians and several nurses present – silent, stunned. Efforts to revive him had failed. The doctor who had been doing the procedure left for home. Devastated, he had lost his first patient. It seemed only a minute before Carrel's wife, Fern, arrived. Then other pastors came to try to comfort the family and then the surgical team.

Before I left the hospital that morning I went back to Carrel's room and picked up Schaffer's book to again read the two passages he had marked. They became the heart of the message, preached later in a memorial service in Carrel's honor, as I reminded all of us that nothing is coincidence, all is according to God's plan and our confusions can be put to rest in Christ.

So You Think You Failed

Reading: 1 Corinthians 15:50-58

"With all this going for us, my dear, dear friends, stand your ground. And don't hold back. Throw yourselves into the work of the Master, confident that nothing you do for him is a waste of time or effort" (1 Corinthians 15:58 The Message).

Dorothy Burough, four days before she died of tuberculosis at the age of eighteen, wrote:

> God, let me lose triumphantly, This is my prayer today
> I, who always prayed to win Along a glorious way.
> God, let me shun all the bitterness
> Of envy or despair,
> That I have run the race and lost While others have gotten there.
> God let me get my breath again, Then Lord, my head still high
> Quite unashamed I did not win
> Glad I had dared to try.

Until I learned to live my meditations (God's Word), not my nerves, failure was a bitter pill to swallow. But as important as my faithfulness is, isn't God's faithfulness the ultimate issue? Therefore, I, like Dorothy, pray for a larger view of God and His plan, despite my feeble attempts and many failures. There's a song whose lyrics embrace: "I've read the back of the book, and we win." No one likes to fail, but what if we had never tried? At this late stage in life, I wonder what might have been, had I only dared to trust God more. Perhaps I should think more about what F. W. Robertson meant when he wrote, "In God's world, for those who are in earnest, there is not failure. No work truly done, no word earnestly spoken, no sacrifice freely made, was made in vain."

The Heart Craves What the Mind Desires

Reading: Philippians 4:1-13

"Summing it all up, friends, I'd say you'll do best by filling your minds and meditating on things true, noble, reputable, authentic, compelling, gracious – the best, not the worst; the

beautiful, not the ugly; things to praise, not things to curse. Put into practices what you learned from me, what you heard and now saw and realized. Do that, and God, who makes everything work together, will work you into his most excellent harmonies" (Philippians 4:8 The Message).

How shall I begin my walk with the Lord today? A crucial strategy for engaging in a good day. Make every effort to look for the best in others, letting God care for what is worst; seek to bring out the beauty in others, forsaking the ugly; search for reason to praise others, rather than something to criticize or condemn.

How do I accomplish this noble task? By reading the Scriptures, following the Apostle Paul's example and practicing the art of meditation on things true, noble, reputable, authentic, compelling, gracious. Practice, practice, practice. One day at a time, one step at a time.

God will make your day. He will work together all things for good and orchestrate your relationship with others with whom you come in contact. By days end, you will be filled with gladness in your walk with Him, having been an encouragement to others. Find the heart's craving fulfilled in your mind's desire.

Prayer:

"I will arise and bless You, Lord my God' You are from everlasting to everlasting.

Blessed by Your glorious name, Which is exalted above all blessing and praise" (Nehemiah 9:5).

"As for me, I will see Your face in righteousness; When I awake, I will be satisfied with Your likeness" (Psalm 17:15).

Tom Younger

Others Coming After

Reading: 1 Kings 18:16-30

"And this was his message: 'After me will come one more powerful than I, the thongs of whose sandals I am not worthy to stoop down and untie'" (Mark 1:7 NIV).

In our youth, full of ourselves, we lean into the wind with a heady view of who we are. Pride soon takes command as we lose our perspective, our relative importance and place in God's economy. As great a person as was Elijah, his self evaluation concluded that he was the one man in Israel who was left standing and who had not bowed his knee to Baal. Imagine Elijah's astonishment when God revealed to him that He had seven thousand Israelites who hadn't bowed the knee to Baal nor kissed him. Indeed, pride goes before a fall; and before we amount to much in God's sight, we must face the fact that we are but one in the stream of God's grace. There will be others coming, as great or greater than we are, so we dare not assume an inflated view of our own importance.

We learned early on as handball players, that no matter how accomplished we became, there was, sitting in the wings, someone eager to jump onto the court and teach us a lesson. Even if that someone wasn't a good enough player to whip us in a match, there would be someone else waiting to take us on.

So, too, in the realm of our service to the Lord, there will always be one more to follow. Keep focused on the task at hand. Don't think more highly of yourselves than is proper. God has someone standing in the wings to take over when our time passes. It will come to pass.

Without Deceit

Reading: John 1:43-50

"Nathanael…in whom there is nothing false" (John 1:47 NIV).

One of our nation's former vice presidents concluded giving an interview, then kicked back to chitchat with the reporter. The vice president started talking about the art of not being himself. He meant the art of being sincere on camera, in front of an audience, without really being sincere. A lot of people practice sincerity because it's not in their makeup to begin with. By any other name it is life based on deceit. Jesus looked upon Nathanael and recognized that in him there was no guile, treacherous cunning, and skillful deceit. Insincerity has no place in our lives. God sees it for what it is; count on it. So do our friends. We can live as Jacob did (Genesis 23:35), deceiving others and get by it for a while, but not for long.

Fortunately, the practice of deceit surfaces its ugly head in many ways. Marshall Pugh, British author wrote in the *Chancer* "[they] exchanged the quick, brilliant smile of women who dislike each other on sight." Thomas Fuller, English physician, once wrote: "With foxes we must play the fox." There are a loft of foxes in the world, some commercial, some political, and some in the church. Must we play the fox and practice deceit in dealing with those who do? Not according to the Bible. "Now this is our boast: Our conscience testifies that we have conducted ourselves in the world, and especially in our relations with you, in the holiness and sincerity that are from God. We have done so not according to worldly wisdom but according to God's grace" (2 Corinthians 1:12 NIV).

You can't beat living life sincere, unaffected, unfeigned, wholehearted. That's the kind of friendship sought after.

Tom Younger

Committed To Our Post

Reading: 2 Corinthians 6:1-13

"We put no stumbling block in anyone's path, so that our ministry will not be discredited" (2 Corinthians 6:3 NIV).

In Christian colleges students agree to attend chapel services. When I attended college, not only were we required to attend chapel, but entered a designated door, registered our presence and sat in a designated seat. I thought that a bit much then.

Years later I became president of a college where chapel attendance was on an honor system. Noticing that some students ignored this commitment, one day instead of attending chapel, I visited the library. Many students were there. I talked to one student who was cloistered away in a private room. Since I was new to the college, this senior student didn't know me well and I didn't know him at all. We talked a while. Then I asked why he wasn't in chapel. His matter of fact reply was that he had more important things to do. "Like what?" I asked. He answered, "Study theology." When asked "What are you planning on doing for a vocation?" He replied that he intended to pastor a church.

I gently suggested perhaps God didn't need pastors who treated commitments lightly. The student heard me out, scooted around in his seat and let me know he'd think about it. I left the library somewhere between being angry and deeply disappointed with this young man's attitude. Later that afternoon, that young man appeared in my office to apologize for his attitude. He explained he'd continued studying but couldn't concentrate, because he was convicted by the Holy Spirit. "I changed my attitude and came to apologize. I was shocked by your suggestion of skipping the ministry. I can't remember somebody telling me I couldn't do something."

Several years later, I was playing a pick-up game of handball at the YMCA with a bearded fellow I didn't know. At the end of the match, he asked, "You don't remember me, do you?" I didn't. He gave me a clue, "Remember talking to a kid in the college library about keeping commitments? Well, I'm the guy." Of course I remembered. "I'm now pastor of a church north of town," he continued, "and of all the lessons I learned in college and seminary, the lesson learned from you that day in the library stands at the top of the list. I'll never forget it!"

"Well, now is the right time to listen, the day to be helped. Don't put it off; don't frustrate God's work by showing up late, throwing a question mark over everything we're doing. Our work as God's servants gets validated – or not – in the details" (2 Corinthians 6:2,3 The Message).

Forgotten

Reading: Acts 10

"In whom we have redemption, the forgiveness of sins" (Colossians 1:14 NIV)

I have known of people who resist forgiving another all the way to their grave. An unforgiving spirit is a dragnet to the soul. It serves no useful purpose and hurts the growth of one's being. There is no freedom in an unforgiving spirit.

Soren Kierkegaard wrote: "Only love never thinks about the latter, about saving oneself, about acquiring confidence itself; the lover in love thinks only about giving confidence and saving another from death. But the lover is not therefore forgotten. No, he who in love forgets himself, forgets his sufferings in order to think of another's, forgets all his wretchedness in order to think of another's, forgets what he himself loses in order lovingly to look after another's advantage: truly, such a person is not forgotten. There is one who thinks of him, God in heaven; or love thinks of him. God is love, and when a human being because of love forgets himself, how then should God forget him! No, while the lover forgets himself and thinks of the other person, God thinks of the lover. The self lover is busy; he shouts and complains and insists on his rights in order to make sure he is not forgotten – and yet he is forgotten. But the lover who forgets himself, is remembered by love. There is One who thinks of him, and in this way, it comes about that the lover gets what he gives."[37]

Is there anyone against whom you harbor an unforgiving spirit that you need to forgive and purge yourself of the evil?

Drowning In Knowledge; Starving For His Presence

Reading: Philippians 3: 1-10

"I want to know Christ and the power of his resurrection and the fellowship of sharing in his sufferings, becoming like him in his death, and so, somehow, to attain to the resurrection from the dead" (Philippians 3:10 NIV).

C.S. Lewis is his work, *A Grief Observed*, tells how he deals with the death of his wife. During times of grief and loneliness Lewis raises the question, where is God? "When you are happy that you have no sense of needing Him, so happy that you are tempted to feel His claims upon you as an interruption, if you remember yourself, and turn to Him with gratitude and praise, you will be – or so it feels – welcomed with open arms. But go to Him when your need is desperate, when all other help is vain, and what do you find? A door slammed in your face, and a sound of bolting and double bolting on the inside."

We Christians sense the need for a keen awareness of God's presence in our lives; but admit to times, as Lewis would say, "a door is slammed in our face." Steadfast faith, at times, stands solely on the knowledge that God is there because He says He is, though we do not sense His presence.

A pastor friend once told me, "As I move about in ministry it appears we're drowning in knowledge, but starving for His presence." He'd just returned from a week long preaching assignment at a seminary, a midyear spiritual life conference. His preaching theme pointed to the relative ease of finding knowledge, compared to the ease of either losing or failing to develop a sense of His presence. Anyone in or near a seminary is sympathetic with the condition. At week's end, my friend asked those who needed to turn attention to His presence, to recommit their life to a balance between seeking His presence and finding knowledge. Many students and faculty, acknowledging the need, rose to strive for a better balance between knowledge and heart for ministry.

Acquiring knowledge was addressed by the Apostle Paul, when he wrote about food sacrificed to idols, "Knowledge puffs up, but love builds up. The man who thinks he knows something does not yet know as he ought to know" (1 Corinthians 8:1,2 NIV).

Years ago a professor of mine wrote a poem about what he knew:

I know that I know little,
But I'm thankful for the little I know;
For the highest knowledge I know
Is to know how little I know.

The issue of "heart , of knowing His presence", is kept in balance when, we take time not only to find knowledge, but also take time to reflect on the presence of Him whom we're learning about. That is to pray, to meditate, to think: how does this affect my relationship to Jesus Christ? How does recognition of His presence in my life influence those with whom I am in relationship? Knowledge of Him is important; so also the knowledge of His presence.

Tom Younger

Clearing the Harbor Of Spiritual Blahs

Reading: Psalm 50:1-15

"Sacrifice thank offerings to God, fulfill your vows to the Most High, and call upon me in the day of trouble; I will deliver you, and you will honor me" (Psalm 50:14,15 NIV).

During the troubled years of the Second World War, Allied forces drove the enemy out of a harbor in North Africa, only to discover that the enemy had filled many barges with concrete and sunk them in the harbor, making it unusable. The Allies came forth with a creative way of clearing the harbor. They simply waited for low tide, and attached huge floatable tanks to the sunken barges. As high tide came in, the inflated tanks floated atop the tide, raising the barges out of the muck. The barges were then towed away, clearing the harbor and making it usable to Allied forces.

Think of the dynamic power of the tide. The barges were chained to the tanks. The tanks were dependent upon the tides. The tides were pulled by the gravitational attraction of the moon, and the moon was moving in accord with the whole cosmos, the great sidereal system.

From this story we learn two lessons, one about tides and how they come and go and the other about how the enemy obstructs the harbor, negating its usefulness. There may also be another lesson when we at times find ourselves mired in the muck of daily activity. Not always is it a matter of unconfessed sin, or even a lack of faith that snarls the harbor of our souls. Sometimes, we just get the spiritual blahs. And how do we clear the harbor? How may we catch the incoming tide? Is it not to remember that God is the great Provider and the great Deliverer? Is it not the floatable tanks of gratitude and trust rising with the tide that clears the harbor? I think so. "Through Jesus, therefore, let us continually offer to God a sacrifice of praise – the fruit of lips that confess his name" (Hebrews 13:15 NIV),

Lord, let me not miss the lesson of the silent power of the tide, because of ingratitude and lack of trust.

As Now, So Then

Reading: Ephesians 4:1-16

"No prolonged infancies among us, please. We'll not tolerate babes in the woods, small children who are an easy mark for impostors. God wants us to grow up, to know the whole truth and tell it in love – like Christ in everything" (Ephesians 4:14,15 The Message).

One day in my first year of college, I questioned a professor, as to why my grade was so average; it didn't reflect the time I devoted to his course. Surely he'd mistaken me for someone else. When I finished pleading my case, he asked: "Did you do your best?" Best? What did he mean? He explained "best" as in "best effort." I lost the case for "best effort." Then he said something I've never forgotten, "AS NOW, SO THEN." Thoughts and actions today will determine the future. My "Prof", a young man, was kind, gentle, generous, but firm. Little did I perceive then, but this encounter turned our relationship into a lifelong friendship, lasting fifty years and still counting. I graduated somewhere during that stretch of time and today, while he is in his eighties, I count my friendship with the "prof" as one of the most beloved I've ever weathered. We are both "old" as far as age goes. We're what society refers to in a variety of ways, young old, old old, nouveau old, muppy, ARRPIES, geezer, gerio, gerri-everything – whatever. We're candidates for "Winkle Towers". But neither of us has the money for it. That doesn't really matter, anyway.

Now nearing the end of my pastoral ministry, I invited my friend for a weekend visit. He preached twice one Sunday at my church; once about caring and once about the prevailing darkness of this world. He encouraged us to care as Jesus did and punch a hole in the darkness of this world, simply by being the light that we are in Jesus Christ. He pointed out that unless we care as Jesus did, we have no possibility of punching holes in the darkness for righteousness' sake.

For three days we talked, prayed, and reminisced about life's journey and talked of the future. Not to my surprise, I found him: AS THEN, SO NOW – still gentle, kind, generous, but firm. He is a man, who combined with no apparent self consciousness, or even difficulty, the warm heart and the clear head. Steady on the go, waiting for the shout! Carrying on this lengthy friendship with him has done me good, and makes my journey more meaningful, like in the Gospel song: "I wouldn't take nothin' for my journey now."

Do you have a friend who makes your journey through life meaningful?

Along Comes the Master.

Reading: Philippians 3:12-4:1

"Not that I have already obtained all this, or have already been made perfect, but I press on to take hold of that for which Christ Jesus took hold of me" (Philippians 3:12 NIV).

Ignace Jan Paderewski, the famous composer-pianist, was scheduled to perform at a great concert hall in America. It was an evening to remember – black tuxedos and long evening dresses, a high-society extravaganza. Present in the audience that evening was a mother with her fidgety nine-year-old son. Weary of waiting, he squirmed constantly in his seat. His mother was in hopes that her boy would be encouraged to practice the piano if he could just hear the immortal Paderewski at the keyboard. So – against his wishes –he had come.

As she turned to talk with friends, her son could stay seated no longer. He slipped away from her side, strangely drawn to the ebony concert grand Steinway and its leather tufted stool on the huge stage flooded with blinding lights. Without much notice from the sophisticated audience, the boy sat down at the stool, staring wide-eyed at the black and white keys. He placed his small, trembling fingers in the right location and began to play "chop-sticks." The roar of the crowd was hushed as hundreds of frowning faces turned in his direction. Irritated and embarrassed, they began to shout:

"Get the boy away from there!"
"Who'd bring a kid that young in here?"
"Where's his mother?"

Backstage, the master overheard the sounds out front and quickly put together in his mind what was happening. Hurriedly, he grabbed his coat and rushed toward the stage. Without one word of announcement he stooped over behind the boy, reached out around both sides, and began to improvise a counter melody to harmonize with and enhance "chop-sticks." As the two of them played together, Paderewski kept whispering in the boy's ear:

"Keep going. Don't quit son. Keep on playing...don't stop...don't quit."

And so it is with us. We hammer away on our project, which seems about as significant as "chop-sticks" in a concert hall. And about the time we are ready to give it up, along comes the Master, who leans over and whispers:

"Now keep going; don't quit. Keep on...don't stop; don't quit", as He improvises on our behalf, providing just the right touch at just the right moment.

Journey

Reading: Exodus 1:18-24

"Come on, let us deal wisely with them; lest they multiply". (Exodus 1:10 KJV).

Make no mistake, the world takes notice and seeks to deal wisely with God's people, generally for their own interests not necessarily God's. The Israelites found themselves in favor in Egypt, but only for a short time and that was for the benefit of the wicked. Egyptian favor turned to slavery. After Israel was delivered from slavery, Jethro, Moses' father-in-law, acknowledged that God was in it. "Now I know that the LORD is greater than all gods: for in the thing wherein they dealt proudly he was above them" (Exodus 18:11). He knew it before, but now he knows it better. In the journey of faith God gives us assurances of His presence along the way; His wisdom outstrips the wisdom of the world. "The LORD bringeth the counsel of the (nations) to nought: he maketh the devices of the people of none effect" (Psalm 33:10 KJV).

Prayer: Lord, help us to depend upon your presence and wisdom when it appears that the wisdom of this world is in charge. Help us to trust You, for "...we know that God causes all things to work together for good to those who love God, to those who are called according to His purpose" (Romans 8:28 NAS).

Fear

Reading: Exodus 1:15-22

"And it came about because the midwives feared God, that He established households for them" (Exodus 1:21 NAS).

The midwives were rewarded for their conduct. A paradox of our walk with the Lord is a cause and effect relationship with Him. Midwives reverenced God; He made them houses. We are not passive instruments in God's hands. There is a reward for fearing God. Furthermore, during difficult times, help arrives from the most unusual people and places. From the depth of our distress we discover God has already been there. Often God's presence and help is in the person of someone we would never have suspected.

What can we say, but "if God be for us, who can be against us?" (Romans 8:31 NIV).

Choices

Reading: Exodus 2:1-10

"...and he became her son" (Exodus 2:10 KJV).

Divine providence is always at work. Pharaoh's daughter is guided to the right place; the baby captures her heart. Risking her own life, she rescues him. Moses becomes her son by adoption. It is her choice which gives him privileges in education, but for far different purposes from what his adopted mother intended. Likewise by an act of God we were adopted, for He "foreordained us unto adoption as sons through Jesus Christ unto himself, according to the good pleasure of his will" (Ephesians1:5). The act of compassion Pharaoh's daughter made was a good but risky choice in the moment of time. Our adoption into the family of God is eternal and far reaching. "His unchanging plan has always been to adopt us into his own family by sending Jesus Christ to die for us. And he did this because he wanted to" (Ephesians 3:5 TLB). "Not only so, but we ourselves who have the firstfruits of the Spirit, groan inwardly as we wait eagerly for our adoption as sons, the redemption of our bodies" (Romans 8:23 NIV).

Little do we realize how important to God our choices are each day.

Groveling

Reading: Hebrews 4:14-16

"Let us come boldly to the very throne of God and stay there..." (Hebrews 4:16 TLB).

Kofil Annan, U.N. leader, tells a fascinating story taken from his days at M.I.T. and his playing days in Ghana, Annan describes his mission in life by relating to an observation he made as a kid while in his father's office. His father didn't smoke, nor did he approve of those who did. One day a junior manager was called into Annan's Dad's office to discuss a business matter. The young fellow stuffed his cigarette, still lit, into his pocket. Certainly it was a stressful time for the lad whose cigarette was burning in his pocket all the time he was in Annan's office. Obviously, he was in pain. Afterward, young Kofi Annan, angrily asked his father why he let the young man suffer so, making him put his cigarette in his pocket.

Lecturing Kofi on the spot, Mr. Annon explained he didn't ask the manager to put the cigarette in his pocket. He could have used an ashtray. He could have excused himself and disposed of the cigarette. He could have continued smoking. The lit cigarette need not have been stuffed in his pocket.

Looking his son in the eye, Annan said, "Today you saw something you should never do. Don't crawl."

Be thankful we don't have to grovel in the presence of God. "Jesus the Son of God is our great High Priest who has gone to heaven itself to help us; therefore let us never stop trusting him. This High Priest of ours understands our weaknesses for he faced all of the same temptations as we do, yet he did not sin. So let us come boldly to the throne of our gracious God. There we will receive his mercy, and we will find grace to help us when we need it" (Heb. 4:14-16 TLB).

Hearing

Reading: Exodus 2:23-25

"God heard their groaning and remembered his covenant with Abraham, with Isaac and with Jacob" (Exodus 2:24 NIV).

Israel's groanings, sighs, and protests were directed to God. "Then we cried out to the LORD, the God of our fathers, and the LORD heard our voice and saw our misery, toil and oppression" (Deuteronomy 26:7). The verb "heard" is to "hear-favorably" – "look with kindness" – "cared for, kept in mind." We can't read the Scriptures without noticing again and again, the Providence of God: hearing our cries, tending to our weaknesses, caring for us. God cares for us when friends sometimes either neglect or forget our need for help. God's Providence is unlimited; is particular and special; is constant; is consistent with His purpose for our lives even when the process seems unintelligible to us; it connects us to Him in a life of trust, patience, hope, and gratitude.

A son decried his little old mother's faith. Upon his return from a university. He declared that she was too old, too small, of little importance in the big picture of affairs. One day she surprised her son by addressing his concerns about her faith.

She conceded that she didn't amount to much, but if God didn't save her, He would lose more than she would. God would lose His name and His character. To deny His Word, God will not do; neither will He forget His promises.

Taking Notice

Reading: Exodus 2:11-25

"God had respect unto them". (Exodus 2:25 KJV).

Just as God took notice of Israel's afflictions, so also, He takes notice of our afflictions. We may, at times, harbor the notion that He fails to notice our trials, sufferings. Not so, for God sees and notices and regards our innermost being. His energy of love and empathy is imparted to us. Luther paraphrased it, "He accepted them." When caregivers tend to our needs with love and empathy, it is God who is at work. We may not think God knows our afflictions, or cares, since sometimes He seems distant and silent. But we are never forgotten or abandoned. He hears, remembers, and He knows our condition. "Cast thy burden upon the LORD, and he shall sustain thee: he shall never suffer the righteous to be moved" (Psalm 55:22 KJV). "For the LORD knoweth (watches over) the way of the righteous: but the way of the ungodly shall perish" (Psalm 1:6. KJV).

"Likewise the Spirit also helpeth our infirmities: for we know not what we should pray for as we ought: but the Spirit itself maketh intercession for us with groanings which cannot be uttered. Who is he that condemneth? It is Christ that died, yea rather, that is risen again, who is even at the right hand of God, who also maketh intercession for us" (Romans 8:26, 34 KJV).

Faithful in Prayer

Reading: Ephesians 1:1-14

"Remembering you in my prayers" (Ephesians 1:16 NIV).

Paul's prayer for his friends in Ephesus wasn't that they be spared persecution or have six tickets to enjoy the next concert with friends. No. He prayed that their understanding be illuminated, that their knowledge of God abound; that they experience deep in their hearts what they knew in their heads.

I was a mere lad of barely fifteen years when I became a Christian. My friend, Fred, was in his fifties. He greeted me one day with a hug and said,: "Tom, before you rise in the morning, I pray for you each day." As college and seminary years passed, and on to my first pastoral experience, every time I'd see Fred, he'd remind me that he prayed for me every day. With a twinkle in his eye, he would add – "before you rise in the morning." Eventually Fred passed on to heaven, but his memory and prayer life is firmly embedded in my mind. I wasn't the only lad Fred prayed for each day. There were a number of us boys on his prayer list, all of whom were called to preach.

It is a challenge today to maintain friendships, since we move about so much. So we often put friends at arms length, on the back burner, out of sight, out of mind. This reminds me of the story of two fellows who had not seen each other for some time. When they did meet, they greeted each other with great enthusiasm. One said to the other, "Since I last saw you, I have heard many things." His friend wasn't too concerned about what was being said about him, only were they mentioning his name.

Like Samuel, who prayed for Israel, we are challenged to pray for one another. "Moreover as for me, God forbid that I should sin against the LORD in ceasing to pray for you: but I will teach you the good and the right way: Only fear the LORD, and serve him in truth with all your heart: for consider how great things he hath done for you." (1 Samuel 12:23-25 NKJ). "Dear brothers, giving thanks to God for you, is not only the right thing to do, but it is our duty to God because of the really wonderful way your faith has grown and because of your growing love for each other. We are happy to tell other churches about your patience and complete faith in God, in spite of all the crushing troubles and hardships you are going through" (II Thessalonians 1:3-4 TLB).

Turn

Reading: Exodus 3:1-4:17

"So Moses said, 'I must turn aside now,'" (Exodus 3:3 NAS).

Moses turned aside and the Lord spoke to him from the burning bush. "When Moses saw it, he wondered at the sight: and as he drew near to behold it, the voice of the Lord came unto him:" (Acts 7:31 KJV). There are occasions in our walk with the Lord that call us to turn aside to contemplate God's extraordinary presence. There are times when we must turn aside, not run, but stop and boldly inquire what it is God wants to teach us. Moses sensed that the burning bush was extraordinary: there was fire, but no human agent to kindle it; a voice, but nobody in sight; a living Being in the flames, who knew him, and called him by name. Our burning bush experience may come because we are in a state of fatigue or burn out. "And He said to them, `Come away by yourselves to a lonely place and rest a while.' (For there were many {people} coming and going, and they did not even have time to eat.) And they went away in the boat to a lonely place by themselves" (Mark 6:31-32 NAS).

We all need time to think and meditate..

The Staff of God

Reading: Exodus 4:18-26

"He took the staff of God in his hand "(Exodus 4:20 NIV).

The staff in Moses' hand - a mark of authority, a scepter - was the instrument of God used to perform the divine miracles (4:17). God chose not to endow Moses with great physical presence to impress people with his leadership prowess, nor did He provide present day cultural marks of success, such as fame and wealth. He simply made His staff available. Sufficient in and of itself is God's presence and authority.

Pharaoh's pride and power would bow before the Staff of God. The power we Christians use in the interest of the Gospel and a world consumed with the pride of life is the power of God's Word and the power of the Holy Spirit in us. With privilege goes responsibility. Moses learned that when he struck the rock a second time it got him in big trouble with God. He also found God's staff to be versatile. It was used to feed, protect and rule his people. There is a great need for balance in our use of God's Word. To handle the Word of God is an honor more important than worldly honors.

Wilderness

Reading: Exodus 4:27-31

"And the LORD said to Aaron, 'Go into the wilderness'" (Exodus 4:27 NKJ).

God directed Aaron into the wilderness to work alongside his brother Moses, God's chosen agent to lead Israel to freedom from bondage. The brothers were so taken with God's providence in bringing them together, they embraced as brothers and friends. Liberating Israel from Pharaoh's grip was a challenge Moses didn't feel up to it at first. Now God had plans to help him. With joy we can trace Aaron's part in this venture. The brothers experienced closeness to God and to each other. God also sends us help to accomplish His will in our lives. He sent His Holy Spirit to dwell in our lives, another comforter of the same kind, who abides with us forever (John 14:16). He provided the church with the gift of "helps" by bringing others to walk alongside us and to aid us in our walk and ministry (John 14:16). "God is our refuge and strength, a tested help in times of trouble" (Psalm 46:1 TLB). To experience God's help we have to go willingly into the wilderness of His choosing. There, we find that God is already at work on our behalf. Years ago, we used to sing a chorus: MY LORD KNOWS THE WAY THROUGH THE WILDERNESS; all we have to do is follow.

Hardened Hearts

Reading: Exodus 6:10-7:13

"And he hardened Pharaoh's heart, as the LORD had said" (Exodus 7:13 KJV).

Pharaoh wasn't the only one to harden his heart against God. The Egyptians hardened their hearts and on occasion Israel did the same. The Israelites refused to listen to God; they plugged their ears so they couldn't hear. The Apostle Paul, speaking of men in general, said they didn't like to retain God in their knowledge and thus God gave them over to a reprobate mind. We are not immune to the behavior that is unyielding to

God's will. It is presumptuous sin. It only takes a moment for us to get off course to begin the process of hardening. We get complacent in our walk with the Lord; it doesn't feel like bondage until we taste freedom again.

Pharaoh made his own heart obstinate against God. Israel did the same. We also can react against God. We can't lay a charge against God because of circumstances in life we don't like or are not to our perceived benefit. In Proverbs we read, "He that being often reproved hardeneth his neck, shall suddenly be destroyed, and that without remedy" (Proverbs. 29:1 KJV). "Wherefore, as the Holy Ghost saith, Today if ye will hear his voice, harden not your hearts, as in the provocation, in the day of temptation in the wilderness" (Hebrews 3:7-8). "But exhort one another daily, while it is called Today; lest any of you be hardened through the deceitfulness of sin (Heb 3:13 KJV).

Digging

Reading: Exodus 7:14-25

"And all the Egyptians dug along the Nile to get drinking water" (Exodus 7:24 NIV).

Pharaoh and the Egyptians had to dig wells along the riverbank because they hardened their hearts against God. The water of the Nile had turned to blood as Moses raised his staff and struck the water. Stubbornness has its price. Contrast that with hearts sensitive to God's direction and will. The prophet Isaiah wrote: "Behold, God is my salvation, I will trust and not be afraid; for the LORD GOD is my strength and song, and He has become my salvation. Therefore you will joyously draw water from the springs of salvation" (NAS). Jesus stunned the woman at the well in Samaria with the good news that if she drank of the water He gave, she would never thirst; that the water He gave would be water springing up into everlasting life (John 4:14). On another occasion, Jesus declared that those who believe in Him would have steams of living water flowing from within. "Whoever believes in me, as the Scripture has said, streams of living water will flow from within him" (John 7:38 NIV). The Psalmist knew about good water when he wrote: "How excellent is thy loving-kindness, O God! Therefore the children of men put their trust under the shadow of thy wings. They shall be abundantly satisfied with the fatness of thy house; and thou shalt make them drink of the river of thy pleasures. For with thee is the fountain of life: in thy light shall we see light (Psalm 36:8,9 KJV). Good water is hard to come by in some parts of the world, but the living water that comes by believing in Jesus Christ as our Lord slakes our thirst for meaning and knowing God. It's available to all that will believe. Consider John W. Peterson's gospel song, SPRINGS OF LIVING WATER:

> I thirsted in the barren land of sin and shame,
> And nothing satisfying there I found;
> But to the blessed cross of Christ one day I came,
> Where springs of living water did abound.
> Drinking at the springs of living water,
> Happy now am I, My soul they satisfy;
> Drinking at the springs of living water,
> O wonderful and bountiful supply.

Vulnerable

Reading: Exodus 8:1-15

"And Moses said to Pharaoh, 'The honor is yours to tell when shall I entreat for you and your servants and your people that the frogs be destroyed'" (Exodus 8:9 NAS.

Pharaoh was up to his eyeballs with frogs everywhere. Yes, everywhere! He cried "Uncle" as if he were a kid conceding he'd lost a wrestling match. Pharaoh wanted to be done with frogs: Get them out of here! Now Moses said something we don't want to miss. "'Be so kind as to tell me when you want them to go,' Moses said, 'and I will pray that the frogs will die at the time you specify, everywhere except in the river'." (TLB)

Moses made himself vulnerable before Pharaoh. Moses told Pharaoh to take the glory for himself by setting the time for the plague to be lifted. For Moses, God's glory was more important than his own glory. So he took the position below Pharaoh. It was if he said, "You want the glory? Go ahead Pharaoh."

The desired result: Moses said to Pharaoh, "The honor is yours to tell me: when shall I entreat for you and your servants and your people, that the frogs be destroyed from you and your houses, {that} they may be left only in the Nile?" Then Pharaoh said, 'Tomorrow.'" So Moses said, "{May it be} according to your word, that you may know that there is no one like the LORD our God" (NAS).

We don't like being vulnerable. It's too uncomfortable. Especially so when we are sharing Christ with someone. We fear the question we may not be able to answer. We fear the possibility of someone taking offense at the Gospel. We fear being rejected. But that's all right. Know that it's all right to say that you don't know. It's all right to say you'll think about their question and get back with an answer. It's all right to become vulnerable, taking the lower seat and letting the Holy Spirit work in his or her heart through the Word of God. Yes, but you ask, doesn't the Bible say that we ought to be "ready always to give an answer to every man that asketh you a reason of the hope that is in you with meekness and fear?" (1 Peter 3:15 KJV) Sure does. But the overriding issue in sharing the Gospel is the power of God's Word and the power of the Holy Spirit. Let the Spirit do His work. Our vulnerability will be of little consequence.

God uses our vulnerability also for His glory (good opinion).

Gathering

Reading: Nehemiah 1:4-2:8

"I will gather them from there" (Nehemiah 1:9 NAS).

Ours is a great gathering God. He scattered the Israelites because of their transgressions. If they were to be gathered from their enemies, God had to do it. Nehemiah confesses Israel's sins and pleads with the Lord to remember Moses' word, that if His people repented and kept His commandments, He would gather them together and bring them to the place He had chosen for them.

The Israelites were more inclined to want the gathering than they were the repenting. This was not unlike us in many ways. We live in a country where gathering is almost the only game in town. We have our homes, our cars, our SUVs, our 401K, our pensions, our stock portfolios. Well, more of us do than any other sizable number of people in the world. Yes, we are in a gathering frenzy.

Yet all we have is not enough; we still need a pay raise six months after we received the last one. Our focus on gathering tends to obscure the habit of giving. Two, the well being of gathering material comforts and dims our vision for that great gathering morning when Christ shall return and take us to be with Him. Question not that the greatest gathering is when God takes us home to the place of His choosing. Until He does, let's keep gathering and giving in balance.

I have a friend who when he goes on an expensive trip, first writes a check of an equal sum for the Lord's work. Now, most of us may not be able to do that, but let us give regularly and at least a tenth of our income to the Lord.

Should you get careless and out of balance by giving more, you will learn that you can't out give God. No, I'm not talking here about the false notion of a prosperity gospel, just the fact that God takes into account our attitude toward giving and chooses to bless us.

Power

Reading: Exodus 8:16-19

"This is the finger of God" (Exodus 8:19 NAS).

The "finger of God" refers to God's power working through the Holy Spirit to bring plagues upon Egypt. Pharaoh's magicians identified that power, as God's; Pharaoh didn't. Magicians confessed God's finger at work; Pharaoh protested. The magicians couldn't rid Egypt of the plagues; God's finger could and did.

God has more power in His little finger than all the world's power, sum total. Why do we then doubt the power of God? Why do we fail to see the finger of God at work in our circumstances, both good and bad? Why are we stricken with terror when the Devil's agents assault us? Can evil overcome the finger of God? Most assuredly, not.

"Who is he that condemns? Christ Jesus, who died— more than that, who was raised to life— is at the right hand of God and is also interceding for us. Who shall separate us from the love of Christ? Shall trouble or hardship or persecution or famine or nakedness or danger or sword? As it is written: 'For your sake we face death all day long; we are considered as sheep to be slaughtered.' No, in all these things we are more than conquerors through him who loved us. For I am convinced that neither death nor life, neither angels nor demons, neither the present nor the future, nor any powers, neither height nor depth, nor anything else in all creation, will be able to separate us from the love of God that is in Christ Jesus our Lord." (Romans 8:34-39 NIV).

Prayer

Reading: Exodus 8:20-32

"Now pray for me" (Exodus 8:28 NIV).

Praying for others is high on our priority list. Man's fallen nature calls for it. Pharaoh was hypocritical when he asked Moses to pray for him, for he hardened his heart against God. Shall we turn away from prayer because hypocrisy lies at the door of the one for whom we pray? Moses didn't turn away from Pharaoh. He prayed for him. Moses also prayed for his own people. They too, were often hypocritical.

Abraham spoke to God about Sodom. Christ prayed for Peter and his disciples. He even prayed for those who crucified Him. After He ascended into heaven He continues to pray for the church. "Therefore he is able to save completely those who come to God through him, because he always lives to intercede for them" (Hebrews 7:25 NIV).

Do we ever search for words when we pray? I'll say we do. Be encouraged that "In the same way the Spirit helps us in our weakness. We do not know what we ought to pray for, but the Spirit Himself intercedes for us with groans that words cannot express. And He who searches our hearts knows the mind of the Spirit, because the Spirit intercedes for the saints in accordance with God's will. (Romans 8:26,27 NIV).

Do you write people off because you are astonished with their behavior? Here again, we are exhorted to pray. "I exhort therefore, that, first of all, supplications, prayers, intercessions, and giving of thanks, be made for all men; For kings, and for all that are in authority; that we may lead a quiet and peaceable life in all godliness and honesty. For this is good and acceptable in the sight of God our Saviour" (I Timothy 2:1-3 KJV).

Distinctions

Reading: Exodus 9:1-7

"But the LORD will make a distinction between the livestock of Israel and that of Egypt, so that no animal belonging to the Israelites will die" (Exodus 9:4 NIV).

God made a distinction between the livestock of Israel and that of Egypt. With regard to people, God is no respecter of persons. He does not distinguish between Jew or Gentile, race or creed. Christ died for all mankind because all men have fallen in sin and need a savior. Salvation is available for all who will believe in the Lord Jesus Christ. Believers are placed into the body of Christ. Jesus said, "And I, if I be lifted up from the earth, will draw all men unto me (John 12:32 KJV).. That is, He will draw all men unto Himself without distinction.

Paul wrote to the Galatian believers that "There is neither Jew nor Greek, there is neither bond nor free, there is neither male nor female: for ye are all one in Christ Jesus" (Galatians 3:28 KJV). On the other hand, the word for distinction in verse 4 actually means "to set apart." In that sense, God set apart the livestock of Israel from that of Egypt. Interestingly, when we come to faith in Christ, we are set apart by God unto Holiness. Just as the Israelites' livestock was set apart in a miraculous way, so too, believers are set apart in a miraculous way. "What? Know ye not that your body is the temple of the Holy Ghost which is in you, which ye have of

God, and ye are not your own?" (I Corinthians 6:19 KJV). It's all right that we are not our own. We belong to the Lord who bought us with His precious blood. In this knowledge we find comfort. "Thou shalt not be afraid for the terror by night; nor for the arrow that flieth by day; Nor for the pestilence that walketh in darkness; nor for the destruction that wasteth at noonday. A thousand shall fall at thy side, and ten thousand at thy right hand; but it shall not come nigh thee" (Psalm 91:6,7 KJV).

Listen Here, Son

Reading: Exodus 9:8-12

"But the Lord hardened Pharaohs heart and he would not listen" (Exodus 9:12 NIV).

I remember my Grandfather who lived with us when I was a child. It didn't take a village; it only took a grandfather! And a mother and father, of course. Gramps often said, "Now, listen here, son!" He thought I was hearing him, but suspicious that I wasn't listening to him. He was right, of course. What he didn't seem to know was that I was listening more than he thought. What Gramps was looking for was obedience. He was my special trainer! Pharaoh heard God, but he wasn't listening.

There are several other distinctions made with the word "listen" in the Bible, that occurs about 1160 times. God wants us to have more than an intellectual relationship with Him. A spiritual hearing of His Word is necessary. We sit at the feet of Jesus, listening to him in order to learn how to walk with Him. For best results we must agree with God when we listen to His Word.

Samuel said, "Hath the LORD as great delight in burnt offerings and sacrifices, as in obeying the voice of the LORD? Behold, to obey is better than sacrifice, and to hearken than the fat of rams" (1 Samuel 15:22 KJV). "In Abraham's seed, all nations would be blessed because he 'heard' (obeyed) God's voice" (Genesis 22:18).

We may hear a lot of things by accident, but the best hearing is intentional, intense and purposeful. It's interesting that both the Hebrew and Greek words for "obey" come from the root "to hear."

Indecision

Reading: Exodus 9:13-35

"He would not let the Israelites go" (Exodus 9:35 NIV).

One moment Pharaoh tells Moses that he (Pharaoh) is wrong, and that he has sinned by not letting the Israelites go. Then Pharaoh turns right around, hardens his heart against God and refuses to let the people go. Make up your mind Pharaoh. How long are you going to kick against God? You've had so many doses of Maalox with all these plagues; you may have to invest in the product, Pharaoh. Don't you get it?

Indecision is not an enviable characteristic. On occasion we sit on the fence because we can't make a decision. Our mug is on one side; our rump on the other side. Sometimes we plead open mindedness, when we're really indecisive and don't want to risk being found out. There are days when our friends may think we graduated with a degree in "practical vacillation". Who wants to claim his spiritual gift, otherwise known as "uncertainty?" Who wants to be tossed about between the fear of death and the hardship of life, unwilling to live, and not knowing how to die? We all admit to being indecisive at times. Mark Twain once said, "I must have prodigious quantity; it takes me as much as a week, sometimes, to make it up." Better to take a week, than not to make up one's mind. On Mount

Carmel, Elijah cried out to the people, "`How long halt ye between two opinions? If the LORD be God, follow him: but if Baal, then follow him'. And the people answered him not a word" (I Kings 18:21 KJV). Jesus said, "No man can serve two masters: for either he will hate the one, and love the other; or else he will hold to the one, and despise the other. Ye cannot serve God and mammon" (Matthew 6:24 KJV). "A double minded man is unstable in all his ways" (James 1:8 KJV). "Watch and pray, that ye enter not into temptation: the spirit indeed is willing, but the flesh is weak" (Matt 26:41 KJV). Be resolute today! Take that step in obedience to God. Humble yourself before God and see what He will do.

First

Reading: Exodus 10:1-20

"...that you may know that I am the LORD" (Exodus 10:2 NIV).

The phrase "I am the LORD," appears 73 times in the Old Testament. God wasn't about to allow the nations and Israel to misunderstand who He was. He is the LORD God who made the heavens and the earth. The first time YHWH, "the LORD" appears is in Genesis. 4:26. Pharaoh and Egypt refused to understand the significance of God as LORD. They persisted in worshiping false gods. Even Israel had to be reminded from time to time that God was LORD; that He was the one to be worshiped; that there was none like Him. The LORD declared Himself to be a jealous God. Meaning that He, as God, would tolerate no rivals between Himself and man. God is still saying to man today, "Know that I am the LORD." Now there is a constant learning of matters to know in this life.

Our daughter was laid aside temporarily for a day and her mother offered to bring dinner to the family. But thirteen year old grandson stepped in and said: "Could we make this a learning experience? I could order a pizza and have it delivered." Pizza took precedence over Grandma's generally prized cooking, I suspect Grandma was expected to foot the bill. Learning experiences? Yes, we're duty bound to keep learning. If we're looking for a marriage partner it's desirable to know our head as well as our heart. If our health is an issue, we'd better be prepared to talk to our doctor. He can't help if we don't talk. If we're in the market to purchase a home, we'd best learn something about quality construction, location, interest rates, cash flow, and other matters. If we're buying a car we had better bone up on price comparison, benefits of new or used, and not be carried away with a persuasive sales pitch that you will regret only too late. If we're planning our estate we'd better know something about wills, taxes, estate and capital gains for starters. But all of that aside, our number one priority is our relationship with Jesus Christ to know that He is Lord. How do you plan to engage God in your journey today?

Darkness

Reading: Exodus 10:21-29

"Then the LORD said to Moses, 'Stretch out your hand toward the sky so that darkness will spread over Egypt— darkness that can be felt.'" (Exodus 10:21 NIV).

This is the ninth plague to besiege Pharaoh and Egypt. Darkness, dreadful, held to the last. The Psalmist may have underscored the devastation of this darkness because he lists it first even though it was near the last (Psalm 105:28). The Bible's main use of darkness is in contrast to light. The darkness got the Egyptian's attention for one of their chief deities was the sun god Ra. The darkness was total, felt, terrifying, and continuous. .

Tom Younger

The most awful and scary darkness I have ever known occurred in the summer before my sophomore year in high school. The place was Harlan, Kentucky. I was helping in a Vacation Bible School for children. One night a call came in for the resident missionary to conduct a funeral of someone who had died in one of those "Hollers" outside of town. Well, the missionary had been suddenly called away to another meeting. So I was asked if I'd drive up that "Holler" and conduct the service. The road up was the creek coming down from the hills. I didn't know anything about funerals and little or nothing about preaching, but two high school kids and I commandeered a beat-up Chevy Carryall and headed up the creek. When we got there I was asked: "Will you wash the body? We do that before wrapping it and placing it in the ground." Would I what? "Wash the body!." You've got to be kidding! Fortunately, someone read my face, drained of all life, and they washed the body. I preached. On the way home, a wheel fell off the suburban. Not to worry, we retrieved it and mounted it on the car. Problem was there were no bolts; they were in the creek somewhere. We were up the creek with no paddle. And it was dark. It was really dark. No lights visible anywhere. Where do we go for help? We couldn't see anything to give direction to find help. So we sat there in total darkness. I tell you, it was scary. Finally, in what seemed an eternity, someone came out of nowhere and got us going again. When I think of darkness, I remember Harlan, Kentucky. When I think of darkness, I think of Hannah's prayer: "He will keep the feet of his saints, and the wicked shall be silent in darkness; for by strength shall no man prevail" (1 Samuel 2:9 KJV). When I think of darkness, I think of our LORD who said "that he would dwell in the thick darkness" (1 King 8:12 KJV). When I think of darkness I remember the scriptures telling about the darkness which covered over all the earth when our Lord was crucified (Luke 23:44).

Are you experiencing a dark hour just now? Look for our Lord. "Unto the upright there ariseth light in the darkness: he is gracious, and full of compassion, and righteous" (Psalm 112:4 KJV).

What Makes for Greatness

Reading: Exodus 11:1-10

"Moses himself was highly regarded in Egypt" (Exodus 11:3 NIV).

God gave Moses the gift of credibility with Pharaoh and Egypt; it was not his own doing. Should we be highly regarded by the world, make sure it's God's doing, not ours, blowing our own trumpet. The proper gift of credibility is a miracle of God, just as it was in Moses' day. Men often climb over the backs of others in order to be looked upon as being great. A strategy we as Christians can engage in, also, but not to our good nor to God's glory.

One of the greatest legacies my father left me as a young man was seen in the way he sought to help others without regard to being noticed. At his wake a lot of people came out of respect for him, as one who had helped them in some way while he was living. I had no idea who the people were and only learned of his quiet ministry from their words of respect. He was highly regarded by his friends. Never bothered Dad to go unnoticed; he always took the low road with regard to his own sense of importance. Dad never exhorted me about the truth: "For by the grace given me I say to every one of you: Do not think of yourself more highly than you ought, but rather think of yourself with sober judgment, in accordance with the measure of faith God has given you" (Romans 12:3-4 NIV). He showed me, he didn't tell me. He always took the low road, as it were. I doubt Dad ever knew how much I learned from him. Jesus introduced this concept of greatness that springs from humility and self-forgetting service.

"Whosoever would become great among you shall be your minister; and whosoever would be first among you shall be your servant: even as the Son of man came not to be ministered unto, but to minister, and to give his life a ransom for many" (Matthew. 20:26-28).

Time Out

Reading: Exodus 11:1-10

"This is what the LORD says" (Exodus. 11:4 NIV).

Suppose we dialogue with Moses before we read about the next plague recorded in Exodus eleven. Imagine saying, if you will, "Hey, Moses, your image isn't showing too good these days. You're supposed to be leading your brothers out of Egypt, but you keep getting into trouble with Pharaoh and his lot. Image is all important, Moses. Those Egyptians may be thinking highly of you at the moment, but they will turn on you, believe me. Another thing you are overlooking is your brothers. They are getting awfully testy about your perceived skills as a leader. Like I say, image or perception is where it's at these days. Then there is God. What do you suppose He thinks about His choice of you as His man to deliver His people out of bondage? You'd better watch Moses, or God will sack you and get him a leader whose image guarantees success. God isn't going to be patient with you forever; He wants results. Right Now! Leaders are expendable, Moses. You can be replaced. Better get humpin'! Soon you'll be getting it in the neck from all sides: Pharaoh, your brothers and God.

Now our fanciful flight of imagination connects us with the culture of today that says, image supercedes substance. Consider what part perception plays in the name of politics and market place advertising. Much is based on illusion, being deceived by a false perception or belief, rather than fact and reality. But now we read Exodus 11:4 and see that Moses is convinced of power, not based on illusion, but on God. Moses is emphatic: "This is what the LORD says:". If we spent more time on the power that really counts, we'd have less time to engage in imaging and with less reason. "Now I have given up everything else. I have found it to be the only way to really know Christ and to experience the mighty power that brought him back to life again, and to find out what it means to suffer and to die with him" (Philippians 3:10 TLB).

Knowing

Reading: Exodus 12:1-13:16

"The LORD brought the Israelites out of Egypt" (Exodus 12:51 NIV).

Israel came out of Egypt by the hand of the Lord, not men. They obeyed God and He brought them out. All too often when we get into hot water, we come up with ingenious reasons to trust man instead of the Lord to bring us out. We're exhorted not to put our trust in princes, in mortal men, who cannot save (Psalm 146:3); that "It is better to take refuge in the LORD than to trust in man. It is better to take refuge in the LORD than to trust in princes" (Psalm118:8-10 NIV). The Prophet Isaiah said, "Stop trusting in man, who has but a breath in his nostrils. Of what account is he?" (Isaiah 2:22 NIV). Jeremiah warned God's people "Thus saith the LORD; Cursed be the man that trusteth in man, and maketh flesh his arm, and whose heart departeth from the LORD" (Jeremiah 17:5 KJV).

Now we all experience times when trust is misplaced. Our neighbor trusted her husband to remove a patch of Heather in their yard while she went shopping. When she returned the Rhododendrons in the yard were missing, but the Heather was still in the yard. He didn't know the difference between Heather and Rhododendron. She assumed he did and trusted him to carry out her request. We all got a laugh out of that, at least the wife and her friends did. That misplaced trust was fairly innocent, perhaps costing a few dollars to correct the mistake. But when it comes to eternal issues we best know the difference between Heather and Rhododendron. Or should we say, know the difference between trusting men and trusting God.

"So we say with confidence, `The Lord is my helper; I will not be afraid. What can man do to me?'" (Hebrews. 13:6).

The Road Less Taken

Reading: Exodus 13:17-14:31

"So God led the people around by the desert road" (Exodus13:18 NIV).

We live in a culture that longs for leaders, but we don't like being led. We prefer not having anyone telling us what road to take. Give us our independence, after all, we deserve it. We work hard. Call the shots our way. Children don't always take to being led very well, preferring to kick against restraints. Israel was no different. They wanted a leader, but they wanted to be led by God most often when they were in trouble. Not unlike us at times. Now as the Israelites leave Egypt God leads them by the desert road toward the Red Sea. The word "road" is well trodden and figuratively, a course of life. A mode of action. The choice of road was God's. Moses gave Israel direction, but only as he got instructions from the Lord. We are a lot better off when we pray for God's guidance as to the road of choice and let Him influence that choice. We are less apt to look back and wonder if we chose the right road. Don't forget the road taken is a walk of faith. Fool yourself by thinking you can design and plan your way independent of God and you will be disappointed for "the way of man is not in himself" (Jeremiah 10:23). In 1

Kings 2:4 the road is applied to one's lifestyle: "If thy children take heed to their way, to walk before me in truth with all their heart and with all their soul, there shall not fail thee... a man on the throne of Israel."

What road has God chosen for you to take today? Are you being led or do you insist on being in charge? Yours to choose.

> I shall be telling this with a sigh
> Somewhere ages and ages hence:
> Two roads diverged in a wood, and I—
> I took the one less traveled by,
> And that has made all the difference.
> Robert Frost

What a Song It Is

Reading: Exodus 15:1-18

"I will sing to the LORD...(he) is my strength and my song; he has become my salvation" (Exodus 15:1-2 NIV).

Moses' song is related directly to God's deliverance from disaster at the hands of the Egyptians. I'm referring to the song of salvation when we receive Christ into our hearts. More people than we care to think about, believe salvation is worked up by our own devices; if we're good enough we will reach heaven; if we don't commit horrific sins we'll stand the test before God; if we belong to a religious family we'll be O.K. There is something to be said for good works, for not killing someone, and for a Christian heritage, but salvation is not found in these things. It is found in a personal relationship with Jesus Christ. "Salvation is found in no one else, for there is no other name under heaven given to men by which we must be saved" (Acts 4:12 NIV).

To Philip, Jesus said: “Have I been so long a time with you, and yet hast thou not known me, Philip? He that hath seen me hath seen the Father; and how sayest thou then, Shew us the Father?” (John 14:9-10 KJV). Salvation is a divine work wrought by a divine Agent, the Holy Spirit, who places us into the Body of Christ. When we trust Christ as Savior and Lord, the Bible comes alive. There’s a new song in our heart. “The Spirit itself beareth witness with our spirit, that we are the children of God:” (Romans. 8:16 KJV). There’s a new song in our heart. Whose song will you sing today?

Here We Go Again

Reading: Exodus 15:22-27

“So the people grumbled against Moses, saying, ‘What are we to drink?’” (Exodus 15:24 NIV).

Little wonder God became provoked with Israel. Praising the Lord one minute, grumbling the next. Sing to the Lord, “What a wonder you are”; fall into the ash pile complaining about our lot. Sound the trumpet of praise one moment, grovel in unbelief the next. We know better than we practice. Swell in our knowledge of God’s provision, but avail ourselves to its resources? Not often enough. “There are three wants which never can be satisfied: that of the rich, who want something more; that of the sick, who want something different; and that of the traveler, who says, `Anywhere but here.’” (Ralph Waldo Emerson). Of dissatisfaction Thomas Carlyle wrote: “No sooner is your ocean filled, than he grumbles that it might have been of better vintage. Try him with half of a Universe, of an Omnipotence, he sets to quarrelling with the proprietor of the other half, and declares himself the most maltreated of men. Always there is a black spot in our sunshine: it is even as I said, the Shadow of Ourselves.”

We can do better. Acknowledge that "godliness with contentment is great gain" (1 Timothy 6:6); "Don't extort money and don't accuse people falsely;-be content with your pay" (Luke 3:14); "I am not saying this because I am in need, for I have learned to be content whatever the circumstances" (Philippians 4:11).

Look Where You Brought Us Now

Reading: Exodus 16:1-36

"You have brought us out into this desert to starve" (Exodus 16:3 NIV).

Thomas Fuller, English cleric, wrote: "Anger is one of the sinews of the soul; he that wants it hath a maimed mind." Anger toward God is foolish. The Bible says "Be not hasty in thy spirit to be angry,: for anger resteth in the bosom of fools" (Ecclesiastes 7:9 NIV). Israel became angry with its leaders and with God. Forget the divine wisdom, goodness and power of God Israel had seen beforehand; forget the sudden wonder of God's majesty and power; forget the well thought out beforehand course of Providence benefiting Israel. Look what you've done to us! You've brought us into the desert to starve! Did Israel learn anything from the passage of the Red Sea? Little if any, for they are now grumbling against Moses and Aaron and ultimately God. My how fickle, impatient, and impious we become with leaders and with God. We get so engrossed in the present we forget past divine aid. It was true of Job for he cursed the day of his birth on one occasion. Jeremiah lamented, "May the day my mother bore me not be blessed!" (Jeremiah 20:14). Jonah once said: "It would be better for me to die than to live" (Jonah 4:8). I reckon that at times we have all engaged in anger or resentment with others and ultimately with our Lord over our present circumstances. Like Israel we fail to take into account that "He humbled you, causing you to hunger and then feeding you with manna, which neither you nor your fathers had known, to teach you that man does not live on bread alone but on every word that comes out of the mouth of the LORD (Deuteronomy 29:5 NIV). We'd better take into account Jesus words "Your forefathers ate the manna in the desert, yet they died. But here is the bread that comes down from heaven, which a man may eat and not die. I am the living bread that came down from heaven. If anyone eats of this bread, he will live forever. This bread is my flesh, which I will give for the life of the world" (John 6:49-51 NIV). "He who has an ear, let him hear what the Spirit says to the churches. To him who overcomes, I will give some of the hidden manna. I will also give him a white stone with a new name written on it, known only to him who receives it" (Revelation. 2:17). No complaints here.

The Eyes of Your Heart

Reading: Ephesians 1:15-23

"I pray also that the eyes of your heart may be enlightened..." (Ephesians 1:18 NIV).

Occasionally Gramps would ask: "What in the name of Sam Hill are your thinking Son?" Now I never could figure out who Sam Hill was; maybe Sam stuck his head up at the wrong time in Battle of Little Big Horn; maybe a friend in Gramp's family tree invoked memories. But I knew he meant me to be more discerning than come to the dinner table without first washing my hands. I tried not showing hands, but it was difficult to eat. Gramps was in hope that the eyes of my understanding would be enlightened concerning good hygiene.

God has an even greater concern about the eyes of our understanding. Most frequently the terms mean the giving of spiritual light to the soul. "The precepts of the LORD are right, giving joy to the heart. The commands of the LORD are radiant, giving light to the eyes." (Psalm 19:8-9 NIV). Enlightened self-interest can't do that. Katherine Tait, daughter of Bertrand Russell, said of her life with Russell: "Reason, progress, unselfishness, a wide historical perspective, expansiveness, generosity, enlightened self-interest. I had heard it all my life, and it filled me with despair." The Psalmist said: "The unfolding of your words gives light; it gives understanding to the simple" (Psalm 119:130 NIV). Adolphe Monod wrote: "Philosophy, taking man for its centre, says *know thyself*; only the inspired word which proceeds from God has been able to say *know God*."

"I pray also that the eyes of your heart may be enlightened in order that you may know the hope to which he has called you, the riches of his glorious inheritance in the saints, and his incomparably great power for us who believe. That power is like the working of his mighty strength, which he exerted in Christ when he raised him from the dead and seated him at his right hand in the heavenly realms, far above all rule and authority, power and dominion, and every title that can be given, not only in the present age but also in the one to come" (Ephesians 1:18-21 NIV).

Presumption

Reading: Exodus 17:1-7

"...Is the LORD among us or not?" (Exodus17:7 NIV).

It hadn't been too long ago that God provided water to quench Israel's thirst in the wilderness. But here we go again; their behavior and language is boldly arrogant. A presumption accepted as truth. God, where's the water? What have you done for us lately? Are you among us or not? Forget your presence in the past; forget your past Providences; forget your great power. Where are you now! Have you abandoned us? You've left us in the lurch, God!

Make no mistake; God is not entertained by arrogance. Such presumption is not alone Israel's problem; it's a current problem today. Oscar Wild once noted in *THE AMERICAN INVASION*, "In America the young are always ready to give to those who are older than themselves the full benefits of their inexperience." Youngsters learn presumptuousness from us oldsters. None of us seem to learn our lessons. Eve said to the serpent, "We may eat fruit from the trees in the garden, but God did say, 'You must not eat fruit from the tree that is in the middle of the garden, and you must not touch it, or you will die.'" But the serpent shot back, "You will not surely die ... For God knows that when you eat of it your eyes will be opened, and you will be like God, knowing good and evil." So what happened? She and Adam disobeyed God, a feat of arrogance for which we have suffered the consequences ever since.

"Therefore, just as sin entered the world through one man, and death through sin, and in this way death came to all men, because all sinned" (Romans 5:12). The only remedy for sin came through the Cross when Christ died for our sins and was raised from the dead so that when we bow to Him as Lord, we are made righteous in Him. Now we need to ask God to keep us from insipid displays of arrogance springing from some perceived oversight of our Lord. Knowing this, he has always been faithful and will continue to be on our behalf.

Many Hands

Reading: Ex 17:8-16

"The LORD is my Banner" (Exodus 17:15 NIV).

Many Hands are involved in victories won. North of the Arlington National Cemetery in Washington, D.C., stands the U.S. Marine Corps War Memorial, commemorating the raising of the U.S. flag on Mt. Suribachi, February 23, 1945, during World War II. The bronze memorial honors the U.S. Marine dead of all wars. The statue by Felix de Weldon has six bronze figures, based on a Photograph taken in March 1945 by Joe Rosenthal. James Bradley in his book, *Flags of Our Fathers,* tells what happened to those six boys who raised the American Flag at Iwo Jima. "History turned all its focus, for 1/1400th of a second, on them. It froze them in an elegant instant of battle: froze them in a camera lens as they hoisted an American flag on a makeshift pole. Their collective image blurred and indistinct yet unforgettable, became the most recognized, the most reproduced, in the history of photography. It gave them a kind of immortality—a faceless immortality."

Following Israel's victory against the war with the Amalekites, Moses built a memorial he called "Jehovah my banner." Christians must always lift up their banners unto the Lord. "We will shout for joy when you are victorious and will lift up our banners in the name of our God" (Psalm 20:5 NIV). Aaron and Hur played a part in the victory as they held up Moses hands during battle.

No matter what part God would have us play in victories, we must stand aside and raise our banner to Him. The world rushes to claim credit for victories; Christians need not do so. God knows whose hands are involved as we pray for His cause worldwide.

Inheritance

Reading: Ephesians 1:15-23

"...that you may know the hope to which he has called you and the riches of his glorious inheritance in the saints" (Ephesians 1:18 NIV).

Usual reference to an inheritance refers to money or material valuables. The bumper sticker read*: Where there is a will, I want to be in it*. Where money is inheritance there is often conflict. Greed surfaces, as does anger, jealousy, and envy. Lord Byron in a fit of humor in his letters and journals: "The way to be immortal (I mean not to die at all) is to have me for your heir. I recommend you to put me in your will and you will see that (as long as *I* live at least) you will never even catch cold." Andrew Carnegie, U.S. industrialist and philanthropist wrote in his album: "I would as soon leave my son a curse as the almighty dollar." John Bunyan, English Baptist preacher making his farewell said: "My sword I give to him that shall succeed me in my pilgrimage, and my courage and skill to him that can get it." Lavater, Swiss divine, poet wrote: "Say not you know another entirely till you have divided an inheritance with him."

There are other matters concerning inheritance of more importance than material possessions. In the study of Biology, there is the process of genetic transmission in families. Of even more importance there is the inheritance Paul writes about to the church at Ephesus. "I pray also that the eyes of your heart may be enlightened in order that you may know the hope to which he has called you, the riches of his glorious inheritance in the saints," (Ephesians 1:18 NIV). "We shall be like him, for we shall see him as he is" (1 John 3:2). "Who, by the power that enables him to bring everything under his control, will transform our lowly bodies so that they will be like his glorious body." (Philippians 3:21).

In a culture where the hysteria of wanting to become millionaires tantalizes us, we best should be concerned about becoming more like Christ.

In-Laws: The Ins and Outs

Reading: Exodus 18

"Jethro, Moses' father-in-law ... came to him in the desert" (Exodus 18:5 NIV).

Look out, Moses, here comes your father-in-law. If all we knew about in-laws is what we read about in Western culture, there might be a case for Moses to run to the hills when he received word of his father-in-law coming. And then there are mothers-in-law, about whom jokes are ubiquitous, casting a pall on that category of women. The English had a proverb: "He that would the daughter win, must with the mother first begin." The fellow who pleads with his wife that he didn't marry her relatives, never read the Irish proverb: "Marry a mountain girl and you marry the whole mountain." James Frazer, Scottish classicist said, "The awe and dread with which the untutored savage contemplates his mother-in-law are amongst the most familiar facts of anthropology." Woe betide the fellow who is unfamiliar with a form of psychotherapy where family problems are identified and dealt with in group sessions after church and following dinner in the home of his father-in-law. All in the name of family therapy of course. Like I say, that's Western culture for you.

Fortunately, I never had to run at the appearance of in-laws. I concede it may have been pure grace on their part. I don't know; I never asked. Now concerning Jethro, Moses' father-in–law, Moses need not run to hide. Moses left Midian to carry out the Divine commission with Jethro's consent (Exodus 4:18). He looked after Moses' wife and children at a crucial time. He visited Moses and took pride in his achievements. He gave Moses wise counsel concerning the government of Israel. Jethro was a man of influence in Moses life because he was a man of character, deeply spiritual, of wise judgment, and well balanced: a man of integrity and truth. Want to be a good in-law? Model the characteristics of Jethro.

Windows

Reading: 1 Timothy 5:17-25

"The elders who direct the affairs of the church well are worthy of double honor, especially whose work is preaching and teaching" (1 Timothy 5:17 TLB)..

Defenestration is the act of throwing someone or something out of a window. The defenestration of Prague in 1618 torched Europe in the Thirty Years' War. Two governors were tossed from the window into a mote. Ditched. Who would believe that in this day and age, churches are resorting to the practice of defenestration with their pastors? Call it firing or forced resignation, preachers are under the gun to measure up to the culture's search for significance. A significance falling under a pastor's inability to please people. The boardroom of company and political life has infected the church. Admittedly, such goings on we are witnessing today, is a complex problem. Nobody ever said pastoral ministry would be easy. But have we taken time to examine the work of pastoring, preaching and teaching? James Earl Massey, venerable Preacher-in-Residence of Park Place Church of God, Anderson, Indiana (1994-95), has this to say about preaching: "I have long looked upon preaching, and graciously experienced it, as a burdensome joy. It is `burdensome' because of the way the preparation and delivery aspects of the pulpit task weigh upon the preacher's selfhood—and with so many unique demands.

But preaching is also `joy' because of the divine purpose that makes it necessary and the redeeming eventfulness that it can effect for those who receive it with faith and openness."

When was last time you hugged your pastor, thanked him for the sermon, told him he is at the top of your prayer list, slipped him a gift to take his beleaguered wife to lunch? Somebody started a "Pastor Appreciation Day" supposedly is to be an annual day of appreciation. Little good that will do when the preacher is lonely, taken for granted and/or unappreciated the rest of the year. Now don't all rush up to the pastor at the same time come Sunday; he may drop over of a heart attack. That would be worse than getting fired. Well, maybe worse for you, better for him. Appreciated or not, preachers must focus energies on the calling of preaching. A.J. Gossip encourages preachers: "The Word of God can grow to be only a hunting-ground for texts; and we can preach, meaning intensely every word we utter, and yet in reality only lost for the moment like an actor in his part, or at least leaving it to the folk to live it out; for us, bless me, we have no time for that, but are already immersed, poor harried souls, in determining what we shall preach on next." Let God take care of your enemies; He will take of you. Preach your meditations, not your nerves.

On Eagles' Wings

Reading: Exodus 19:1-25

"I carried you on eagles' wings and brought you to myself" (Exodus19:4 NIV).

Some birds carry the young by their talons. The eagle carries its young on its wings. "He spreads his wings over them, Even as an eagle overspreads her young. She carries them upon her wings— As does the Lord his people! When the Lord alone was leading them, And they lived without foreign gods,

God gave them fertile hilltops, Rolling, fertile fields, Honey from the rock, And olive oil from stony ground!" (Deuteronomy. 32:12-13 TLB). I've never witnessed an eagle carrying its young, but I've seen scores of eagles while fishing in Alaska. They soar high, are swift of speed with ease and strength. There is tenderness in the care of young eaglets. Their nests often measure as much as nine feet across. It is said that when time comes for the young eagle to leave the nest, the mother boots him out and watches so as to fly under him to catch him on her wings. This powerful bird shows great tenderness to its own.

God brought Israel into a state of liberty and honor and communion. It wasn't Israel reaching for God, but the Lord bringing them to Him. It was purely the Lord's doing. So also it is that God brings us to Himself by Christ, in that He died the just for the unjust. In the law a symbol of power is the eagle. In the Gospels a contrast is made distinguishing it from the Law. It is "a hen." "Jerusalem, Jerusalem, thou that killest the prophets, and stonest them which are sent unto thee, how often would I have gathered thy children together, even as a hen gathereth her chickens under her wings, and ye would not!" (Matthew 23:37 KJV). Power brought God's people out of Egypt and into the Promised Land. Grace brings us out of the slave market of sin, manifested when Christ came in humility, took the form of a servant and became obedient unto death, even the death of the Cross.

By Whose Choice?

Reading: Ephesians 1:1,2

"Chosen by God to be Jesus Christ's messenger" (Ephesians 1:1 TLB).

"You did not choose me but I chose you. And I appointed you to go and bear fruit, fruit that will last—" (John 15:16). God sings to the world the song of redemption with a full complement of instruments in the orchestra. Every one of us who are in Christ is a member of that orchestra. The music is not ours, but God's. He is the composer. It was His choice. We, the honored members of that band, sing the song of the redeemed. We didn't audition the part; God chose us. We had no voice for the part; God gave us voice. It springs from a melody deep down in our hearts. We learn to sing the song of redemption only if we practice it. The best of our hymns expresses the music of faith. The world sees all this as unnecessary. There is such a variety from which to choose, but the world chooses not to follow God. That God would care enough to choose is foreign to the thinking of the world. Not so with our Lord. The Apostle Paul wrote the greatest hymn which was said to be sung by the early church: "Your attitude should be the same as that of Christ Jesus: Who, being in very nature God, did not consider equality with God something to be grasped, but made himself nothing, taking the very nature of a servant, being made in human likeness. And being found in appearance as a man, he humbled himself and became obedient to death- even death on a cross! Therefore God exalted him to the highest place and gave him the name that is above every name, that at the name of Jesus every knee should bow, in heaven and on earth and under the earth, and every tongue confess that Jesus Christ is Lord, to the glory of God the Father" (Philippians. 2:5-11 NIV)

Jealousy

Reading: Exodus 20:1-17

"You shall have no other gods before me" (Exodus 20:3 NIV).

"You shall not bow down to them or worship them; for I, the LORD your God, am a jealous God, punishing the children for the sin of the fathers to the third and fourth generation of those who hate me, but showing love to a thousand [generations] of those who love me and keep my commandments" (Exodus 20:5-7.)

The word jealous means an intolerance of a rival. There is a good jealousy and a bad jealousy depending on how the word is used. Jealous as a word is neutral as is the gear in an automobile. The car doesn't move until it's in forward or reverse gear. When two people come together and exchange vows in matrimony they give each other the right to be jealous of their union: not to tolerate a rival to come between them. A good and proper jealousy. On the other hand an example of a bad jealousy would take place if a basketball player were jealous of the presence of his opponent on the court. What makes basketball a game is the presence of a rival; whereas, what makes for a good marriage is an amicable agreement that there shall be no rival. Now regarding God, He has no legitimate rival. "For even if there are so-called gods, whether in heaven or on earth (as indeed there are many "gods" and many "lords"), yet for us there is but one God, the Father, from whom all things came and for whom we live; and there is but one Lord, Jesus Christ, through whom all things came and through whom we live" (1 Corinthians. 8:5-7 NIV).

We should not tolerate any rival between our Lord, Jesus Christ and us. We are His possession.

Tests

Exodus 20:18-21

"God has come to test you" (Exodus 20:20).

Culture is awash with tests: test of endurance, test driver, test data, test case, Test Ban Treaty, Standard Achievement Test for college entrance, test pattern, test tube, test tube baby, test tube fertilization, beta test, psychological tests, health tests and on and on. A test is a procedure for critical evaluation. One doesn't live long without facing tests of some sort. We test a ball point pen to see if it works; we test to be enrolled in college; we test for heart disease; we test for cancer; we test for aptitude; we resort to psychological testing. W.C. Sellar, British author, in "Test V" wrote:" Do not on any account attempt to write on both sides of the paper at once."

Most tests require a lot of courage, the kind that C. S. Lewis writes of, "Courage is not simply one of the virtues but the form of very virtue at the testing point, which means at the point of highest reality." They probably didn't have colonoscopy testing in Lewis' day, but that was a high point of reality for me when I submitted that particular test. Some test that was! Now the purpose of God's testing Israel was that they might not sin against him through distrust, disobedience, resistance to his will and commands. The proving of Israel was that they might adore his majesty, respect his authority, obey his commands, and dread his wrath. It didn't take long before Israel flunked the test. Israel fell into the habit of wanting to test God. They liked that better than being tested by God. Moses asked Israel: "Why do you quarrel with me? Why do you put the LORD to the test?" (Exodus 17:2).

After the church was established in the book of Acts a council was held, "Now then, why do you try to test God by putting on the necks of the disciples a yoke that neither we nor your fathers have been able to bear?" (Acts 15:10). There is a proper testing Christians are held accountable for: "Examine yourselves to see whether you are in the faith; test yourselves. Do you not realize that Christ Jesus is in you, unless, of course, you fail the test?" (2 Corinthians 13:5 NIV).

"Dear friends, do not believe every spirit, but test the spirits to see whether they are from God, because many false prophets have gone out into the world" (1 John 4:1 NIV). "Blessed is the man who perseveres under trial, because when he has stood the test, he will receive the crown of life that God has promised to those who love him" (James 1:12 NIV).

Saints

Reading: Ephesians 1:1-10

"To the saints" (Ephesians 1:1 NIV).

The use of the word "saint" is all over the map in our times. Some recognize people thought worthy of canonization, capable of interceding for people on earth. Others think of a saint as one who has died and gone to heaven. Still others think a saint is an extremely virtuous person. Just take note of present day eulogies of the dead, where we are prone to celebrate one's life ignoring the need for a relationship to Jesus Christ. Marva Dawn expressed it well: "We are saints, declared so by God through the merits of Jesus Christ and transformed by the Spirit at work within us to live out our sainthood..."

We must not ignore the fact that while we may be saints in position, we are still sinners. Martin Luther gave us insight into simul justus et peccata – that we are totally saints and totally sinners at the same time. Beware of the insidious danger of celebrating how good you are or what an awful sinner you are, lest the sin of pride trip you up and you go down with a thud. As Victor Hugo addressed this issue, "A saint addicted to excessive self-abnegation is a dangerous associate; he may infect you with poverty, and a stiffening of those joints which are needed for advancement— in a word, with more renunciation than you care for— and so you flee the contagion."

Gratification

Reading: Ephesians 2:1-10

"All of us also lived ... , gratifying the cravings of our sinful nature and following its desires and thoughts" (Ephesians 2:3 NIV).

We live in a culture that seeks unrestrained gratification of self, the wilder the better. The advertising industry subtly persuades us to please one's self, whether at the expense of pleasing loved ones, employers or God. However nothing is new, for Job said long ago: "They sing to the music of tambourine and harp; they make merry to the sound of the flute. They spend their years in prosperity and go down to the grave in peace. Yet they say to God, 'Leave us alone! We have no desire to know your ways Who is the Almighty, that we should serve him? What would we gain by praying to him?' But their prosperity is not in their own hands, so I stand aloof from the counsel of the wicked." (Job 21:12-16 NIV). Wrong self-indulgence fosters a condition of mental or moral decay. The "will of the mind" referred to here relates to the wicked "thoughts and purposes" of the unrenewed nature—the sins which relate rather to the `intellect' than to the gross passions. Such, for instance, are the sins of pride, envy, ambition, covetousness, etc.; and Paul means to say, that before conversion they lived to gratify these propensities, and to accomplish these desires of the soul.

Another red flag in unrestrained gratification is its hostility. "The sinful mind is hostile to God. It does not submit to God's law, nor can it do so. Those controlled by the sinful nature cannot please God" (Romans 8:7,8 NIV). Self-gratification may be pleasurable to us, but hostile to God. Furthermore, self-indulgence rejects accountability, while hungering for entitlement. The tensions between accountability and entitlement loom large in the political philosophies of our nation. We are better served when we live lives accountable to God and let the pleasure be that of pleasing Him who became accountable for our sins and gave His life a ransom for us that we might have newness of life. "...dear friends, let us purify ourselves from everything that contaminates body and spirit, perfecting holiness out of reverence for God." (2 Corinthians.7:1 NIV).

Heaven

Reading: Exodus 20:22-26

"... I have spoken to you from heaven". (Exodus 20:22 NIV).

Evelyn Waugh, British novelist, wrote, "The human mind is inspired enough when it comes to inventing horrors; it is when it tries to invent a Heaven that it shows itself cloddish." God said to Israel, "I have talked to you from heaven." Isaiah wrote, "'Heaven is my throne, and the earth is my footstool. What kind of house will you build for me? says the Lord. Or where will my resting place be? Has not my hand made all these things?'" (Isaiah 66:1 NIV). Heaven was already there; man didn't or couldn't invent it. Israel knew God was around since He manifested Himself by fire, earthquake, lightning, thick darkness. Now He speaks to them from heaven. The Egyptian magicians couldn't counterfeit God's voice.

Heaven is a real place. It is the eternal dwelling place of God. It is the place from which God descended to become incarnate. It is the place where Jesus ascended and sat down on the right hand of the throne of the Majesty in the heavens. It is the place where Jesus always lives to make intercession for us who are His children. It is the eternal dwelling place of saints gone on to glory. It is the place from which Jesus will come again to receive His own at the rapture. Nothing cloddish about God's heaven. Our citizenship is in heaven. We have an inheritance that can never fade, kept in heaven. Paul wrote to the Corinthians, "Now we know that if the earthly tent we live in is destroyed, we have a building from God, an eternal house in heaven, now built by human hands" (2 Corinthians 5:1 NIV). Storing up treasures on earth? What better investment than to "...store up for yourselves treasures in heaven, where moth and rust do not destroy, and where thieves do not break in and steal" (Matthew 6:20-21 NIV).

Role

Reading: Ephesians 2:8-10.

"For it is by grace you have been saved, through faith, and this not from yourselves, it is the gift of God..." (Ephesians 2:8 NIV).

We love the idea of playing a major role in what we do. People make a career out of play acting in a dramatic performance. Oscars and Emmys are their reward, not to overshadow money paid for services. But, as Irish novelist Brian Moore, observed, "There comes a point in many people's lives when they can no longer play the role they have chosen for themselves. When that happens, we are like actors finding that someone has changed the play." *Role* dates back in English to 1606, coming from French with a sense of playing a part. It's important to know that the Christian life is not based on playing a part.

Coming to faith in Christ is not play-acting; it is to become a new creation in Christ Jesus. Furthermore, we can't take credit for it; the major role is credited to Christ who died on the cross to pay the penalty for our sin. In my view the faith by which we come to Christ is a grace gift as well. No boasting here, only gratitude. Yes, there is an attempt at posturing the Christian life on the assumption that enough good works will land us in heaven when we die. Man may appreciate good works, but Jesus rebuked those who depended on such to get them to heaven. "Many will say to me on that day, 'Lord, Lord, did we not prophesy in your name and in your name drive out demons and perform many miracles?' Then I will tell them plainly, 'I never knew you. Away from me, you evildoers!'" (Matthew 7:22-23 NIV). Better that we humbly admit to being sinners and placing our faith in Jesus Christ. For by grace (surprise gift) are we saved.

Love

Reading: Exodus 21:1-22:15

"...I will not go out as a free man" (Exodus 21:*3* NAS).

Just after the giving of the Ten Commandments, God instituted the law concerning social issues. The law concerning master and servant relationships. A slave by law could go free after seven years, if he so chose. If because of his love for his master, wife and children he would not go free, his master would bore his ear through with an awl. The slave would serve his master forever. Now think about this: the Lord Jesus Christ came to earth to take upon himself our humanity. This humanity was in the slave market of sin. Jesus knew no sin. He could have rejected the idea of death and leave man to God's just judgment. But Jesus willingly died; therefore, "Let us fix our eyes on Jesus, the author and perfecter of our faith, who for the joy set before him endured the cross, scorning its shame, and sat down at the right hand of the throne of God" (Hebrews 12:2 NIV). Why did Jesus die? He loved the sinner.

He left the splendor of Heaven,
Knowing His destiny
Was the lonely Hill of Golgotha,
There to lay down His life for me.
If that isn't love, the ocean is dry;
There's no stars in the sky
and the sparrow can't fly!
If that isn't love, then Heaven's a myth,
There's no feeling like this, If that isn't love.
Dottie Rambo. John T. Benson Publishing Company

The Kindness of God

Reading: Ephesians 2:6-8

"...the incomparable riches of his grace expressed in his kindness" (Ephesians 2:7 NIV).

Kindness is not to be confused here with leniency, softness, or laxity toward us as sinners. How could we think of a Holy God as lenient or lax concerning sin? Oh no, God could not even look upon sin! Yet, Christ became sin for us in order that we might become righteous in Him. Christ was anything but soft on sin, for He gave His life on the cross in order that we might be freed from the penalty and power of sin. God's same power that raised up Christ from the dead, "... raised us up with Christ and seated us with him in the heavenly realms in Christ Jesus in order that in the coming ages he might show the incomparable riches of his grace, expressed in his kindness to us in Christ Jesus" (Ephesians 2:6-8 NIV). God's kindness toward us cost Christ's life on the Cross.

The Apostle Paul raised the question with the Romans: "... do you show contempt for the riches of his kindness, tolerance and patience, not realizing that God's kindness leads you toward repentance?" (Romans 2:4 NIV) We must practice kindness toward others and not take it for granted. P.D. James, British mystery writer, wrote: "Human kindness is like a defective tap, the first gush may be impressive but the stream soon dries up."

When we walk in the light of God's Word and the leading of the Holy Spirit, we need not fear that kindness toward others will dry up. The supply is unlimited. "Whoever believes in me, as the Scripture has said, streams of living water will flow from within" (John 7:38 NIV).

Abuse

Reading: Exodus 22:16-23

"Do not take advantage of a widow or an orphan" (Exodus 22:22 NIV).

My wife announced: "I will not continue working for a company who takes advantage of a widow because she fails to ask what about her rights when she has a legitimate claim coming." God laid down moral regulations to Israel because the heart of man is deceitful and desperately wicked. Isaiah wrote to the nations: "Learn to do right! Seek justice, encourage the oppressed. Defend the cause of the fatherless, plead the case of the widow" (Isaiah 1:17 NIV).

We must learn how to treat people properly; it's not a genetic trait. History is replete with examples of the poor deprived of their rights, the oppressed denied justice, widows and fatherless robbed. Fortunately, a good many of the abused rise above it and go on to great things. Samuel Johnson once said: "A fly, Sir, may sting a stately horse and make him wince; but one is but an insect, and the other is a horse still." He who makes a life out of abusing others is the loser. As James Baldwin observed: "People who treat other people as less than human must not be surprised when the bread they have cast on the waters comes floating back to them, poisoned." Let us not become abusers of any kind. We live in a culture that is throwaway. Beware of putting a loved one in a nursing home and failing to care for them by neglecting to even visit them. "Religion that God our Father accepts as pure and faultless is this: to look after orphans and widows in their distress and to keep oneself from being polluted by the world" (James 1:27 NIV).

Be Careful

Reading: Exodus 23:10-19

"Be careful to do everything I have said to you" (Exodus 23:13 NIV).

God wasn't dealing small talk when He said to Israel, "Be careful." They were not to invoke the names of other gods or even let them be heard on their lips. He knew Israel's penchant for carelessness. They often turned to the left or the right when they should go straight away in obedience. Israel needed the Book of the Law. The LORD exhorted Joshua "Do not let this Book of the Law depart from your mouth; meditate on it day and night, so that you may be careful to do everything written in it. Then you will be prosperous and successful" (Joshua 1:8 NIV).

Sometimes I protest my carelessness as inadvertent, an unintentional lack of care. Or actions taken without due thought or consideration. For these sins I must also confess. Like the spiritual: "Not my brother, not my sister, but it's me, O Lord, standing in the need of prayer."

Lord, help me be cautiously attentive to you: careful to remember that I am not in charge, you are; heedful of the danger of taking lightly the power of Satan; mindful of my heritage, seated in heavenly places in Christ Jesus; observant to help bare the burdens of those less fortunate than I; watchful to avoid giving offense; diligent to confess my sins; eager to share the Gospel with others. God forbid I should dance with careless grace. Amen.

Be Humble, Gentle and Patient

Reading: Ephesians 4:1-7

"*Be completely humble and gentle; be patient, bearing with one another in love"* (Ephesians 4:2 NIV).

Will we ever be worthy of our calling, exhorted, as we are to be completely humble, gentle and patient in relation to others? We manifest these characteristics on occasion depending on whom we are bearing in love. Sometimes easy, at other times difficult. Humility — low-mindedness is a voluntary trait. When we're quick to open our mouth, it comes across as being high minded, and haughty, the opposite of low mindedness. The Greco-Roman world looked upon humility as contemptible. Nothing has changed; the same is true today in our culture, whereas God exalts the humble. The Psalmist, David, recognized the trait of humility in God: "You give me your shield of victory, and your right hand sustains me; you stoop down to make me great" (Psalm 18:35 NIV). Gentleness is a willingness to waive one's rights, disregarding our personal reputation or gain. Gentleness is sympathetic generosity. At times we are generous, but not sympathetic; at other times we are sympathetic, but not generous. Patience is that characteristic willing to cut slack for another's shortcomings, making sure a provocation doesn't overtake patience. Humility, gentleness and patience are qualities produced by the Holy Spirit. "Humble yourselves, therefore, under God's mighty hand, that he may lift you up in due time" (1 Peter 5:6 NIV).

Reliability and Accurate Knowledge

Reading: 1 Corinthians 4:1-5

"Now it is required that those who have been given a trust must prove faithful" . (1 Corinthians 4:2 NIV)

I agree with Muriel Spark, British novelist: "Being over seventy is like being engaged in a war. All our friends are going or gone and we survive amongst the dead and the dying as on a battlefield." Samuel Johnson, English author wrote: "At seventy-seven it is time to be in earnest." At seventy-three what does one do out of a sense of duty? Ah yes, "duty," the sense of duty that drove the engine for so many years. Admittedly, carrying out one's duty included a slowness to learn or understand. I didn't find it difficult to be obtuse. "When a stupid man is doing something he is ashamed of, he always declares that it is his duty," wrote George Bernard Shaw, about Apollodorus, in Caesar and Cleopatra, act 3.

I always pushed myself as one given to a sense of duty which usually involved doing something for the kingdom of God. I'm not ashamed of that, but when I passed "three score and ten," the realization hit that time was running out; health isn't what it once was; one's get up and go, got up and went. Sometimes before noon. So, what does one do, at this stage in life? Well, we don't want to check out ahead of time; neither do we sit down and quit for "There is no discharge in this war" (Ecclesiastes. 8:8). The Apostle Paul defended his honor by declaring to his critics, reliability as a must, given the trust that God gave him. (I Corinthians 4:2) "Now it is required that those who have been given a trust, must prove faithful." Faithful in what sense?

Prayer: Lord, with whatever time is left, sharpen my focus on being certain, genuine, as good as my word, dependable, resolute, constant, proven. Forbid that I should be embarrassed to own your name or share the mysteries of your grace. Amen.

The soul's dark cottage, batter'd and decay'd,
Lets in new light through chinks that Time has made;
Stronger by weakness, wiser, men become
As they draw near their eternal home.
-Edmund Waller (1606-1687)

To Cause To Shine

Romans 12:1-12

"Is anyone among you suffering? Let him pray. Is anyone cheerful? Let him sing psalms" (James 5:13. NKJV).

There is more heroism in a smiling face sometimes than in half the deeds that are chronicled in battle" (George Morrison). I complimented Annette for her smile, saying it cheered me so. Her response: "Thank you. You took me back to my high school days by commenting on my smile. My geometry teacher had felt so bad that all the students were having such a tough time with the subject matter that he gave us all awards. Mine was for the nicest and friendliest smile. I thought maybe I had lost that along with a lot of other things!" Proverbs says, "A merry heart makes a cheerful countenance," (15:13). Friends, Ed and Fran, octogenarians, sign their notes "Cheerily." Many people lose their cheerfulness with age.

Friend Rachel writes: "Even before hitting seventy, a person thinks about what is required of him (or her).

Sometimes what is required is simply that we hold on. I'd like to think that God wants us to "hold on" with a certain amount of cheerfulness or positive attitude—to be an encouragement to others. So often older people (I'm dipping down into the 40s, 50s and 60s) seem so crabby and cranky about life. When a person meets a cheerful person, it's as if the sun shines. And, according to my idea and my father's talk, `holding on cheerfully' can be harder than anything in the world." Rachel is right, God gives grace and peace and cheerfulness when the swirling clouds close down on us. The most cheerful people I know at the moment are those who are suffering from cancer. In the Septuagint, the verb "hilaruno" translates a Hebrew word: "to cause to shine," in Psalm 104:15. Joseph Addison, English essayist wrote: "cheerfulness keeps up a kind of daylight in the mind, and fills it with a steady and perpetual serenity." Give others the gift of a smile today. Be delighted with the response.

Slow to Speak

Reading: Exodus 24:1-8

"...everything the LORD has said we will do" (Exodus 24:3 NIV).

Ever vow to do something, but didn't? Caught saying a second time you'd do something when you hadn't done it the first time? That you'd do something before receiving all the information about what you pledged? If so, you weren't the first; Israel experienced that long before you appeared on the scene. Culture labels it "foot in mouth disease." We are better at talking than listening. Wolfgang Amadeus wrote, "My great-grandfather used to say to his wife, my great-grandmother, who in turn told her daughter, my grandmother, who repeated it to her daughter, my mother, who used to remind her daughter, my own sister, that to talk well and eloquently was a very great art, but that an equally great one was to know the right moment to stop."

The Bible offers plenty of instruction concerning speech and the making of vows. We are charged to obey the Lord, keep his commands, tell others about the good news of the Gospel and be willing to give an answer for the hope that is within us. At the same time the Scriptures tell us to "Let your speech be always with grace, seasoned with salt, that ye may know how ye ought to answer every man" (Colossians. 4:6). "It is a trap for a man to dedicate something rashly and only later to consider his vows" (Proverbs 20:25 NIV). "My dear brothers, take note of this: Everyone should be quick to listen, slow to speak and slow to become angry, for man's anger does not bring about the righteous life that God desires" (James 1:19:20 NIV).

It's a wonder that God didn't scrub his plan of redeeming man considering our sinfulness, but we thank God that he keeps his promises: "The Lord is not slow in keeping his promise, as some understand slowness. He is patient with you, not wanting anyone to perish, but everyone to come to repentance" (2 Peter 3:9 NIV).

Balance

Reading: Philippians 1:27-30

"Whatever happens, conduct yourselves in a manner worthy of the Gospel of Christ" (Philippians 1:27 NIV).

The word "balance" brings to mind the late, Paul R. Jackson. He was president of the seminary I attended in my youth. Paul was amiable, gentle, lovable, a big man with a big heart. Balance was his watchword. As a young man it was not easy to keeps one's equilibrium; the need for balance between exercise and eating, wealth and its use, work and play, healthy relationships with family and friends. Age brings additional challenges to keeping one's balance: use and abuse of medications, finding a pace that enables a healthy rhythm of productiveness. We feel like the Apostle Paul at times: when he said: "I know that nothing good lives in me, that is, in my sinful nature. For I have the desire to do what is good, but I cannot carry it out" (Romans 7:18 NIV). Another word for balance is "congruence." Paul puts it this way: "Only live your daily life congruent with the Gospel..."

Earl Palmer says concerning Philippians 1:27: "To live a balanced life is our goal. At times we bend in the wind of adversity. Through no fault of ours, balance is lost. But we need not stay bent. We recover our balance. That by grace. "But by the grace of God I am what I am, and his grace to me was not without effect" (1 Corinthians 15:10 NIV).

Age and Aging

Reading: Psalm 92

"They will still bear fruit in old age, they will stay fresh and green, proclaiming, 'The LORD is upright; he is my Rock...'" (Psalm 92:14,15 NIV).

Charles Kuralt, once said: "I tell stories about old people because old people are interesting. I'd tell stories about young people, too, if only they were interesting. But since they're not, I don't." There are plenty of old people among us, and the number is growing for whom there is no lack of stories. Life expectancy has gone from 46 to 77 in less than a century. In our country, 77 million baby boomers are beginning to show their age. Perhaps for some boomers, T. S. Eliot is right: "I don't believe one grows older. I think that what happens early on in life is that at a certain age one stands still and stagnates." Count on it, boomers will not be satisfied merely with senior citizen discounts or standing still. They will push for every enviable lifestyle within reach, proving Eliot wrong. Observed Henry Wadsworth Longfellow, "For age is opportunity no less than youth itself, tho' in another dress and as the evening twilight fades away the sky is filled with stars, invisible by day."

The Psalmist said that in old age the righteous should flourish and bring forth fruit. Because we may be aged doesn't mean we can't be fruitful. There is something appropriate for us to do. It is up to us to find out that something and do it. God didn't give us the experiences and wisdom we've gained in younger years for us to sit on, but rather to influence others for good. So, as we age, we must exercise our minds and bodies to make full use of what is left. Remember that God is not dead like idols. Just as he promised to sustain Israel in every circumstance, so he will sustain us who get up and start moving.

Beyond Measure

Reading: Genesis 41:48-49

"... he stopped keeping records because it was beyond measure" (Genesis 41:49b. NIV).

Many are the matters in life beyond measure. Like the time Davina and I decided to finish the trim on a room addition. Trim that dealt with various angles. We measured and cut; measured and cut; measured and cut, until the trim board was too short! So also were our tempers. It came near requiring a counselor before I lumbered out for another board. The kind of counselor who takes the measure of a marriage and repairs it. I hadn't heard of the old Scandinavian carpenter, who when he noticed an error in measurement, said: "Son, it is better to measure ten times and cut once than to measure once and cut ten times."

Now Joseph's grain harvest was so huge he couldn't measure it. The Apostle Paul probably found his sins beyond measure, causing him to say he was indeed, chiefest of sinners. While none of us dare upstage Paul, who would offer a disclaimer about our many sins? Or who would presume to know more than the Psalmist does, who said: "My mouth will tell of your righteousness, of your salvation all day long, though I know not its measure" (Psalm 71:15 NIV). How would you begin to measure Paul's statement in Philippians 4:19? (NIV), "And my God will meet all your needs according to his glorious riches in Christ Jesus." Or Jesus words: "Give, and it will be given to you. A good measure, pressed down, shaken together and running over, will be poured into your lap. For with the measure you use, it will be measured to you" (Luke 6:38 NIV).

We'd best not be taken up with measuring ourselves by ourselves, as Paul warned the Corinthians, for that is not wise (2 Corinthians 10:12 NIV). But rather, devote our time to being "filled to the measure of all the fullness of God" (Ephesians 3:19 NIV). It is amazing that we can be filled with God. How great it is to be filled with the fullness of God; and still greater it is to be filled with *all* the fullness of God. Will we ever plumb the depths of God's fullness? Perhaps not in this lifetime, but what joy there is in the pursuit.

Blindness

Reading: John 9

"The LORD gives sight to the blind, the LORD lifts up those who are bowed down, the LORD loves the righteous" (Psalms 146:8 NIV)

In our efforts to relate to one another, one way or another we contend with blindness. There is the blindness that comes with lack of background information, like taste tests. There are loved ones blinded to the faults of their lover. There is blind faith in a leader. There can be a blind seam in sewing. In Botany, flowers may have a blind bud. Duck hunters often sit in blinds. We may enter into a business agreement blind. Prejudice may blind us to the merits of proposal. Occasionally, the world is staggered by an account of blindness. When Lieut. Captain Dimitri Kolesnikov, Russian sailor, sat in the black chamber of the doomed submarine Kursk, at the bottom of the ocean, he wrote a note to his wife describing his last moments in life: "I am writing blindly."

Now there is a spiritual blindness all of us experienced before we came to faith in Christ. Paul refers to this blindness in his letter to the Corinthians. He said the natural man perceived not the things of God. In our unsaved state we are blind to the spiritual. Jesus called the Pharisees blind guides who strained at gnats but swallowed camels. Jesus gave sight to the blind. He gave sight to the blind man in the Gospel of John. Afterward, Jesus was accosted by religious leaders who sought to entrap him, calling him a faker. When they summoned the man who had been blind, they said, `Give glory to God'....`We know this man is a sinner.'" The poor fellow replied, "Whether he is a sinner or not, I don't know. One thing I do know. I was blind but now I see!" (John 9:24,25).

Where would we be was it not for the Holy Spirit opening our eyes to the truth of the Gospel?

But God

Reading: Exodus 24:9-11

" But God did not raise his hand against these leaders of the Israelites" (Exodus 24:11 NIV).

God could have raised his hand and harmed the leaders of Israel, but he didn't. We are continually amazed at the presence of God in the lives of his chosen. We abandon positions important to God, but God whose purposes will not be frustrated, is faithful. "In all my prayers for all of you, I always pray with joy because of your partnership in the gospel from the first day until now, being confident of this, that he who began a good work in you will carry it on to completion until the day of Christ Jesus" (Philippians 1:4-6 NIV).

We fall in love with money, but God says be content with what you have, "`Never will I leave you; never will I forsake you'" (Hebrews 13:5 NIV). We experience aloneness, but are never alone: "Lo, I am with you always" (Matthew 28:20 NIV). We are tempted to please men, but God tests our hearts (1 Thessalonians 2:4 NIV). We pray amiss, but God knows what is best. We disregard God, but God never ignores us. We neglect to pray, but Jesus ever lives to make intercession for us. We are guilty of not caring for God, but God cares for us. We vote, but God controls. We refuse to pay attention to God, but God pays attention to us. We sin, but God forgives. We get down on ourselves, but "If God is for us, who can be against us?" (Romans 8:31 NIV).

Ceremony

"...`this is my body, which is for you; do this in remembrance of me . . .'" (1 Corinthians 11:24 NIV).

Over the years I've worked at appreciating the celebration of ceremony. Eventually, I discovered the finer points of etiquette. But then, having grown up where breakfast consisted of a pork chop, eggs, gravy and homemade biscuits, sometime grits on the side, served in plain style and eaten with a tin fork and a knife, I admit I was behind the curve learning to celebrate pomp and circumstance. Perhaps my circumstances lacked pomp.

Since I didn't grow up with Shakespeare on my mind, I hadn't heard of Timon of Athens:

> Ceremony was but devised at first
> To set a gloss on faint deeds, hollow welcomes,
> Recanting goodness, sorry ere 'tis shown;
> But where there is true friendship, there needs none.

Ah, friendship and ceremony, about the only celebration was to get to a county fair. E.B. White pictured it: "at a fair your front pocket can be picked by a trotting horse looking for sugar, and your hind pocket by a thief looking for his fortune."

Then I became a Christian, and suddenly I saw ceremony everywhere. Pharisees celebrating something they weren't themselves even trying to live up to; weddings costing a small fortune to celebrate sending a young couple out into the world in a rental house; buying things thinking there was some link to happiness by their possession, only to find later that the memory was etched on a credit card statement. There was then, and is now, plenty of pomp and circumstance to go round. Both good and bad.

But we lose if we throw out all ceremony. I'm reminded of our Lord when he set the table known as The Lord's Supper: "`this is my body, which is for you; do this in remembrance of me . . .' in the same way, after supper he took the cup, saying, `This cup is the new covenant in my blood; do this, whenever you drink it, in remembrance of me. For whenever you eat this bread and drink this cup, you proclaim the Lord's death until he comes'" (1 Corinthians 11:24-26 NIV).

Connections

Reading: Luke 10:25—27

"...when he saw the man, he passed by on the other side" (Luke 10:31-32 NIV).

Connecting with someone is usually inspired by what we can get from him or her, some advantage to carry us along in life; whereas the Gospel of Christ is best served when we look for some connection in which we can serve others. When we do look for those whom we can help, it's often to those already attractive, not the unlovely or broken. Our culture encourages us, if we do take time to connect, to get on with it and get out as soon as possible, lest we get too involved and life passes us by. The priest and the Levite in our story had something else in mind when they passed by the other side of him who needed help. What their aim was that day we'll never know.

Our problem is we don't get near enough to people to see them in their need. Helmut Thielicke rightly observed: "Love always seizes the eyes first and then the hand. If I close my eyes, my hands remain unemployed. And finally my conscience too falls asleep, for this disquieting neighbor has disappeared from my sight."

We are awash with dysfunctional relationships in our society, largely because our aim is self-centered, therefore self-serving. Anne Tyler's novel *Accidental Tourist,* characterizes the marriage of Macon and Sarah: "They were already moving toward their last edgy, miserable year together, toward those months when anything either of them said was wrong, toward that sense of narrowly missed connections. They were like people who run to meet, holding out their arms, but their aim is wrong; they pass each other and keep running."

As we make up our "to do" list today, perhaps we should pray first that God will give us eyes to see someone in need, someone we can help without thought of personal benefit other than the satisfaction that we've connected in a loving way with someone in need.

Decisions

Reading: Psalm 37:1-4

"Delight yourself in the LORD and he will give you the desires of your heart" (Psalm 37:4 NIV).

I've often been asked by friends, "How do you determine the will of God?" If they were hoping for surefire direction, they didn't get any. I don't have any pat answers. Nor do I have any no-fail, safe answers for myself. Not that I've had no experience in decision making, neither do I wish to imply that God is unconcerned about my decisions. When I do something contrary to the Word of God, I need not ask: "Is it the will of God?" Have I ever made bad decisions? Oh yes, I learned a long time ago to look back only to say: "Well, that wasn't one of my better decisions." Have mistakes in decision making dampened my judgment? No, not really. Being of simple faith, I've rested major decisions in my life on Psalm 37:4, paraphrased by Eugene Peterson: "Open up before Yahweh, keep nothing back; he'll do whatever needs to be done. He'll validate your life in the clear light of day and stamp you with approval at high noon." Don't misunderstand, I don't engage in unbridled desire for that only leads to tragedy in the making. I am grateful for peace that God gives through his Word, through the Holy Spirit, through the church, through the counsel of friends, and through the influence of good books.

"I don't doubt that the Holy Spirit guides your decisions from within when you make them with the intention of pleasing

God. The error would be to think that He speaks only within, whereas in reality He speaks also through Scripture, the Church, Christian friends, books etc." (C. S. Lewis).

Dislocation

Reading: Acts 1:1—11

"And surely I am with you always, to the very end of the age" (Matthew 28:20 NIV).

Anomie is a sense of dislocation. A child strays from his mother while in a crowd of people. When he realizes he is not near his mother his assurance and comfort narrows. He cries.

Cedarville University President, Dr. Paul Dixon, is planning ahead to the day in the foreseeable future when he will hand over the reins of day to day administration to another president. Dixon, a godly and gifted leader, will assume the role of chancellor of the university. To prepare for all that will eventually transpire, the subject of transition was being discussed in a meeting of the trustees.

"You will miss your president and experience anomie in his absence." So said Dr. Warren Armstrong, former president of Wichita State University as he addressed the trustees at Cedarville University. God's blessing has been on the university and her president under the leadership of Dr. Dixon in spectacular ways for more than two decades. It's only wise that the trustees be much in prayer and careful in their search for a new leader.

Several thoughts strike me as important to matters of dislocation. We experience dislocation when we walk ahead of the Spirit's leading, as seen in Peter's impetuousness when he struck a soldier and severed his ear. That's a kind of anomie we don't want. We experience dislocation, when we simply walk away from God to satisfy the desires of the flesh as the

Prodigal Son did. God forbid that we go there. We experience dislocation when we hold on to our will and fail to yield to God's will, as seen in Mary's dislocation when she realized it was the risen Christ who spoke to her at the tomb. She held on to him. Jesus said to her "Do not hold on to me, for I have not yet returned to the Father."

When it's all said and done, we continue to walk by faith, not by sight.

Displeasure

Reading: Ephesians 4:17-5:4

"And do not grieve the Holy Spirit of God, with whom you were sealed for the day of redemption" (Ephesians 4:30 NIV).

None wish to have his good evil spoken of. Unfortunately, good men go down because they bring a great deal of displeasure to those with whom they work. It was true of the brilliant General George S. Patton of World War II fame. His superior, General Dwight Eisenhower, wrote, "I am at a loss to find words with which to express my chagrin and grief at having given you, a man to whom I owe everything and for whom I would gladly lay down my life, cause for displeasure with me." Patton was grateful to Eisenhower for his mercy. However, Stephen Ambrose in his book "*Comrades*," quotes Eisenhower: "After a year and half of working with him it appears hopeless to expect that he [Patton] will ever completely overcome his lifelong habit of posing and self-dramatization which causes him to break out in these extraordinary ways." What is it in the nature of man to act with hubris?

Posing and self-dramatization is longstanding in history. Daniel prayed: "O Lord, in keeping with all your righteous acts, turn away your anger and your wrath from Jerusalem, your city, your holy hill. Our sins and the iniquities of our fathers have made Jerusalem and your people an object of scorn to all those around us" (Daniel 9:16). Paul urged Ephesian believers, "And do not grieve the Holy Spirit of God, with whom you were sealed for the day of redemption" (Ephesians 1:13). Who can say he has never grieved the Holy Spirit? Paul's message is to "Cease grieving," or "do not practice the habit of grieving." For sure, we had all better resort to prayer for the Holy Spirit's help.

Ephemeral

Reading: 2 Corinthians 4:7-18

"...for what is seen is temporary, but what is unseen is eternal" (2 Corinthians 4:18 NIV).

Something ephemeral is a markedly short-lived thing, whose use is fleeting, throwaway, temporary or disposable. Strange that we hang on to such things, until the garage, the attic, the shed, every available space is used to store things temporary. Occasionally we may garage sale stuff out the door, but then hit the trail Saturday mornings to our neighbor's garage sale. We justify our squirreling tendencies with such "may need it some day; too good to throw away; or we'll give to the kids." Now there are some things we dispose of that later we wish we had stored. But for the most part we play along with the disposable culture that says we need this, if only to store in case of a rainy day. It may become a good investment if we keep it long enough.

As Christians we are to differentiate between the transient and the eternal, those matters that "do not last long" and "last, or endure forever." The Apostle Paul wrote that some people "mind earthly things" when their concern should be about heavenly things; that is, to consider things of this world from heaven's viewpoint. To do this we turn to the Scriptures, which reveal the mind of God about things both temporal and eternal. Observe Eugene Peterson's poignancy: "Within the large, capacious context of the biblical story we learn to think accurately, behave morally, preach passionately, sing joyfully, pray honestly, obey faithfully." But we don't do these things by abandoning the story else "we walk right out of the presence and activity of God and set up our own shop." Only to collect stuff that lasts but a short time.

Futility

Reading: Lamentations 3:22—27

"So I tell you this, and insist on it in the Lord, that you must no longer live as the Gentiles do, in the futility of their thinking. They are darkened in their understanding and separated from the life of God because of the ignorance that is in them due to the hardening of their hearts" (Ephesians 4:17,18 NIV).

There may be moments in life when we experience a sense of futility, thinking our life may have served little useful purpose; a sense of uselessness; a lack of importance. Some people run straight out of the starting blocks of life thinking all is futile. In the year 2000, the race horse, Invisible Ink, came down with an infection that sapped 200 pounds off his body. The veterinarian in charge recommended putting the horse down; it was futile to try save his life. A year later, Invisible Ink ran in the Kentucky Derby, listed last in the odds to win: 50-1. It appeared futile for Invisible Ink to run the race, but he did. He placed second in the Kentucky Derby.

Some people seem to hit the wall at some mid-life point, feeling they have not measured up to their own expectations or the expectations of those for whom they work. Then there is the point in life when we get near the finish line and feel that we've run out of time to fulfill our dreams. Perhaps that is why not all of us end up well. We lose perspective and fail to cope with the reality of our own purpose and mortality. Now the world despairs from a sense of uselessness. Jean-Paul Sarte in *Being and Nothingness, Doing and Having*, wrote: "Man is a useless passion." Along comes Mark Twain with his razor sharp wit in *Pudd'nhead Wilson*, writing: "He is useless on top of the ground; he ought to be under it, inspiring the cabbages."

To be sure, it is useless for man to think he can make any sense out of life and get to heaven by his own efforts. Paul wrote: Titus 3:3-7 (NKJV) "not by works of righteousness which we have done, but according to His mercy He saved us, through the washing of regeneration and renewing of the Holy Spirit, whom He poured out on us abundantly through Jesus Christ our Savior, that having been justified by His grace we should become heirs according to the hope of eternal life."

Christians need not wallow in the slough of futility. We embrace Christ as Lord and are introduced into the family of God. Jesus Christ becomes a friend "who sticks closer than our brother" (Proverbs 18:24).

Just as the Lord had a plan for Israel, so also for us "'For I know the plans I have for you', declares the LORD, 'plans to prosper you and not to harm you, plans to give you hope and a future'" (Jeremiah 29:11 NIV).

Grudges

Reading: 1 Corinthians 13:4-7

"A man's wisdom gives him patience; it is to his glory to overlook an offense" (Proverbs 19:11 NIV).

Bearing grudges not only is an injustice toward others, but also to one's own soul. God told Israel: "Do not seek revenge or bear a grudge against one of your people, but love your neighbor as yourself. I am the LORD." Grudge bearing, like bad breath, alienates us not only from those against whom we bear a grudge, but also our friends. It is not pleasing to God. Yet, we insist at times on bearing a grudge. It is said "when Callas carried a grudge, she planted it, nursed it, fostered it, watered it and watched it." The very possibility of grudge bearing has a deleterious effect upon on our souls. "When Joseph's brothers saw that their father was dead, they said, `What if Joseph holds a grudge against us and pays us back for all the wrongs we did to him?'" (Genesis 50:15 NIV). When the story unfolded the brothers were dismayed that their brother Joseph was not holding a grudge against them. Sport has been made of grudge bearing as seen in the relationship between two great composers, Toscannini and Puchinni. The two had a fallen out that lasted a long time. One year Puchinni, who had a tradition of sending Christmas cakes to friends, sent one to Toscannini. Soon after, Puchinni remembered that he was not on speaking terms with Toscannini. He sent a telegram saying: "Cake sent by mistake." Puchinni. The next day Toscannini sent a telegram to Puchinni saying: "Cake, eaten by mistake." Laughing about grudges is one way we see through our weaknesses. Excusing our grudge holding is another.

Now we may say, "I'm not easily provoked." Emphasis on the word "easily." We may even quote the love passage in 1 Corinthians 13 that is translated in some of our Bibles: "love is not easily provoked." But we can't get by with that excuse for the word "easily" does not appear in the original language. Love is not provoked. End of excuses. So we must remember to call forth any grudges we are holding against others, seeking God's forgiveness and deliverance from the power of such a debilitating practice.

He Came

Reading: John 1:1-12

"He came to that which was his own, but his own did not receive him" (John 1:11 NIV).

As promised, Jesus came, but what had He never come? He promised eternal life to those who believe in Him, but what had He never come? He promised to rob the grave of its victory, but what had He never come? He promised never to leave us nor forsake us, but what had He never come? Did He promise too much? Was His promise sincere? George Shelley wrote: "Let your promises be sincere, and so prudently confided as not to exceed the reach of your ability; He who promises more than he is able to perform, is false to himself; and he who does not perform what he has promised, is a traitor to his friend." It was said by Luc Vauvenargues Marquis de: "One promises much, to avoid giving little."

The Savior's reach was not beyond His grasp for He was God; Neither was it too little to accomplish our redemption. Many children learned the song:

> "Every promise in the book is mine,
> Every chapter, every verse, every line,
> All the blessings of his book divine,
> Every promise in the book is mine."

True, not all promises were directed to us; many were directed only to Israel, but there is a wealth of promises in the Bible for us who are his children. In either case, God's promises are faithful and good. They will be carried out. Paul wrote the Galatian Christians: "The promises were spoken to Abraham and to his seed." The Scripture does not say `and to seeds,' meaning many people, but `and to your seed,' meaning one person, who is Christ." To the Church at Corinth, he wrote: "Since we have these promises, dear friends, let us purify ourselves from everything that contaminates body and spirit, perfecting holiness out of reverence for God" (2 Corinthians 7:1 NIV). "My eyes stay open through the watches of the night, that I may meditate on your promises" (Psalms 119:148 NIV).

Hospitality

Reading: Romans 16:22-27

"Share with God's people who are in need. Practice hospitality" (Romans 12:13 NIV).

I was disappointed the day I had to cancel a plane flight cross-country to attend a meeting. Why disappointment when it was easier to stay home? Missing the opportunity to be with friends and enjoying their hospitality is the answer. Now hospitality — the generous reception of guests — is an ancient practice dating back to Bible times. Christine Pohl writes: "The practice of hospitality is always located within the larger picture of Jesus' sacrificial welcome to all who come to him". Wrote Samuel Johnson (18th Century), "In a commercial country, a busy country, time becomes precious, and . . . hospitality is not so much valued."

"Surprisingly, as early as the mid-sixteenth century, John Calvin mourned the demise of ancient hospitality. `This office of humanity has . . . nearly ceased to be properly observed among men; for the ancient hospitality celebrated in histories, is unknown to us, and inns now supply the place of accommodations for strangers.'" Quote by Christine D. Pohl in her book *Making Room*.

Thoreau wrote: "Nowadays the host does not admit you to *his* hearth, but has got the mason to build one for yourself somewhere in his alley, and hospitality is the art of *keeping* you at the greatest distance." Practicing hospitality to strangers was likened sometimes to entertaining angels unawares. Of course I am not a stranger to my friends nor is there anything angelic about my presence so far as I know. But it gives pause to reflect on what we miss when we settle for a motel and isolation from friends. I am reminded of Peter's word to "Offer hospitality to one another without grumbling." And from John who wrote: "We ought therefore to show hospitality to such men so that we may work together for the truth." Perhaps he is right who said: "We are all guests of life. We have to learn to be guests and to treat each other as guests, to make each other welcome, or we are in danger of extinction" (George Steiner).

Meanwhile I am looking for ways to practice hospitality and for the day soon when there will be another trip to visit friends.

Slow Down

Reading: Psalm 27

"But those who wait on the LORD Shall renew their strength; They shall mount up with wings like eagles, They shall run and not be weary, They shall walk and not faint" (Isaiah 40:31 NKJV).

Regrettable decisions frequently occur when we are in a hurry. There are times and places for hurrying, but often the choice brings less than satisfying results. We hurry to a doctor's appointment only to be stalled in the waiting room until our name is called. We hurry around another car in order to be first in line at the next stoplight. We gobble our food in haste to prove Robert Louis Stevenson right: "He sows hurry and reaps indigestion." We hurry our pace in a foot race but burn out before the finish line. We're in a hurry to marry. Sancho Panza said to Don Quixote, "Does the devil possess you? You're leaping over the hedge before you come at the stile." Eric Hoffer in *Reflections on the Human Condition,* wrote: "The feeling of being hurried is not usually the result of living a full life and having no time. It is on the contrary born of a vague fear that we are wasting our life. When we do not do the one thing we ought to do, we have no time for anything else—we are the busiest people in the world."

Lord Chesterfield wrote his son: "Whoever is in a hurry, shows that the thing he is about is too big for him." We'd all be better off if we slowed down, contemplating God as the Psalmist did when he said: "I wait for the LORD, my soul waits, and in his word I put my hope."

Double-mindedness

Reading: I Kings 18

"He is a double minded man, unstable in all his ways" (James 1:8 NIV).

According to the Yiddish Proverb, "You can't dance at two weddings at the same time." To be irresolute is to stand in the middle of the road, a sure place to get run over. We all have difficulty making up our minds on occasion; however, it becomes a flaw in our thinking, when we raise vacillation to the aura of statesmanship. Julius Hare wrote: "Half the failures of this world arise from pulling in one's horse as he is leaping." For the Christian there is plenty of opportunity for indecision. It was Martin Luther's belief that "The human heart is like a ship on a stormy sea driven about by winds blowing from all four corners of heaven." That's bad enough, but worse yet is what Nicolai A. Berdyaev, Russian Christian philosopher, describes: "We find the most terrible form of atheism, not in the militant and passionate struggle against the idea of God himself, but in the practical atheism of everyday living, in indifference and torpor (a state of mind or physical activity or insensibility). We often encounter these forms of atheism among those who are formally Christians." When Israel struggled with indecision by mixing the worship of God and the worship of Baal together, Elijah sliced through the smoke of indecision by calling to the people, "How long will you falter between two opinions? If the LORD is God, follow Him; but if Baal, follow him." But the people answered him not a word" (1 Kings 18:21 NKJV). For the most part, I've found that a bad decision was better than indecision. I never liked the after taste of "What if?"

Insiders

Reading: Ephesians 2:11-22

"But now in Christ Jesus you who once were far away have been brought near through the blood of Christ" (Ephesians 2:13 NIV).

Have you ever felt like an outsider? You just didn't belong to the group? Or perhaps you belonged, but still felt like an outsider. Didn't feel like you were worth much? Little to offer? Merely tolerated, but not really accepted? The Gospel is for outsiders. The Christians at Ephesus were at one time, outsiders, strangers to the Gospel of Jesus Christ. They were separate from Christ, excluded from citizenship in the family of God, foreigners to the covenant of promise, far away, without hope and without God. "But now," Paul says, "in Christ Jesus you who once were far away have been brought near through the blood of Christ." You are not just tolerated, but accepted in Christ, welcomed in the household of God. Brought near by the blood of Christ.

When Israel was in bondage in Egypt, God told them: "On that same night I will pass through Egypt and strike down every firstborn—both men and animals—and I will bring judgment on all the gods of Egypt. I am the LORD. The blood will be a sign for you on the houses where you are; and when I see the blood, I will pass over you. No destructive plague will touch you when I strike Egypt" (Exodus 12:12,13 NIV). Christ is our Passover. When we receive Christ as Savior, the blood of Christ cleanses us from all sin.

> O great compassion! O boundless love!
> O loving kindness, faithful and true!
> Find peace and shelter under the blood,
> And I will pass over you. (J. F. H.)

Insight

Reading: Ephesians 3:1-4

"In reading this, then, you will be able to understand my insight into the mystery of Christ" (Ephesians 3:4 NIV)

Insight is the ability to size up a situation. We may have better insight into some things, but not in others, depending upon the field of judgment. Insight, in and of itself, doesn't guarantee anything, if we do not act upon what we have grasped. Furthermore, whatever insight we have must be turned over to God for his direction.

There is also the matter of hindsight, where our perception is weighed against an event after it has occurred. Sometimes even our hindsight doesn't show much insight. The opposite of insight (to grasp, perceive, to know, to understand) is foolishness. Paul cites mankind's lack of insight: "For although they knew God, they neither glorified him as God nor gave thanks to him, but their thinking became futile and their foolish hearts were darkened" (Romans 1:21 NIV).

Elsewhere, Paul writes: "The man without the Spirit does not accept the things that come from the Spirit of God, for they are foolishness to him, and he cannot understand them, because they are spiritually discerned" (1 Corinthians 2:14

NIV). Now you may think that for those in Christ, spiritual discernment is a given. Not necessarily so, for who has not made foolish decisions despite his insight? The cleverest of all, in my opinion, is the man who calls himself a fool at least once a month. (Dostoyevsky) However insight aids us, we still must walk by faith.

Knowledge

Reading Philippians 3:1-10

"They knew not the Lord" (1 Samuel 2:12 NIV).

We like to be around people whose knowledge is great, even greater than ours for it is stimulating and challenging to listen to people who know a lot. We may never grow if we surround ourselves solely with friends who know little and care less. George Gurdjieff said: "A man can only attain knowledge with the help of those who possess it. This must be understood from the very beginning. *One must learn from him who knows."*

At the same time one's knickers twist if he lingers long in the presence of him who knows more answers than there are questions and loves to prove his superiority by the display of his knowledge. We can take a page from Lord Chesterfield, English Statesman, who observed: "Never seem wiser, nor more learned, than the people you are with. Wear your learning, like your watch, in a private pocket: and do not merely pull it out and strike it; merely to show that you have one." William Cowper thought:

> "Knowledge, a rude unprofitable mass,
> The mere materials with which wisdom builds,
> Till smoothed and squared and fitted to its place,
> Does but encumber whom it seems to enrich.
> Knowledge is proud that he has learned so much;

Wisdom is humble that he knows no more."

When the Apostle Paul addressed the Corinthian church about food sacrificed to idols, he wrote: "Knowledge puffs up, but love builds up. The man who thinks he knows something does not yet know as he ought to know. But the man who loves God is known by God." Paul's heartbeat was to know Christ and the power of His resurrection. That is to have a living, experiential relationship with Him who is Lord and Savior.

Mature Faith

Reading: Ephesians 4:11—16

"Therefore, since we have a great high priest who has gone through the heavens, Jesus the Son of God, let us hold firmly to the faith we profess" (Heb 4:14 NIV).

"Mature faith is a lack of appetite for proof," commented Alan Bittel during the course of a lecture on the book of Exodus. Now that's a statement to chew on. Wouldn't we all like to be in possession of a mature faith? Paul prayed for the Ephesians that they would experience "unity in the faith and in the knowledge of the Son of God and become mature, attaining to the whole measure of the fullness of Christ." Nipping at our heels in pursuit of the will of God is a yearning for proof. Gideon agonized over the need for proof that God wanted him to defeat the Midianites. So he played a sign game with the Lord. God told Gideon what he wanted done and gave him a sign, the Spirit of the Lord was upon him, but Gideon wanted more signs. We're often like Gideon wanting our fleece wet if it's dry and dry if it's wet. Oh how we long to know what the will of God is. Just give us a sign, Lord.

Recently, Davina and I felt we ought to find a home on one floor instead of two, so we put our home up for sale. In so doing, we agreed not to buy another home until the one we had, sold. We lived comfortably with that agreement for a year while waiting for a buyer, even though we had our eye on a suitable home we wished to purchase. Then one day the owner of the home we desired phoned and offered an attractive option if we'd go ahead with the purchase. We agreed to go ahead, despite our previous agreement not to buy another home until we sold the one we owned. So much for the sign or proof that we were in the will of God. That went by the board. However, within three weeks our home sold. I look back on that year and wonder whether God bailed us out or was it just a matter of faith? Perhaps, both. I don't know the answer to that question, but I do know that seeking proof or signs isn't as much fun as is stepping out in faith.

Spiritual Maturity

Reading: Ephesians 4:11-16

"...until we all reach unity in the faith and in the knowledge of the Son of God and become mature, attaining to the whole measure of the fullness of Christ" (Ephesians 4:13 NIV).

Maturity is, in the minds of many, associated with middle age. Marie Dressler wrote: "By the time we hit fifty, we have learned our hardest lessons. We have found out that only a few things are really important. We have learned to take life seriously, but never ourselves." Alexander Herzen, Russian Journalist thought: "Every man who has lived for fifty years has buried a whole world or even two; he has grown used to its disappearance and accustomed to the new scenery of another act: but suddenly the names and faces of a time long dead appear more and more often on his way, calling up series of shades and pictures kept somewhere, `just in case,' in the endless catacombs of the memory, making him smile or sigh, and sometimes almost weep." G.K. Chesterton opined that "Youth is the period in which a man can be hopeless. The end of every episode is the end of the world. But the power of hoping through everything, the knowledge that the soul survives its adventures, that great inspiration comes to the middle-aged." Now William Shakespeare wrote of Falstaff, to the Lord Chief Justice, in King Henry IV, "Your lordship, though not clean past your youth, have yet some smack of age in you, some relish of the saltiness of time."

Turning to the Bible we hear the writer of the book of Hebrews say that maturity, spiritual in nature, requires solid food, for that's how we are trained to distinguish good from evil. James ties together maturity with perseverance making us complete. Paul sighted Epaphras as one who wrestled in prayer for the Colossian believers in order that they find maturity, being fully assured. Paul wrote the Ephesians believers about "unity in the faith and the knowledge of the Son of God" that they become mature, "attaining to the whole measure of the fullness of Christ" (Ephesians 4:12,13 NIV). So spiritual maturity involves faith in Christ, perseverance, feeding on the Word of God and prayer. Perhaps those who view maturity as something attainable by the time of middle age are right. The Christian's walk is one of faith and it's best accomplished in course of time.

Nostalgia

Reading: Philippians 3:12-21

"But our citizenship is in heaven. And we eagerly await a Savior from there, the Lord Jesus Christ, who, by the power that enables him to bring everything under his control, will transform

our lowly bodies so that they will be like his glorious body" (Philippians 3:20, 21).

In recent months I've seized opportunity to once again pare down my library holdings. It's rather painless in that I have access to a great library near at hand. While sorting books I was curious to find so many personal journals. They are of all shapes and conditions. Many entries tell about days when ministry seemed much simpler. Other entries recall regrets. Still others, remorse. But all of the journals held certain entries in common: good and bad; a mere sentence here, great detail there; large gaps between entries, often months at a time. Events and people long since forgotten evoked vivid memories once again. William Wordsworth called it: Nostalgia

> What though the radiance which was once so bright
> Be now for ever taken from my sight,
> Though nothing can bring back the hour
> Of splendour in the grass, of glory in the flower;
> We will grieve not, rather find
> Strength in what remains behind.

I found interesting that one thread weaving its way through the pages of first one journal then another was not concerning my memory, but God's. It is of God's memory, which John MacArthur identifies as, "the covenant basis on which he exercises his grace." Oh, the many entries of God's grace in days gone by. Entries that make one homesick. Not a yearning to live `back when' in order to relive old days of the past, but rather to enjoy this day, one day at a time. We are citizens of this world but also of another world.

Nostalgia of times past is good for the soul. But I concluded that nostalgia in and of itself is like a fragrant rose, enough to enjoy a whiff of its perfume, but not to eat the rose itself. There is something else to consider as well as the past. Nostalgia. It struck me that God's memory is better than mine for which I am thankful. By that I'm not referring to his memory of anything I may have said or done. Rather I'm thinking of the covenant basis on which he exercises his grace.

Why do we ask God to remember us? Or remember something we may have done? Are we afraid God's memory will fade or fail completely with time? Do we think God remembers us in short term memory? Let us not forget what God has done for us. "I will remember the deeds of the LORD; yes, I will remember your miracles of long ago" (Psalms 77:11 NIV).

Haughty Eyes and a Proud Heart

Reading: Proverbs 21:1-7

"Pride goeth before destruction, and an haughty spirit before a fall" (Proverbs 16:18 KJV).

The Bible says that haughty eyes and a proud heart, the lamp of the wicked, are sin! I am haughty when I lift myself up high, when I exalt myself above my God-given station, when I steal honor not belonging to me. My haughtiness dishonors God. On the other hand, when I am proud, my heart becomes wide, broad, spacious, and greedy. John Calvin wrote of men with proud hearts: they "are never satisfied unless they swallow up the whole world." Why is it that we sniff haughtiness and pride in others, but fail to detect it in us? We then are written off as snobs, arrogant, conceited, and as Logan Pearsall Smith writes, "The word snob belongs to the sour-grape vocabulary." Not to say there's no room for a proper sense of dignity or self-respect; pleasure in some achievement; or a soldier wearing his country's pride. Paul wrote the Corinthians: "I have great confidence in you; I take great pride in you. I am greatly encouraged; in all our troubles my joy knows no bounds." To the Galatian Christians, Paul noted: "Each one should test his own actions. Then he can take pride in himself, without comparing himself to somebody else, for each one should carry his own load." It's scornful pride and a condescending look that runs us out of bounds, placing us in company with the wicked. None have so much to brag about, but that there's enough in our lives to make us weep. Therefore, we should walk humbly before our God and fellow man, not to think more highly of ourselves than we ought to think.

Of Trumpets and Trumpery

Reading: 1 Corinthians 15:42-58

"For the trumpet will sound, the dead will be raised imperishable, and we will be changed" (1 Corinthians 15:52 NIV).

On Christmas night 1776, George Washington and 2400 men crossed the Delaware River on their way to Trenton. In the early morning hours, Washington and his men surprised a Hessian garrison of a thousand men and soundly defeated them, taking nearly 900 prisoners. Afterward, Henry Knox, Continental General, wrote his wife that "the hurry, fright, and confusion of the enemy was [not] unlike that which will be when the last trump shall sound." Indeed, there will be confusion when the trumpet sounds that Paul writes about. There will be confusion of the enemy Satan; confusion of men who will bow the knee to confess Jesus is Lord; confusion of those who thought they could get to heaven by any other way than through Jesus Christ, for "Salvation is found in no one else, for there is no other name under heaven given to men by which we must be saved" (Acts 4:12 NIV).

There shall be no confusion for those who are in Christ "For the Lord himself will come down from heaven, with a loud command, with the voice of the archangel and with the trumpet call of God, and the dead in Christ will rise first. After that, we who are still alive and are left will be caught up together with them in the clouds to meet the Lord in the air. And so we will be with the Lord forever. Therefore encourage each other with these words" (1 Thessalonians. 4:16-18 NIV).

On Special Assignment

Reading: 1 Timothy 1:1-14

"I, Paul, am an apostle on special assignment for Christ, our living hope" (1 Timothy 1:1 The Message).

Our God is the God of special assignments. Abraham was on special assignment to get out of his country to another where God would make him a great nation. Moses was on special assignment to deliver Israel from Egyptian bondage. Job was on special assignment "in a cosmic test, a contest proposed in heaven but staged on earth" (The Student Bible). Jesus was on special assignment to make his dwelling among us, to die for our sins, in order that "whoever believes in him shall not perish but have eternal life" (John 3:16). The Apostle Paul was on special assignment "by the command of God our Savior and of Christ Jesus our hope."

The study of Paul's assignment and how he handled it has always challenged me. Paul was mindful that his calling came from God, not from man. He considered himself a servant, not a volunteer. He served the Lord with great humility and with tears. To the Galatians he wrote: "... If we or an angel from heaven should preach a gospel other than the one we preached to you, let him be eternally condemned!" Paul wasn't serving his own self interest for he "considered everything a loss compared to the surpassing greatness of knowing Christ Jesus my Lord, for whose sake I have lost all things. I consider them rubbish, that I may gain Christ." Near the end of his life, Paul assessed his assignment as he wrote young Timothy: "I have fought the good fight, I have finished the race, I have kept the faith. Now there is in store for me the crown of righteousness, which the Lord, the righteous Judge, will award to me on that day — and not only to me, but also to all who have longed for his appearing" (2 Timothy 4:7,8 NIV).

"And what does the Lord require of you? To act justly and to love mercy and to walk humbly with your God" (Micah 5:2).

Pedestrian

Reading: Psalm 84

"For you have delivered me from death and my feet from stumbling, that I may walk before God in the light of life" (Psalm 56:13 NIV).

Our grandson, Mike, wrote a paper about Scotland for his middle school class assignment. After much research that included personal incidents in the life of his great grandfather who reigned as lightweight champion boxer in Britain for six years, Mike practiced his speech before his Dad. Dressed properly, wearing his Wallace plaid tie, well written speech in hand, he covered several Scottish themes. When he came to religion, Mike, said: "The predominant religion in Scotland is pedestrian." He meant Presbyterian, of course, but hadn't realized what he said. Dad laughed. We laughed when the story came to us. Mike probably didn't know much about Presbyterians or pedestrians. He does now. A pedestrian travels by foot.

Mark Twain, said: The true charm of pedestrianism does not lie in the walking, or in the scenery, but in the talking. The walking is good to time the movement of the tongue by, and to keep the blood and the brain stirred up and active; the scenery and the woodsy smells are good to bear in upon a man an unconscious and unobtrusive charm and solace to eye and soul and sense; but the supreme pleasure comes from the talk". There is a sense of the spiritual that every Christian is a pedestrian. We walk with the Lord. The Psalmist wrote: "For you have delivered me from death and my feet from stumbling, that I may walk before God in the light of life" (Psalm 56:13). Paul wrote the church at Ephesus: "For you were once darkness, but now you are light in the Lord. Live as children of light (for the fruit of the light consists in all goodness, righteousness and truth) and find out what pleases the Lord." John the Apostle reminds us, "If we claim to have fellowship with him yet walk in the darkness, we lie and do not live by the truth. But if we walk in the light, as he is in the light, we have fellowship with one another, and the blood of Jesus, his Son, purifies us from all sin" (1 John 1:6,7 NIV).

Prompted to Give

Reading: Exodus 25:1-7

"Tell the Israelites to bring me an offering. You are to receive the offering for me from each man whose heart prompts him to give" (Exodus 25:2 NIV)

When God asked Israel to bring an offering for the building of the Temple, they responded willingly, giving so much, Moses had to call off the giving. Considering that God blessed Israel with the spoils of Egypt, it seems quite right that they would be generous. However, Israel could have turned up absent, thereby missing the opportunity to give. Replacing the joy of giving with the habit of buying leads to poverty of spirit. Earl Palmer quotes John Updike on the problem of having too much money. "The superrich make lousy neighbors – they buy a house and tear it down and build another, twice as big, and leave. They're never there. The essence of the superrich is absence. They're always demonstrating they can afford to be somewhere else. Don't let them in. Their money is a kind of poverty."

Fortunately, most all those whom I've known to be rich have also been generous givers. When the call goes out to give, we must step up spontaneously and give as God prompts our hearts. "One man gives freely, yet gains even more; another withholds unduly, but comes to poverty. A generous man will prosper; he who refreshes others will himself be refreshed" (Proverbs 11:24,25 NIV).

Purpose

Reading: 2 Timothy 1:8-10

"With this in mind, we constantly pray for you, that our God may count you worthy of his calling, and that by his power he may fulfill every good purpose of yours and every act prompted by your faith" (2 Thessalonians 1:11 NIV).

I'm staring out the window this afternoon watching the grass grow. It's green and vibrant appearing, having absorbed a long drink of water last evening. The sun is shining through the heavens to the west with a mixture of gray, blue and dark clouds. Dark clouds looming in the background from the Pacific Ocean signal another shower coming. The air is so clean. At the same time I'm thinking about writing. Writing about God's purpose in hardening Pharaoh's heart. God purposed to make known in all the earth His power that His name might be proclaimed. Pharaoh didn't get it. In the New Testament, the Pharisees rejected God's purpose for themselves. When Jesus was nailed to the cross, with the help of wicked men, the world didn't comprehend the purpose and foreknowledge of God. There are times when the best of us wonder for what purpose

God makes all things work together for the good of those who love Him. Yes, I know and believe Paul when he wrote the Roman Christians: "...We know that God causes all things to work together for good to those who love God, to those who are called according to His purpose" (Romans 8:28 NAS).

But perhaps Richard Dawkins, British biologist and author of *River Out of Eden*, makes a point: "We humans have purpose on the brain. We find it hard to look at anything without wondering what it is 'for,' what the motive for it is, or the purpose behind it. When the obsession with purpose becomes pathological it is called paranoia—reading malevolent purpose into what is actually random bad luck. But this is just an exaggerated form of a nearly universal delusion. Show us almost any object or process, and it is hard for us to resist the 'Why' question—the `What is it for?' question."

I don't believe there is such a thing as "random bad luck," but I do ask "why" on occasion, knowing full well that God is not without purpose in everything He does; it is left for us to trust Him. At times it also helps to stare out the window and watch the grass grow.

Raised Up and Seated

Reading: Ephesians 2:4-10

"And God raised us up with Christ and seated us with him in the heavenly realms in Christ Jesus" (Ephesians 2:6 NIV).

American citizens shell out money in multi-million dollar amounts for a seat in government. Whether the winner is best qualified for such a seat, is left to the judgment of the electorate. It's the way we do it, as imperfect the process. Seats in congress bring power and prestige. Now the Bible tells us King Xerxes honored Haman, who was not worthy of honor, by "giving him a seat of honor higher than that of all the other nobles" (Esther 3:1 NIV). When Evil-Merodach became king of Babylon, he released Jehoiachin from prison and gave him a seat of honor higher than other kings. (2 Kings 25:27-29)

The Psalmist tells us we shouldn't be found in the seat of the mockers (Psalm 1). James wrote: "My brothers, as believers in our glorious Lord Jesus Christ, don't show favoritism. Suppose a man comes into your meeting wearing a gold ring and fine clothes, and a poor man in shabby clothes also comes in. If you show special attention to the man wearing fine clothes and say, `Here's a good seat for you,' but say to the poor man, `You stand there' or `Sit on the floor by my feet,' have you not discriminated among yourselves and become judges with evil thoughts?" (James 2:1-4). The seat we occupy is of great importance. Now when Paul writes that "God raised us up with Christ and seated us with him in the heavenly realms in Christ Jesus," we are into high honor. An honor bestowed on us by God. It's cost? Christ's death on the cross. Favored? Yes, we are all favored, who are in Christ. "The Lord is not slow in keeping his promise, as some understand slowness. He is patient with you, not wanting anyone to perish, but everyone to come to repentance" (2 Peter 3:9 NIV). Our challenge is use our influence to tell others about Christ.

Reality

Reading: Colossians 2:16—3:1

"...the reality, however, is found in Christ" (Colossians 2:17 NIV).

Facing reality is a constant challenge in life at every stage. "Human kind cannot bear very much reality," wrote, T. S. Eliot. Serge Daney, observed, "In an age of synthetic images and synthetic emotions, the chances of an accidental encounter with reality are remote indeed." We think our child is a star athlete when he's not, but we deny reality. He may well be the star in our family, but not the team. We imagine ourselves worthy of being boss, but are disappointed when our superiors don't agree. Culture says: "We can be everything and do anything we want." The closer we get to reality the specter of denial hounds our every step. Now all of us admit we are capable of doing or being more than we are, but this "do it yourself philosophy" is dangerous to our well being, for it often crashes in the face of reality. We want to win so badly that when we lose, we see ourselves as "losers." We can spend a lifetime chasing shadows, often capturing them, only to find there's little substance gained. The captured shadow causes us to miss the substance of the life found in our relationship with Jesus Christ. The Colossian believers chased shadows. The law was but a shadow of things to come. Paul said that reality, substance, and body is to be found in Christ. "My counsel for you is simple and straightforward: Just go ahead with what you've been given. You received Christ Jesus, the Master, now live him" (The Message).

Reason

Reading: Ephesians 3:1-4

"For this reason..." (Ephesians 3:1 NIV).

Paul moved about with reason for what he believed or preached. He hears of the Ephesians' faith and writes: "For this reason I have not stopped giving thanks for you and your love for all the saints" (Ephesians 1:16). He is concerned that the Gentiles in Ephesus know that the gospel is for them as well as the Jews and writes: "For this reason, (this cause), I am a prisoner of Jesus Christ". He cautions them not to feel sorry for him because he is in prison: "For this reason I kneel before the Father...I pray that out of his glorious riches he may strengthen you with power...so that Christ may dwell in your hearts by faith" (Ephesians 3:14,15). He instructs Ephesian believers about the importance of the church: "For this reason a man will leave his father and mother and be united to his wife, and the two will become one flesh...I am talking about Christ and the church" (Ephesians 5:31,32 NIV). Paul did not discount the reason for suffering for the sake of the gospel.

We agree with Eric Hoffer: "We need not only a purpose in life to give meaning to our existence but also something to give meaning to our suffering. We need as much something to suffer for as something to live for." Now, lest we live by reason alone, let us remember the necessity for passion. As Paul said to Timothy: "For this reason I remind you to fan into flame the gift of God, which is in you through the laying on of my hands" (2 Timothy 1:6 NIV).

Reruns

Reading: Ex 27:21-28:1

"This is to be a lasting ordinance among the Israelites for the generations to come" (Exodus 21:28 NIV).

Someone wrote a book taking up the plight of child stars in the entertainment world whose star became lost with age and the passing of time. The writer concluded that: "In the end, though, there is absolutely nothing "former" about a former child star. They could get lost; we could give them up. But they'd always be found. They are, and always will be. Reruns, after all, are forever." I enjoy seeing reruns, especially of the Andy Griffith Show, but as successive generations appear, tastes for entertainment and reruns change. So even the reruns fade away.

God gave Israel instructions of a lasting nature. Some were for a period of time, God's time. Some were of an eternal nature. So too, God gives Christians directions of a lasting nature. It's always right to love and enjoy God, to pray without ceasing, to love one another, to love one's enemies, to be forgiving, to be generous, to be kind, to be ready to give an answer for the hope which lies within us. When the reruns of our life are played, what will we be known for?

Riches

Reading: Ephesians 1:15-23

"The seed that fell among thorns stands for those who hear, but as they go on their way they are choked by life's worries, riches and pleasures, and they do not mature" (Luke 8:14 NIV).

Think riches and we usually picture dollar signs. We never seem to have quite all the money we deserve or wish to acquire. We compare our lifestyle with our neighbors only to feel we are more deserving than they are. Theodore Roosevelt observed: "Probably the greatest harm done by vast wealth is the harm that we of moderate means do ourselves when we let the vices of envy and hatred enter deep into our own natures." Six months after we receive a pay increase, we need more. We soon learn that riches cannot buy happiness. Arnold Schwarzenegger once said: "Money doesn't make you happy. I now have $50 million but I was just as happy when I had $48 million." He probably said it in jest, but there is an element of truth in our relative assessment of wealth. A professional basketball player, playing on an $18 million contract, was asked why his team is so inconsistent? His response: "If I knew the answer, I'd be a rich man." The challenge of wealth is to bring all that we have into the care and direction of God who makes possible our wealth. Now there is more to riches than money. Paul the Apostle, said: "Oh, the depth of the riches of the wisdom and knowledge of God." To the Ephesians, Paul wrote:

"In him we have redemption through his blood, the forgiveness of sins, in accordance with the riches of God's grace...I pray also that the eyes of your heart may be enlightened in order that you may know the hope to which he has called you, the riches of his glorious inheritance in the saints" (Ephesians 1:7 & 18 NIV).

"... in order that in the coming ages he might show the incomparable riches of his grace, expressed in his kindness to us in Christ Jesus" (Ephesians 2:7).

Ice

Reading: Psalm 147

"The breath of God produces ice, and the broad waters become frozen." (Job 37:10; NIV); 'Who gives birth to the frost from the heavens when the waters become hard as stone, when the surface of the deep is frozen?"(Job 38:29-30 NIV).

Most substances contract when cooled. Not so water—and we should be grateful that's so. Since ice is less dense than its liquid counterpart, it floats. If it sank, the oceans of the world would freeze solid and make life as we know it impossible. A world covered by ice and snow would reflect most of the sunlight that struck it, the average temperature of our planet would plunge to minus 128 degrees Fahrenheit. About three quarters of the earth's fresh water is stored in glaciers that cover about 11 percent of the world's land area.[38] (from *How Majestic is Thy Name*).

I have stood on or near many glaciers in New Zealand and Alaska. They are spectacular and the frozen ice is blue. What a dramatic creation of God. "He spreads the snow like wool and scatters the frost like ashes. He hurls down his hail like pebbles. Who can withstand his icy blast? He sends his word and melts them; he stirs up his breezes, and the waters flow" (Psalm 147:16-18 NIV).

Gold

Reading: Revelation 21

"The fear of the LORD is pure, enduring forever. The ordinances of the LORD are sure and altogether righteous. They are more precious than gold, than much pure gold; they are sweeter than honey, than honey from the comb. By them is your servant warned; in keeping them there is great reward" (Psalm 19:9-11 NIV).

Gold comes out of the earth; it is a combination of chemical and physical properties. God has ensured perfect performance over a long period of time. This indestructible metal is completely recyclable and virtually immune to the effects of air, water, and oxygen; it will not tarnish, rust or corrode. There are many medical, industrial, and electrical applications using gold; resistance is just one. North America is one of the world's leading producers of gold producing nearly 16.4 million ounces of gold, representing 20 percent of the world's gold. The United States is the world's second largest gold producing nation, and Canada is the fourth largest producer. Mexico, an emerging gold producer, is amongst the top 20 producing countries.

Computers are dependent upon gold connectors. Doctors use gold in the treatment of rheumatoid arthritis and skin ulcers. Gold-coated visors worn by astronauts on the moon reflect 98 percent of the sun's infrared radiation; otherwise their eyes would be scorched. We are dependent upon gold to open parachutes, receive radio transmissions, components for airbags and ejection seats.

You may not think you possess much gold now, but there is coming a day when Christians will settle down in a city made of pure gold: "The wall was made of jasper, and the city of pure gold, as pure as glass. The twelve gates were twelve pearls, each gate made of a single pearl. The great street of the city was of pure gold, like transparent glass. Nothing impure will ever enter it, nor will anyone who does what is shameful or deceitful, but only those whose names are written in the Lamb's book of life" (Revelation 21;18, 21, 27 NIV).

Sowing Seed

Reading: 1 Corinthians 9:19-23

"The fruit of the righteous is a tree of life, and he who wins souls is wise" (Proverbs 11:30 NIV).

It was Saturday morning. I boarded a flight out of Portland, Oregon, to Spokane, Washington, to speak at a dinner meeting that night. I proceeded to find my seat in the economy section at the back of the plane. On my way past people already seated in the business section, I noticed a fellow holding a pamphlet that I recognized as the *Four Spiritual Laws*. He was talking to the fellow next to him about what was in the pamphlet.

I had prayed that morning that I could sit next to someone to whom I could encourage along the way in his or her own spiritual journey. We were seated and the flight headed northeast to Spokane. The young man sitting next to me was a manager at Delco Remy, a General Motors Company. In a few minutes we were sharing our own spiritual journey with each other. He was familiar with the Gospel and the Bible, but had spurned any serious attempt to understand it. Toward the end of our friendly exchange, wanting to put something in his hand to read later on, I excused myself and walked up to the front of the plane to see the fellow I had noted earlier who held a copy of the Four Laws.

"Excuse me, but do you happen to have another copy of your pamphlet that you could give me?" Without any introduction, he smiled a knowing smile, reached into his shirt pocket and handed me a copy of the Four Laws. I thanked him and went back to my seat. I gave the pamphlet to my seatmate. He thanked me and asked, "Your friend?" To which I replied, "Well, yes and no, he's my friend, but we've not met as yet."

After the flight while waiting for our luggage, I looked up the young man who gave me the pamphlet and discovered that he was the Campus Crusade Rep on the campus of Gonzaga University. He told me that the fellow to whom he was talking was a line coach for the San Diego Chargers pro football team. He went on to tell me that after he handed me the pamphlet, the coach turned to watch you go to the back of the plane. Then he asked, "How many guys like you are on this plane anyway?"

The Campus Crusade Rep had no way of knowing the answer to that question, but he did know that there were at least two ordinary looking fellows on the plane that day, sowing the seed of the Gospel of Jesus Christ.

Spirituality

Reading: Ephesians 5:15-21

"Do not get drunk on wine, which leads to debauchery. Instead be filled with the Spirit" (Ephesians 5:18 NIV).

The move about us today is a search for spirituality. In part it's due to the discovery that the affairs of this world are temporal and material and thus not fulfilling; and in part it's because we thirst for something better and more satisfying. We grow tired of being completely absorbed and preoccupied with ourselves. As Ron Rosenbaum said: "He was already pretty full of himself". In his address to the Irish Senate, Oliver St. John Gogarty, Irish Physician, said of lawyer and politician Lord Carson: "His spiritual life has been exaggerated by a chronic attack of mental gallstones."

Now the Bible tells us that God, the Holy Spirit, is directly involved in things spiritual. Communication with God is by the Holy Spirit. Becoming a Christian means we are baptized into the body of Christ by the Holy Spirit. We are indwelt by the Holy Spirit. In Ephesians Paul commands us to be filled with the Spirit. That is, to be continually in control of the Spirit. There is the anointing of the Holy Spirit that John writes about: "But you have an anointing from the Holy One, and all of you know the truth...As for you, the anointing you received from him remains in you and you do not need anyone to teach you. But as his anointing teaches you about all things and as that anointing is real, not counterfeit—just as it has taught you, remain in him" (1 John 2:20,27 NIV). Spirituality is not a "do it yourself" exercise.

To Inspire

Reading: Exodus 24:12-18

"To the Israelites the glory of the LORD looked like a consuming fire on top of the mountain" (Exodus 24:17 NIV).

In the presidential election year 2000, the late Missouri Gov. Mel Carnahan, died during his race for a seat in the U.S. Senate. Even though dead, Carnahan won the election. Carnahan's widow, Jean, indicated she would accept an appointment to take her husband's place in the senate if he were elected. After announcing her willingness to serve, Jean Carnahan didn't campaign on behalf of her deceased husband, except to film one TV commercial with the slogan: "Don't let the fire go out." The constituents of Missouri didn't let the fire go out, for Carnahan won the senate seat even though dead.

We use the symbol of fire to inspire intensity of effort. God used the symbol of fire as a means of inspiring Israel to serve him with reverence and godly fear for our "God is a consuming fire" (Hebrews12:29 NIV).

The symbol of fire inspired Job: "But he knows the way that I take; when he has tested me, I will come forth as gold. My feet have closely followed his steps; I have kept to his way without turning aside (Job 23:10-11 NIV). Job was confident that being tested by fire he would come forth as gold. The more pure the gold, the more intense is the heat. Trials test us under fire, bringing forth intense effort to pursue holiness of life. We need not dread afflictions. They will not hurt us. As gold is for the application of heat, so we are as we undergo trials.

Achieving

Reading: Philippians 3:7-16

"Not that I have already obtained all this, or have already been made perfect, but I press on to take hold of that for which Christ Jesus took hold of me" (Philippians 3:12 NIV),

Whenever I see a young minister struggle in his pursuit of maturity, a struggle he himself may not even be aware of, I remember my own struggles when I was young. And then I remember some of those same struggles at middle age. Dare say, I still, at the age of 74, still long for the maturity that is in Christ Jesus.

When we are young we are like a wild stallion that has never been ridden. The very nature of our ministry as Pastor-Teacher, Shepherd, or Bishop demands more from us than we are able to deliver. I see it more clearly now from this perspective in life than in my youthful days. I see myself in young men, and it draws me to pray for them, lest they fall by the way because they are not achieving everything fast enough that goes together to produce maturity.

I think it would be good to have another shot at life and benefit from what little I now know about achieving the graces needed to minister to others. But then, all is not lost for I am convinced that maturity takes time. There is no such thing as instant maturity. Oh yes, there are those who knew us when we were young who may have said: "My, isn't he mature for his age!" However, there were probably more friends than we know of, who prayed: "Lord, we love him, but help him grow (faster) in grace and in the knowledge of Jesus Christ - lest we kill his spirit. Amen!"

Maturity demands change, and we change slowly. At whatever rate of change, time is in the equation. The final tape at the end of the race isn't reached at an early age. As we get older we see more clearly the final tape, the finish line. Paul wrote the Philippian believers: "I press on to take hold of that for which Christ Jesus took hold of me" (Philippians 3:12 NIV). It is, as Earl Palmer says: "Jesus' acceptance of the man, Paul, enables Paul to focus his personality-unlike the person who is uncertain of acceptance and who desperately runs in every direction in an attempt to find a place where he or she will feel accepted and secure." We run to the finish line not to make the team; we are on the team and running to finish that which God has begun in us when we received Christ into our lives.

John Henry Newman is right when he said: "May it be to our blessedness, as years go on, to add one grace to another, and advance upward, step by step, neither neglecting the lower after attaining the higher, nor aiming at the higher before attaining the lower. The first grace is faith, the last is love; first comes zeal, afterwards comes loving-kindness; first comes humiliation, then comes peace; first comes diligence, then comes resignation. May we learn to mature all graces in us;—fearing and trembling, watching and repenting, because Christ is coming; joyful, thankful, and careless of the future, because he is come....In a higher world it is otherwise, but here below to live is to change, and to be perfect (mature-my insert) is to have changed often."

If you are in the ministry, be patient, keep on running the race. If you have a pastor, be patient, pull alongside him and keep on running the race. God is at work.

Admirer or Follower

Reading: Luke 7:36-50

*"My purpose is that they may be encouraged in heart and united in love, so that they may have the fullest riches of complete understanding, in order that they may know the mystery of God, namely, Christ, in whom are hidden all the treasures of wisdom and knowledge" (*Colossians 2:2,3 NIV).

James E. Gilman in his work, *Fidelity of Heart, An Ethic of Christian Virtue*, argues that the story in Luke 7:31-50 is a study of two different types of commitment: Admirer or Follower. I think he makes a good point. The story line in Luke tells how that Jesus is invited by a Pharisee to have dinner. Jesus accepts the invitation and goes to the Pharisee's home. A woman of ill repute unexpectedly shows up during the dinner and breaks out a jar of expensive perfume. She stands behind Jesus, weeping, wets his feet with her tears and pours the perfume on his feet.

Gilman observes two different forms of commitment in the story. The Pharisees commitment was intellectual, that of an admirer. The woman's commitment was of the heart, a follower of Christ. One is intellectual; the other is of the heart. Both involve the mind, but there is a significant difference. Gilman goes on to argue his point that fidelity of heart requires one to be a follower of Christ, not a mere admirer.

What makes a true follower of Christ? The Greeks considered three words important, relating to the mind:

knowledge, prudence, and understanding. A true follower of Christ pursues knowledge, the knowledge of things both human and divine. Paul writes the Church at Corinth: "I didn't try to impress you with polished speeches and the latest philosophy. I deliberately kept it plain and simple: first Jesus Christ and who he is; then Jesus and what he did - Jesus crucified ... it's not popular wisdom of high priced experts ... God's wisdom is something mysterious that goes deep in the interior of his purposes" (Eugene Peterson, The Message).

A true follower of Christ who hunts down prudence, goes beyond the theoretical to find what is practical. "Therefore if there is any consolation in Christ, if any comfort of love, if any fellowship of the Spirit, if any affection and mercy, fulfill my joy by being like-minded, having the same love, being of one accord, of one mind" (Philippians 2:1,2 NKJ). A true follower of Christ gives chase to understanding Christ and his purpose for our lives. We have a choice every day, whether we will be a mere admirer of Christ, one who lives by a bumper sticker theology, or a true follower of Christ.

Appearances

Reading: Isaiah 53

"Who is like the wise man? Who knows the explanation of things?" Wisdom brightens a man's face and changes its hard appearance" (Ecclesiastes 8:1 NIV).

Appearances are not always what they are cracked up to be. The old King James rendering of 1 Thessalonians 5:22 read: "Abstain from all appearance of evil." The word should read: "from every form of evil," as it does in the New King James translation. Nevertheless, appearances play an important part in our perception of both good and evil. We make judgments often by appearances. John Buchan, British author wrote: “Civilization is a conspiracy. ... Modern life is the silent compact of comfortable folk to keep up pretences.” I remember walking into a farmer’s barn once when he was sacking potatoes for market. A rig set-up held a big sack in place. In the middle of the sack was a large sized stovepipe. The farmer poured his biggest and best bakers in the sack but around the outside of the stovepipe, then filled the pipe with runt potatoes, removed the pipe and tied the sack, ready for market. To this day when I buy potatoes I wonder what’s in the middle of the sack. Have you had the notion that some people may look at you and wonder if what appears on the outside is genuine and consistent with what’s in your heart? Are you for real or just a façade? Is it truly a Christian they are seeing or something with a front? We live in a culture knee deep in pure hype. We are confronted with a gigantic PR job promoting one thing or another. Often the hype is deliberately misleading. The Apostle Paul wrote the Corinthians: “For we commend not ourselves again unto you, but give you occasion to glory on our behalf, that ye may have somewhat to answer them which glory in appearance, and not in heart.” Paul wasn’t worried about his motives or his integrity. His motives were clean and right. We may well pay attention to behavior that in both appearance and in the heart there is truth not evil.

Applause

Reading: Proverbs 31:10-31

“Let another praise you, and not your own mouth; someone else, and not your own lips … man is tested by the praise he receives” (Proverbs 27:2, 21b)

This poignant lesson about applause in Proverbs was written by Solomon. When it comes to applause we are conflicted. It's fashionable to applaud the boisterous, the inane, lacking significance, meaning or point. We glory in "making a statement" by the way we dress or don't dress, by our conduct without regard for others, by doing what is legal but without ethical consideration. Greil Marcus asserted: Applause that comes thundering with such force you might think the audience merely suffers the music as an excuse for its ovations.

We expect applause without due regard for merit. We associate applause with noise. Ralph Waldo Emerson in 1838, at a Divinity College address, Harvard University, said: "The silence that accepts merit as the most natural thing in the world is the highest applause."

"The purity of human hearts is tested by giving them praise" (Proverbs 27:21 The Message). Our works, not our tongues, should praise us at the gates. "Give her the reward she has earned, and let her works bring her praise at the city gate." (Proverbs 31:31). Is there no room for praise? Yes there is, but let it come from others.

Caring For Others

Reading: Matthew 25:31-40

"I was a stranger and you welcomed me" (Matthew 25:35 NIV).

Christine Pohl's grandmother exercised a remarkable show of hospitality to strangers and friends. Grandma often became upset that others did not share her passion to reach out to others. On one occasion, Christine told grandma that one person to whom she brought food seemed to have more than he needed. Grandma answered: "It's not just about food, you know, it's about knowing someone cares."

Caring for others is healthful. It lifts the spirit of the one to whom care is shown. We become engaged in helping someone who may not be able to reciprocate. We are reminded that to whom much is given, much is required. The love of God is manifested. Our ever-willing pride is kept in check. It blocks the tendency to think only of us. Hospitality demonstrates to family and friends a spirit of selflessness.

Climbing the Mountain

Reading: Isaiah 30:15-22

"Although the Lord gives you the bread of adversity and the water of affliction, your teachers will be hidden no more; with your own eyes you will see them. Whether you turn to the right or to the left, your ears will hear a voice behind you, saying, 'This is the way; walk in it'" (Isaiah 30:20-22 NIV).

More than once has a new believer been aghast at the prospect of suffering adversity. But a wise old Southern lady once said: "If the mountain was smooth, you couldn't climb it."

"But he said to me, `My grace is sufficient for you, for my power is made perfect in weakness.' Therefore I will boast all the more gladly about my weaknesses, so that Christ's power may rest on me. That is why for Christ's sake, I delight in weaknesses, in insults, in hardships, in persecutions, in difficulties. For when I am weak, then I am strong" (2 Corinthians 12:9,10).

Suffering and hard times will strengthen us if we accept it as Paul did and ask for God's help. He does not always answer our prayers to remove the difficulty but He does give grace which is sufficient for the time..

His love has no limit,
His grace has no measure,
His power has no boundary known unto men,
For out of His infinite riches in Jesus,
He giveth and giveth and giveth again."

Annie Johnson Flint

Conversion

Reading: Acts 9:1-9

"As he neared Damascus on his journey, suddenly a light from heaven flashed around him. He fell to the ground and heard a voice say to him, 'Saul, Saul, why do you persecute me?' 'Who are you Lord?' Saul asked. 'I am Jesus..." (Acts 9:3-5 NIV)

Conversions happen in all sorts of different ways: some sharp and catastrophic (like St. Paul, St. Augustine, or Bunyan) some very gradual and some intellectual (like my own).

How exactly does this take place? C.S. Lewis writes that he knows "when" it happened but not exactly "how." He was on a motorcycle heading to the zoo. He writes, "When we set out I did not believe that Jesus Christ is the Son of God, and when we reached the zoo I did. Yet I had not exactly spent the journey in thought. Nor in great emotion . . ." He then uses a rather striking yet familiar metaphor: "It was more like when a man, after a long sleep, still lying motionless in bed, becomes aware that he is now awake."

Psychiatrist, Armond M. Nicholi, Jr, writes "Lewis is careful to explain, 'I had not exactly spent the journey . . . in great emotion'. Emotion is perhaps the last word we can apply to some of the most important events. As a psychiatrist, I find it difficult to believe that these events were entirely unemotional, even for Lewis. We feel more easily than we think, and our feelings often control our decisions and behavior than our thoughts.

Harvard Medical School and the Massachusetts General Hospital. Quoting

Lewis in the *Question of God.* p 92

Conviction

Reading: Job 1:11-13

"Surely, O God, you have worn me out; you have devastated my entire household. You have bound me - and it has become a witness; my gauntness rises up and testifies against me. God assails me and tears me in his anger and gnashes his teeth at me; my opponent fastens on me his piercing eyes" (Job 16:7-9 NIV).

If we had lost our entire family, health, possessions, and emotional perspective, given such loss, we wonder if we would have done any better than Job who actually experienced it? He was so devastated with loss that his opinion of God suffered. Job's opinion of God, who seemingly was not moved enough to hear him, was wrong. Of course, God's anger wasn't directed at Job for he had previously held him up before Satan as one who fears God and shuns evil.

Job in desperation looked around for someone to understand his plight. He found no earthly friend who knew all and could vouch for him. But then he declared with strong conviction to his misguided friends, "Even now my witness is in heaven; my advocate is on high" (Job 16:19). With the full revelation of Scripture, we know that our advocate in heaven is Jesus Christ. (Hebrews 9:24)

It's important that we form our convictions about God and his ways with us before we cast our opinion about what's going on in our lives and whether God is aware of our troubles. Like we say, would we have done any better than Job? Probably not.

Credit

Reading: Philippians 2: 1-11

"I will sing to the Lord, for he is highly exalted".(Exodus 15:1 NIV).

"There is no limit to what a man can do so long as he does not care a straw who gets the credit for it," observed English author, C. E. Montague.

Ah, credit, to praise someone for an act, ability, or quality; that is the challenge. Lurking in our minds is this notion: "Why should he get all the credit?" It is interesting at times, we struggle to make a credit entry on behalf of another person when we are the beneficiaries of the greatest attribute of credit that a person can receive. Referring to the stroke of attribution when God credited to our account, the righteousness of Christ. We, who deserved no credit were made righteous by virtue of Christ's death and resurrection on behalf of us who believe. As the old gospel song says: "The old account was settled long ago."

Rather than looking to take credit for our actions, we could best spend our time seeking to credit others for something good. There lies the greatest satisfaction, crediting someone else rather than us.

Wilson Greatbatch, who developed the implanted pacemaker, shared a prize of $500,000 with Earl Bakken, inventor of the wearable pacemaker. According to the Washington Times, Greatbatch "had been asked for a letter recommending Bakken for the award, and did so not knowing he was up for the prize himself."

When the Israelites went through the Red Sea on dry ground Moses could have done a bit of chest thumping about his skills as a leader. A perfect opportunity for the Israelites to exalt Moses! After all, this came on the heels of victory over the Egyptians. "Take a bow, Moses, you're the man! Long live Moses! We'll never have a better leader than you, Moses! Give credit where credit is due." But what did Moses do? Why, he sang a song, a song giving God the credit: "I will sing to the Lord, for he is highly exalted" (Exodus 15:1). Better we should sing songs giving God credit for any good done, than to be seeking credit from one another. God keeps the books anyway. If there is any credit to be handed out, He who knows us will administer the credit properly and in due time. Count on it.

Edifice and Edification

Reading: Hebrews 3:3—6

"Jesus has been found worthy of greater honor than Moses, just as the builder of a house has greater honor than the house itself" (Hebrews 3:3 NIV).

An edifice is a building, whereas edification is spiritual improvement, enlightenment. We are hoodwinked if we confuse edifice with edification. We traveled in Europe one summer and saw many beautiful cathedrals, but I daresay, there was little edification going on inside those works of art for they seemed attended by a handful of patrons. Does that mean we ought to not appreciate art and architecture in its resplendent beauty? I appreciate true art and architecture. I have been involved in times past in more than a dozen church building projects, most of great beauty. It's easy to fall in love with an edifice; especially one you had a hand in building. But real building is of a spiritual nature. It's the building Paul speaks about in Ephesians 2:19-22: "Consequently, you are no longer foreigners and aliens, but fellow citizens with God's people and members of God's household, built on the foundation of the apostles and prophets, with Christ Jesus himself as the chief cornerstone. In him the whole building is joined together and rises to become a holy temple in the Lord. And in him you too are being built together to become a dwelling in which God lives by his Spirit."

Harry Blamires says: "[Such metaphors] shed light on the world around us and how it has been involved, object by object, in the Christian revelation.... We have no need to search the stars and the vast regions of space in the desire to contact the untouchable world of God's presence...Do [this] meditatively. And . . . next time you see a building being built, think of how we Christians are all being built, brick by brick, into the fabric of God's temple." My friend Phil is completing an edifice to seat 1200. He implored his people: "Don't mistake this building more highly than you do ministering to the poor." So the congregation went on record to add another $30,000 quarterly to give those in need. Enjoy the edifice, but neglect not edification.

Our Source of Energy

Reading: 2 Corinthians 12:9—10

"Likewise, we are weak in him, yet by God's power we will live with him to serve you" (2 Corinthians. 13:4).

It is of little surprise that we have an energy crisis in our country since Americans consume a high percentage of the world's energy. Massive rolling blackouts stretching from Central California to the Oregon border cast 675,000 homes and businesses in the dark for hours at a time, according to U.S. News and World Report. I've never understood much about electricity, except to be careful when I'm exposed to it. Yet I use electrical energy so much and I think little about it. As a kid I remember what electrical energy did to a friend who stuck his scissors in a wall plug. I remember when my father was checking spark plugs on our car and he reached down to hold my hand. I had energy! For Christmas my wife gave me a flashlight. I have two of them now. I can never remember where I last used the first one. When I went to purchase batteries, I was reminded of how much we rely on energy. Batteries of all sizes for a host of appliances: flashlights, computers, cameras, TV remote control, clocks, locks, toys, games, radios, drills, mowers, cars, golf carts, hearing aids. I've used most of them.

Now I'm told I need to become acquainted with the battery pack of a pacemaker so my heart can keep time with a metronome. Not while playing a musical instrument mind you, but simply to keep one's head out of the dinner plate and on top the ground, not in it. The doctor said the batteries last about ten years and they're smaller than a breadbox. Comforting. Thinking of piling another ten years on top of what I've already had, I asked if that was a guarantee. He smiled, meaning no guarantees. Indeed, as Hawthorne would have it, "Is it a fact—or have I dreamt it—that, by means of electricity, the world of matter has become a great nerve, vibrating thousands of miles in a breathless point of time?"

Aha, there is another energy source of a spiritual nature, more pervasive and continual, lacking nothing. Paul refers to the energy that is in Christ. He links it to the power of Christ's resurrection. He ties the power of Christ generally in the church and individually. "To this end I labor, struggling with all his energy, which so powerfully works in me" (Colossians. 1:29). I can do all because Christ makes it possible for me or makes me able to do it. The power that is ours is closely related to the hard work and toil mentioned in verse 29. The energy of the might of Christ's strength keeps us on the road serving him and others.

"I pray also that the eyes of your heart may be enlightened in order that you may know the hope to which he has called you, the riches of his glorious inheritance in the saints, and his incomparably great power for us who believe. That power is like the working of his mighty strength" (Ephesians 1:19).

Escaping Futility

Reading: Joshua 1:1-9

"Be strong and very courageous. Be careful to obey all the law my servant Moses gave you; do not turn from it to the right or to the left, that you may be successful wherever you go. Do not let this Book of the Law depart from your mouth; meditate on it day and night, so that you may be careful to do everything written in it. Then you will be prosperous and successful." (Joshua 1:7-9 NIV).

This is the Lord's command to Joshua as he is ready to lead the children Israel across the Jordan River and into the promised land.

Many a person has no quality of having a useful purpose. They see themselves lacking in importance, a futile act "The Jews had no 'thoughts of peace,' but only of 'evil' (misfortune, because they could not conceive how deliverance could come to them). The moral malady of man is two-fold, at one time vain confidence, then, when that is disappointed, despair. So the Jews first laughed at God's threats, confident that they should speedily return; then, when cast down from that confidence, they sank in inconsolable despondency". (Jamieson, Fausset, and Brown Commentary).

There is no reason for the Christian to live life without purpose for God has a plan for his life. "'For I know the plans I have for you' declares the LORD, 'plans to prosper you and not to harm you, plans to give you hope and a future'"(Jeremiah (29:11 NIV).

Tom Younger

Following By Faith

Reading: Exodus 13:17—22

"And the LORD went before them by day in a pillar of a cloud, to lead them the way; and by night in a pillar of fire, to give them light;" (Exodus 13:22).

It's a good thing we don't know ahead of time what's ahead in our life. We'd probably react much worse than Moses. Probably run for our life. In spite of our emphasis on planning, projecting, goal setting, strategizing. Were God to lay before our eyes His plan for our life and how it would be played out, we might want to check out, break our contract, lose ourselves. Moses must have felt like that when God called him to lead the children of Israel out of Egypt. He tried to get out of it: "Who am I? I tried once and my people wouldn't let me lead. What shall I say? Behold, they will not believe me. Oh my LORD, I am not eloquent. Send someone else, anyone but me." But then Moses surrendered to the LORD and agreed to lead the Israelites out of slavery to the Promised Land.

Now can you imagine Moses seeking out a confidant to talk over what procedures to take to get Israel moving? They were to head out into the wilderness. Imagine Moses' friend asking: "Moses, are you sure it was God who called you to this task? Do you have any idea what it will take to make this happen?"

"What are you thinking, friend?"

"Well, for starters there are roughly two million men, women and children involved in this move. That's not counting flocks and herds and very many cattle. Feeding these people alone at one pound of food per person each day would require 900 tons of food per day. That's two trainloads each day just for food and we don't have tracks in the desert! Of course we'd have to cook the food which means we'd need 2,400 tons of firewood per day. Remember, Moses this is desert; it's not the National Forest. Take water, just for drinking and cooking. We'd need one gallon per person per day, meaning we'd be in need of a hundred wheel wells at every halting place to produce 72,000 gallons of water per twelve-hour day. And that's not all, Moses, think of it. We go up out of Egypt harnessed five in rank that forms a column 230 miles to pass a given point. The first Israelite out of camp would be on the road 10 days before the last left Egypt. Now, that's not all, consider camping at night. We would occupy 500 square miles each night. Think of the nightmare on getting word to the people: `we're moving on out.'

"Hello, Moses, are you listening?"

"Yes. I'm listening. Now let's get moving."

And they moved out of Egypt harnessed five in a rank. There was never another prophet like Moses who had seen the Lord face to face.

Flight

Reading: Psalm 11

"Therefore, since we are surrounded by such a great cloud of witnesses, let us throw off everything that hinders and the sin that so easily entangles, and let us run with perseverance the race marked out for us. Let us fix our eyes on Jesus, the author and perfecter of our faith, who for the joy set before him endured the cross, scorning its shame, and sat down at the right hand of the throne of God. Consider him who endured such opposition from sinful men, so that you will not grow weary and lose heart" (Hebrews 12:1 NIV).

Flight creates a lot of images in our minds. Deadbeat parents failing to take responsibility for their children. Drug and alcohol abuse used as an escape. Mothers and children abused by spouses. Criminals running from the law. Infidelity considered acceptable in the marriage relationship. Refugees suffering insurmountable conditions in any effort to seek a safe haven. The erasure of values, moral and ethical. Suicide, thinking that reality is worse than death. As vile as are such evils and not to be indulged by Christians, there are flights we must take.

Flee to the right refuge. "The name of the LORD is a strong tower; the righteous run to it and are safe" (Proverbs 18:10 NIV).

"In the LORD I take refuge. How then can you say to me: 'Flee like a bird to your mountain?' For look, the wicked bend their bows; they set their arrows against the strings to shoot from the shadows at the upright in heart. When the foundations are being destroyed, what can the righteous do?' The LORD is in his holy temple; the LORD is on his heavenly throne" (Psalm 11:1-4 NIV).

Flee to take hold of hope. "Because God wanted to make the unchanging nature of his purpose very clear to the heirs of what was promised, he confirmed it with an oath. God did this so that, by two unchangeable things in which it is impossible for God to lie, we who have fled to take hold of the hope offered to us may be greatly encouraged. We have this hope as an anchor for the soul, firm and secure" (Hebrews 6:17-19. NIV).

Resist the devil. "Submit yourselves, then, to God. Resist the devil, and he will flee from you. (James 4:7 NIV).

Take comfort in God's refuge. "If I rise on the wings of the dawn, if I settle on the far side of the sea, even there your hand will guide me; your right hand will hold me fast" (Psalm 139:9-10 NIV).

Footwear

Reading: Ephesians 6:10-19

"How beautiful on the mountains are the feet of those who bring good news, who proclaim peace, who bring good tidings, who

proclaim salvation, who say to Zion, 'Your God reigns!'" (Isaiah 52:7 NIV).

There's no substitute for good fitting pair of shoes of the right kind. Encarta Encyclopedia says about the Foot: lowest structure on the leg, in human beings containing 26 bones. Seven tarsal bones form the heel and back of the instep; five metatarsal bones form the front of the instep and the ball of the foot. Fourteen smaller phalanges make up the toes. All the bones are connected by ligaments. Two flexible arches absorb pressure and shock from walking and jumping. The plantar arch runs from the heel to the ball, and the metatarsal arch stretches across the ball.

Our sophomore grandson, Aaron, placed third in a 1500-meter race in a track meet involving runners from two high schools. Everybody else sported the proper spiked running shoes, except Aaron, who wore an old pair of Nike's. Whether he would have done better with the proper shoe we will never know, but it is likely that he would have cut considerable time off his run. Wearing the right shoes can make a difference in how we walk or run.

During the Civil War, Confederate forces ventured out one night in search of better shoes; shoes with leather soles like the Union soldiers wore. Confederate issue shoes were of wooden soles. The Confederate army suffered a resounding defeat that night. The Time-Life series on Gettysburg included this comment: ""before he (General Early) left he noticed that the town possessed a shoe factory, and he sent word back to A.P. Hill that Gettysburg might be a good place to get some badly needed shoes."

Now in the letter of Paul to the Ephesians, he includes footwear as an important part of the Christian's warfare against evil. "and with your feet fitted with the readiness that comes from the gospel of peace" (Ephesians 6:15 NIV). The gospel of peace refers to that "peace with God through our Lord Jesus Christ" (5:1). With properly shod feet we are confident of our union with Christ, knowing that He is alongside to fight for us. "The weapons we fight with are not the weapons of the world.

On the contrary, they have divine power to demolish strongholds" (2 Corinthians 10:4 NIV).

The Grip

Reading: Luke 9:57—62

"Jesus replied, 'No one who puts his hand to the plow and looks back is fit for service in the kingdom of God.'" (Luke 9:62 NIV).

Losing one's grip in the reality of the faith is a perilous venture in our daily walk with the Lord. Peter once told the Lord, "I am ready to go with you to prison and to death." A short time later, he was seen standing at the enemy's fire warming his hands. When asked if he was one of Jesus' disciples, Peter denied it, saying, "I am not."

When we loosen our grip on the reality of our faith - the content of the Christian gospel - we begin role playing before God. Effective prayer vanishes, feet go astray, we become scriptwriters instead stagehands, and we lose our sense of contentment. We become restless, lose our tenacity for the battle, and stagger in the face of difficulties or obstacles. Paul wrote young Timothy: "There are some, you know, who by relaxing their grip and thinking anything goes have made a thorough mess of their faith Hymenaeus and Alexander are two of them...Keep a firm grasp on both your character and your teaching. Don't be diverted. Just keep at it. Both you and those who hear you will experience salvation." (1 Timothy 1:19,20 The Message)

Of leaders in the church, Paul insists that "They must keep hold of the deep truths of the faith with a clear conscience. In this way they will lay up treasure for themselves as a firm foundation for the coming age, so that they may take hold of the life that is truly life." How firm is your grip?

Hitting the Ground

Reading: John 18:1-6

"They drew back and fell to the ground" (John 18:6).

Ira Hayes, marine paratrooper, was one of the boys who raised the American Flag on Iwo Jima during World War II. William Faulkner, his buddy, remembered their first jump from a plane. "He went from brown to white and I went from white to green. He hit the ground hard, like sack of wet cement. We were both scared, but we did it." Hitting the ground in a life situation can be terrifying. Witness the Transfiguration when Peter was talking to Jesus, "a voice from the cloud said, `This is my Son, whom I love; with him I am well pleased. Listen to him!' When the disciples heard this, they fell facedown to the ground, terrified."

Saul fell to the ground one time and heard a voice: "Saul, Saul, why do you persecute me?" When he got up from the ground he was blind. For Saul, renamed Paul, hitting the ground was a life changing experience. Hitting the ground can kill you. Poor Eutychus slept during one of Paul's sermons and fell from the third story. He was DOA (Dead on arrival). A lot of people have slept during my sermons, but none ever died from hitting the ground. Maybe it's because I usually preach from the ground floor.

What is there to be gained from hitting the ground because of some devastating experience? One, we never hit the ground unnoticed. Two, God cares about our hard falls. For if God is aware and concerned when a sparrow hits the ground, will He not notice and care about us? "Are not two sparrows sold for a penny? Yet not one of them will fall to the ground apart from the will of your Father."

Furthermore, it's not a bad idea to walk close to the ground. We never fall too far when we walk close to the ground. "He has showed you, O man, what is good. And what does the LORD require of you? To act justly and to love mercy and to walk humbly with your God" (Micah 6:8 NIV).

Imitation

Reading: Ephesians 4:22-5:2

"You became imitators of us and of the Lord; in spite of severe suffering, you welcomed the message with the joy given by the Holy Spirit" (1 Thessalonians 1:6 NIV).

Imitation is something copied from an original. Some people mimic others with such skill that makes it look easy. But if copying another's voice or mannerism is something like playing a piece of music on the piano, it takes a lot of repetition. Children are best at imitating. One Sunday morning the daughter of a pastor came late into the worship service, sauntered down the aisle mimicking a habitually late church member in her walk and sat in the second row up front. The congregation, noticing the pastor's daughter, struggled to stifle an outburst of laughter. That is, everyone, except the church member whose walk was being imitated. Afterward, it was the pastor who got the embarrassing credit for his daughter's skill of mimicry. The daughter had picked up at home, her father's habit of mimicking his church member. Isn't it ironic that we sometimes imitate the less desirable traits of someone we admire?

Despite the desire to "be our own man," or to "be independent," as our culture dictates, we usually keep to the tracks of others and imitate those whom we admire. And that's not bad. British poet James Fenton, wrote: "Imitation, if it is not forgery, is a fine thing. It stems from a generous impulse, and a realistic sense of what can and cannot be done." However, as Samuel Johnson observed: "Almost all absurdity of conduct arises from the imitation of those whom we cannot resemble." Which leads us to conclude that in imitating someone, we'd best seek to being "imitators of God, therefore, as dearly loved children" (Ephesians 5:1), rather than the peculiar walk of another church member. It's not only safe, but also apt to be more accurate.

Music

Reading: Ephesians 5:15-21

"You will go out in joy and be led forth in peace; the mountains and hills will burst into song before you ..." (Isaiah 55:12 NIV).

When I was in my teens and still at home we often gathered around the piano and sang. After we became Christians we learned to sing hymns and Gospel songs. During that time Red and Lin Lindquist joined us with their accordion and stringed instruments. The Lindquist brothers were from Minnesota. My sister, Dorothy was an accomplished pianist who could play anything she had heard played. and was excellent in sight reading music. Those were memorable days.

I treasure a copy of the hymnal; Congregational Praise published for the Congregational Church in England and Wales. I refer to it often. At times I've used it for meditation and prayer, such as Thomas Toke Lynch's lyrics:

Truthful Spirit, dwell with me,
I myself would truthful be;
And with wisdom kind and clear
Let Thy life in mine appear;
And with actions brotherly
Speak my Lord's sincerity.

Luther considered music "next to theology. The Devil hates music because it drives away temptation and evil thoughts." Jacques Barzun observed: "In the schools Luther wanted to see established that he would allow no man to teach who could not sing, `nor would I let him preach either'."

Need

Reading: 1 Corinthians 12:21—28

"Do your best to present yourself to God as one approved, a workman who does not need to be ashamed and who correctly handles the word of truth" (2 Timothy 2:15).

"I live in a (converted) one-room schoolhouse here. You don't need more than you need," said Wilson Greatbatch, inventor of the implanted heart pacemaker and reported by Douglas Turner, News Washington Bureau Chief and picked up by the Buffalo Evening News. I now wear one of those pacemakers, as millions of people do worldwide. Greatbatch, holder of 220 patents, "will receive half of a $500,000 prize that is described as the Nobel Prize of engineering." Yet, he and his wife have chosen to give most of their money away to charitable causes.

"You don't need more than you need," a challenge to us who live quite well, even beyond our needs. It's not that we are never in need for there are needs we all have.

<u>1. We need one another.</u>

The Apostle Paul: "The eye cannot say to the hand, "I don't need you! And the head cannot say to the feet, I don't need you...so that there should be no division in the body, but that its parts should have equal concern for each other. If one part suffers, every part suffers with it; if one part is honored, every part rejoices with it."

2. We need God's grace

in order to abound in every good work. The writer of Hebrews states: "Let us then approach the throne of grace with confidence, so that we may receive mercy and find grace to help us in our time of need."

3. We need contentment.

during adverse conditions, says Paul. "I am not saying this because I am in need, for I have learned to be content whatever the circumstances. I know what it is to be in need, and I know what it is to have plenty. I have learned the secret of being content in any and every situation, whether well fed or hungry, whether living in plenty or in want. I can do everything through him who gives me strength."

4. We need something to share

with others in need. "He who has been stealing must steal no longer, but must work, doing something useful with his own hands, that he may have something to share with those in need."

5. We need to perseverance

in our walk with the Lord. "You need to persevere so that when you have done the will of God, you will receive what he has promised." As for material things: "You don't need more than you need," but you do need what is needed.

Rebuke

Reading: Job 21:22-34

"My troubled thoughts prompt me to answer because I am greatly disturbed . I hear a rebuke that dishonors me, and my understanding inspires me to reply" (Job 20:2, 3 NIV).

The wicked have no sense of shame; their spirit will not let them stop their drive.. They have no capacity to recognize the error of their thinking. So true of Zophar in his relentless attack upon Job. Certainly Job's words were straightforward, but Zophar did not get it. Typical of the blindness that wickedness clouds a person's thinking. Sin is subtle and insidious in obscuring the real issue of godless thinking. Salt smarts in the wounds of the ungodly. Zophar could not locate the nature of his shame. The most Zophar could muster in this dialogue was to take offense at what Job said. How easily do we miss the point of our own ill gotten behavior and faulty thinking.

There is enormous power in feeling. Dallas Willard points that out when he writes: "Now, one thing quickly becomes clear when you think of the power of feeling. No one can succeed in mastering feelings in his or her life who tries simply to take them head-on and resist or redirect them by "willpower" in the moment of choice. To adopt that strategy is to radically misunderstand how life and the human will work, or - more likely - it is to have actually decided, deep down to lose the battle and give in. This is one of the major areas of self-deception in the human heart. The very "giving in" can be among the most exhilarating feelings known to man, though it can also be one of complete despair and defeat."[39]

It is remarkable that Job stood his ground in the face of such a diatribe. Unperturbed in his right thinking, Job spoke truth and dismissed the issue like a used Kleenex napkin. No cause for worry here. A much needed message today.

Respect

Reading: Romans 13:1-7

"They have harps and lyres at their banquets, tambourines and flutes and wine, but they have no regard for the deeds of the LORD, no regard for the work of his hands." (Isaiah 5:12 NIV).

One of the many missing characteristics in our world today is the lack of respect; to esteem others higher than us; to show deferential regard for others; to show concern. Not that we don't know how to respect others. Our nation's response in helping those who suffered first hand in the September terrorist strike showed we could. Normally however, we are taken up with grasping for our own self-respect and self-esteem. Now to lose the character trait of respect is not new as the Prophet Isaiah spoke of Israel.

The writer of Proverbs juxtaposed two contrasts when he said: "A kindhearted woman gains respect, but ruthless men gain only wealth." One can seize wealth by any means, but "honor" is the reward for the gracious person. The Proverb goes on to say "A kind hearted man benefits himself, but a cruel man brings trouble upon himself...he who sows righteousness reaps a sure reward." We are all better off when we concentrate on respecting others, esteeming them better than ourselves.

"Give everyone what you owe him: If you owe taxes, pay taxes; if revenue, then revenue; if respect, then respect; if honor, then honor" (Romans 13:7 NIV).

Tom Younger

Righteously Mean Christians

Reading: 1 Timothy 6:1-13

"Command them to do good, to be rich in good deeds, and to be generous and willing to share. In this way they will lay up treasure for themselves as a firm foundation for the coming age, so that they may take hold of the life that is truly life" (1 Timothy 6:18,19 NIV.)

One of the products of Christianity as we know it today is the practice of producing mean and angry Christians. Just broach the subject to Christian leaders today, who have experienced assaults on the soul. Dallas Willard points to the reason for such sickness in much of the Western church. "It takes as its basic goal to get as many people possible ready to die and go to heaven. It aims to get people into heaven rather than get heaven into people."

A friend recently told me of his reaction to such judgment on the part of evangelical Christians. He, a liberal, sees it for what it is: "They have found ways of being `Christian' without being Christlike." Willard goes on to relate to how they engage in them as he writes: "They rarely get along with one another, much less those `outside.' As a result, they actually fall short of getting as many people who may be ready to die, because the lives of the `converted' testify against the reality of 'the life that is life indeed' (ontos zoas, 1 Timothy 6:19, PAR). . . .When we are counting up results we, also, need to keep in mind the multitudes of people (surrounded by churches) who will not be in heaven because they have never, to their knowledge, seen the reality of Christ in a living human being." Which raises the question of where are we in relation to being "righteously mean?"

Second Fiddle

Reading: Matthew 16:21-28

"Lord, it is good for us to be here. If you wish, I will put up three shelters-one for you, one for Moses and one for Elijah" (Matthew 17:4).

"It needs more skill than I can tell to play the second fiddle well."—Spurgeon

We were fishing in Alaska. There were fifteen distinguished men, leaders in their fields of endeavor. Few were experts in hooking and landing fifty pound King Salmon. One fellow had never caught a fish of any kind. He hoped he wouldn't embarrass himself. Midway through the week another fellow sat on a large rock on the riverbank with his pole resting against a bush. He had not so much as attracted the attention of a salmon. He was pondering why he left his successful business to engage in a week of frustration. A thought occurred to me that to catch fish, one must have his line in the water, but I was careful to sympathize, not preach. Still another fellow, a noted surgeon, landed a prize King and while watching the guide strip out the filets, observed how much fun he was having, not being in charge. He was used to being in charge, referring to the operating room, where he did his best work. You wouldn't want anybody else in charge during surgery. My concern was not about catching fish, but whether or not these successful men who were used to being in charge, could withstand the challenge of playing second fiddle without slinging a hook in somebody's ear, or throwing me in the river. Not to worry. By week's end all fears were allayed; everyone had his fish story. I've since reflected upon how important it seems for us (men especially) to be in charge and yet, how often Jesus worked with his disciples in order to teach them the importance of playing second fiddle. To quote Eugene Peterson's paraphrase, THE MESSAGE: "The Son of Man is no lackey to the Sabbath; he's in charge ... anyone who intends to come with me has to let me lead. You're not in the driver's seat, I am."

Sensitivity

Reading: Ephesians 4:17—24

"Having lost all sensitivity, they have given themselves over to sensuality so as to indulge in every kind of impurity, with a continual lust for more" (Ephesians 4:19 NIV).

Decades after seeing the horrors of the death camp first hand at Buchenwald, it is told that Andy Rooney saw the movie, "Schindler's List." Rooney was seated next to a young girl who was digging into a box of popcorn. He commented: "How strange, I thought, that we could be sitting side by side, strangers, she with her thoughts, me with mine, so close and yet so distant." There were reasons for their sensitivity or the lack thereof. Rooney's sensitivity was because he had seen the evil of the Buchenwald death camp first hand. The girl's insensitivity, if indeed she was, may have been more a matter of the ignorance of history or the entertainment injected into Speilberg's moving account. Outrageous it is that some would deny that Buchenwald and other death camps ever existed in World War II.

Paul in his letter to the Ephesian believers wrote: "Having lost all sensitivity, they have given themselves over to sensuality so as to indulge in every kind of impurity, with a continual lust for more." The idea is "being past feeling, to throw off all sense of shame." Now I am reminded of being sensitive as I enjoy a beautiful flowering orchid, a gift from a friend. Thoreau commented about sensitiveness: "The finest qualities of our nature, like the bloom on fruits, can be preserved only by the most delicate handling. Yet we do not treat ourselves nor one another thus tenderly." We all need to pray that God will make us sensitive to maintaining a good relationship with Him, with fellow Christians and with those who need Christ. Prayer is essential for when we are insensitive, we are last to notice.

Spurs

Reading: 2 Corinthians 8:7—9

"For I know your eagerness to help, and I have been boasting about it to the Macedonians, telling them that since last year you in Achaia were ready to give; and your enthusiasm has stirred most of them to action" (2 Corinthians 9:2 NIV).

The speaker at commencement grew up in Eastern Oregon on a ranch. His horse was named "Ready to Go." Our speaker spoke fondly of his horse and the many memories of growing up on the ranch. Whenever he climbed into the saddle the horse's ears perked up and he'd be ready to go. After field chores were finished they would head to the barn. Ready to Go, ears dropped, head relaxed, would lope back, seeming to know he'd done another good job that day. Occasionally, a gate may have been left open and it was necessary to go back into the field. So he'd gently rub his spurs along the belly of Ready to Go, turn his head and lead him back toward the field. His horse was always ready to go. Our speaker challenged the college graduates with the words of Hebrews 10:24, "And let us consider how we may spur one another on toward love and good deeds."

Now I don't know much, if anything, about spurs as related to horses; however, I do have a daughter-in-law and a son-in-law, both of whom know a lot about horses and spurs. Gundi, is a horsewoman from Germany who now lives in England and owns a special show horse named Tip Top. Timm, grew up on a ranch in Central Washington and is an expert in training horses. So I asked them to tell me what they knew about spurs.

They both knew quite a lot. There are many different kinds of spurs depending on the horse, its age and purpose for which it is ridden. Spurs are best used sparingly, lest the horse find their use too commonplace. Spurs are meant to get the attention of the horse so he will rise to a higher level of running. They are an aid in giving instructions, like pointing in another direction. Spurs can do harm if used by an inexperienced rider.

Getting back to the writer of Hebrews, the challenge is to "consider how we may spur one another on toward love and good deeds." He's talking about encouraging one another. Different translations help here: "help one another" (TEV); "Outdo each other" (TLB); "Stimulate" (NAS); "Provoke" (ASV).

Encouragement requires experience, a sense of timing, a purpose to help, a sense of direction. Sometimes it requires words, at other times it requires that we just be there with full attention.

Talk

Reading: Job 16:18-22

"Should a wise man answer with empty knowledge?....Should he reason with unprofitable talk?" (Job 15:2,3 NKJ).

Our world is awash with talk, talk, talk. The tides of talk crash the shores of our mind relentlessly. Talk shows, scream therapy, talk in national and international forums. As though all differences between men is the result of not understanding one another. The late A.W. Tozer conjectured that we need a new decalogue: "Thou shalt not disagree"; and a new set of Beatitudes: "Blessed are they who tolerate everything, for they shall not be made accountable for anything."

"How long will you say such things? Your words are a blustering wind." (Bildad). (Job. 8:2).

Israel's sin was noted in Hosea 11:12: "Ephraim has surrounded me with lies, the house of Israel with deceit. And Judah is unruly against God, even against the faithful Holy One." 12:1 "Ephraim feeds on the wind; he pursues the east wind all day multiplies lies and violence."

Mozart, the Austrian composer, in a letter to his family wrote: "My great-grandfather used to say to his wife, my great-grandmother, who in turn told her daughter, my grandmother, who repeated it to her daughter, my mother, who used to remind her daughter, my own sister, that to talk well and eloquently was a very great art, but that an equally great one was to know the right moment to stop." Wolfgang Amadeus Mozart (1756–91), Austrian composer. Letter, 4 Nov. 1787 (published in *The Letters of Mozart and His Family,* 2nd ed., ed. by Emily Anderson, 1966).

Tempests

Reading: John 4:39—41

"They were terrified and asked each other, 'Who is this? Even the wind and the waves obey him?'" (Mark 4:41 NIV).

According to the dictionary a tempest is "A violent windstorm, frequently accompanied by rain, snow or hail." I've been in windstorms, rain, snow and hail of the natural kind, but I'm thinking of a tempest of another kind: a tempest in the teapot – furor over a matter of little or no importance. It's the uproar in spirit that devastates our common sense and usual calm spirit. It's "*The tempest in my mind/Doth from my senses take all feeling*" (Shakespeare). Why do we lose composure? Sometimes it's worry. A friend said: "I think I must be an expert on high wind over small matters. I am a born worrier, so I start worrying before anything ever happens - and most of the time it doesn't ever happen." There is a fine line between concern and worry. A tempest can be incubated in immaturity due to inexperience or a lack of discipline when we know better. Cynicism also breeds a tempest. Sydney J. Harris describes a cynic as one who "is not merely one who reads bitter lessons from the past; he is one who is prematurely disappointed in the future."

A cynical spirit hatches immense distrust of other's motives and actions. Still again, anger is a nemesis that destroys our inner tranquility and the peace of others. Psychology has a word for extreme tempestuousness: Aggression-frustration hypothesis," a theory contending that when we are deeply frustrated, we vent our anger on others. We see it as an exploding temper tantrum in children —. "It's your fault, not mine; you caused me to lose my cool." Until we deal with the causes of tempestuous outbursts, we're in danger of damaging relationships with others. Something we need is to be aware of the problem and work at it..

The Art of Leadership

Reading: Acts 1:17-26

"And when Philip ran up, he heard him reading Isaiah the prophet, and said, 'Do you understand what you are reading? And he said, 'Well how could I unless someone guides me?' And he invited Philip to come up and sit with him" (Acts 8:30,31 NAS).

When the Ethiopian said to Philip, "I don't understand what I'm reading", he raised the question of how can I except someone guide me? The word is not explain, but guide. They share the same verbal root "to lead." It is one thing to lead the meaning out of a text, quite another to guide or lead you in the way of the text. Philip is faced with a choice: to stand alongside the chariot of the Ethiopian providing information, answering the Ethiopian's questions or will he involve himself in a spiritual explanation with this stranger.

Eugene Peterson makes the point that herein is the difference between the shopkeeper who sells maps of the wilderness and the person who goes with you into it, risking the dangers, helping to cook the meals, and sharing the weather. Philip decides to climb in the chariot and shares the journey. That's leadership at its best.

The Yoke

Reading: Matthew 11:25-30

"Come to me, all you who are weary and burdened, and I will give you rest. Take my yoke upon you and learn from me, for I am gentle and humble in heart, and you will find rest for your souls. For my yoke is easy and my burden is light" (Matthew 11:28-30 NIV).

What is the implication of bearing the yoke of Christ? I've often pondered that question. Dallas Willard aptly point out that "What we most learn in his yoke, beyond acting with him, is to abandon outcomes to God, accepting that we do not have in ourselves-in our own heart, soul, mind, and strength-the wherewithal to make this come out right, whatever `this is'. Even if we suffer according to the will of God, `we simply `entrust our souls to a faithful creator in doing what is right' (I Peter 4:19).Now, this is a major part of that meekness and lowliness of heart we also learn in his yoke. And what rest comes with it!"

This gives little cause to strain against the yoke of Christ. Are you prepared to wear the yoke? Not as a restraint, but rather as an aid to accomplishing what God has for us today.

Anxiety

Reading: John 16:17-33

"In this world you will have trouble, but take heart! I have overcome the world" (John 16:33 NIV).

Shortness of breath is one of the symptoms of heart failure, a condition I have experienced myself in recent years. It is tied to anxiety. Helmut Thielicke calls out attention to the nature of anxiety. It is the root word from the Latin angustia which means shortness of breath: the feeling of constriction which occurs in the maximum state of fear – in connection, for example, with angina pectoris. It is the indefinable character of feeling threatened.

When we bring a child into the world, we risk shortness of breath as we watch our children grow. We are caught up in anxiety sometimes at the birth of a child who has an incurable disease. At other times in the growth process, we experience anxiety when they choose to jump from a bridge eighty feet high spanning the river below. The same child also provides an antidote in anxiety by showing great love for life and for his parents. Jesus promises that He has overcome the world and we need not fear,

The opposite of fear and anxiety is love. "There is no fear" – one could just as well translate "anxiety" – in love. Perfect love drives out fear," says the First Letter of John 4:18. We often observe this in our children as they grow.

Beginnings

Reading: Mark 1:1-8

The beginning of the gospel about Jesus Christ, the Son of God (Mark 1:1 NIV).

Life is a series of beginnings. From our time in the womb until we draw our last breath, there is the dawn of a new day with a host of beginnings. Some beginnings were planned, others unplanned; some ill advised, others steeped in wisdom; and some downright disastrous, others successful. Are we not thankful for a fresh start? Have we not, at times, wished we knew enough to stop something we had launched, but continued pursuing long after we realized our mistake? We savor those startups in which we persevered to the end and tasted the joy of finishing that which we had begun.

This beginning of the gospel about Jesus Christ includes the life, death and resurrection of Christ. Had there been no beginning about Jesus Christ in our lives, where would we be who know Christ as our Lord? There is duration and completion in this beginning.

Since nothing can separate us from the love of God and His presence, what beginnings are we facing today we need fear? "...I always pray with joy because of your partnership in the gospel from the first day until now, being confident of this, that he who began a good work in you will carry it on to completion until the day of Christ Jesus" (Philippians 1:6 NIV).

Books

Reading: 2 Timothy 4:1—13

"Bring my winter coat I left at Troas with Carpus; also the book and the parchment notebook" (2 Timothy 4:13 The Message).

Over the years various authors and books have meant a lot to me. My recent love for books and those I value are contained in series and individual writings. Books that have enriched my life and ministry. The reading of books has drawn the curtain back so we can learn from the mistakes and successes of people. I have made it a practice to read books daily in my half century career, much to my profit.

1. *An Introduction to Five Spiritual Classics*
2. *Works of Love* by Soren Kierkegaard
3. The George Morrison collection of sermons
4. *Speaking for Themselves: The Personal Letters of Winston and Clementine Churchill Edited by their daughter* Mary Soames
5. *Truman* by David McCullough
6. *Alexander Botts and The Earthworm Tractor*
7. The collection of Eugene Peterson
8. The collection of Philip Yancey
9. The collection of C.S. Lewis
10. *Radical Christianity* by Vernon C. Grounds

Bo Who? Bozos!

Reading: Romans 10:1-15

"But how can people call for help if they don't know who to trust? And how can they know who to trust if they haven't heard

of the One who can be trusted? And how can they hear if nobody is sent to do it?" (Romans 10:14 The Message).

We are apt to know more about Bo Jackson of baseball and football fame, than we know about the Bozos of this world. Jesus knew all about Bo and the Bozos. Long before they were born – eternity past – Christ died so that all the Bo's and Bozos of this world might come to a saving knowledge of Jesus Christ. I first learned there were people known as Bozos through missionary friends. The following letter draws the curtain back on the missionaries; arrival to a remote tribe in West Africa.

"We will be at the bush station at Mana, an hour's drive southeast of Bamako. No electricity, no telephone, but there will be three fellow missionaries. The BOZO (yes, Bozo!) tribe – a group yet to be reached with the good news of Jesus Christ – live in a near by village. Our prayer is to be a part of the evangelistic outreach of these people. There has been much planning and preparation. We are raising financial support to send out the missionaries. But, it will take prayer to reach this tribe with the gospel. Good-byes are hard. Please remember our loved ones we leave behind – for the Lord's comfort as we will miss each other a lot.

"Our love for one another comes from our God who mercifully and graciously speaks to us in love through Jesus on the cross. Remembering that the heart of man is changed 'not by might, nor by power but by my Spirit says the Lord of Host.' It is our prayer that we will use the gifts that God has given our family to plant churches among the unreached peoples of Mali, West Africa. Praise God for all the help we've had in making this move; for the necessary support that continues to come in; the good home we've found for our dog, Digger. Pray that God will move the hearts and minds of those he would have us meet and that we'll live lives that mirror the Lord Jesus. AW NI FAAMA! (Bambara for 'We haven't seen you in a while – welcome!')"

God forbid that we're more interested in the stats of a Bo Jackson than we are in reaching the Bozo tribes of this world.

Perhaps we should think about Paul's question: "...How can they hear if nobody is sent to do it?"

Engraved

Reading: Isaiah 49:13—18

"...I bear in my body the marks of Jesus Christ" (Galatians 6:17 NIV).

Why people sport tattoos is a mystery to me. Those permanent designs carved on the skin are said by some to be a love of art. For others it is to make a statement. Still others get tattoos to impress a lover. Would you believe that some see in tattooing a thing of beauty? We could hardly ascribe tattooing as art. Today the usual statement made is one of rebellion. Impressing a lover is hazardous, especially when one lover is exchanged for another. I agree in this case with Jean Rostand, "Beauty in art is often nothing but ugliness subdued." Many people tattooed wish they had never submitted to the procedure in the first place. Jews practiced a form of tattooing on their hands or arms to show their affection and zeal for the temple or the city. When the Jews became discouraged during the time of captivity, thinking they were abandoned, God affirmed them: "Behold, I have graven thee upon the palms of my hands; thy walls are continually before me." The Apostle Paul wrote the Galatian Christians, "the scars I have on my body show that I am the slave of Jesus" (TEV). Better to engage in that form of engraving reflecting our love as a servant of Jesus Christ than to be tattooed with the ways of the world.

So, do you really wonder why tattoos make some of us uneasy? For the believer remember 1 Corinthians 6:19. "Do you not know that your body is a temple of the Holy Spirit, who is in you, whom you have received from God. You are not your own; you were bought at a price. Therefore honor God with your body."

Friend

Reading: Proverbs 18:14-24

"A man of many companions may come to ruin but there is a friend who sticks closer than a brother" (Proverbs 18:24 NIV).

In ancient usage the word "friend" had much deeper implications than our casual usage. Aristotle indicated that a person might be called on to sacrifice his life for that of a friend. According to that famous Greek philosopher: "To a noble man there applies the true saying that he does all things for the sake of his friends" (*Theological Dictionary of The New Testament* IX p 153). This concept of friendship lays the basis for the New Testament use of this word. The word philos (friend) appears 29 times in the New Testament: 17 of these references are in the culturally Greek writings of Luke. He attaches many shades of meaning to this basic word.

First, "friend" speaks of social contact. Jesus was accused of loose behavior, because He ate with the collectors and sinners (Luke 7:34). When the shepherd of Jesus' parable found his one lost sheep, he summoned his friends to celebrate the event with him (15:6).

Second, a friend can also refer to a neighbor. People invited friends and neighbors to their feasts, for this was normal (Luke 14:21). When the Prodigal Son returned home, his overjoyed father fetched his friends and neighbors for a party (15:29). Here again, friends are found among one's neighbors. The same truth is seen in the parable of a neighbor who came late at night to ask for help (Luke 11:5-8).

Third, allegiance to Christ outweighs fidelity to one's family. Jesus urged His disciples to obey him, even if they had to leave friends and family (21:16). This is a hard teaching when one considers the depth of feeling attached to oriental friendships.

Fourth, the disciples were called friends by Jesus. The Lord prefaced His most serious teaching about martyrdom by calling the disciples, "My friends" (12:4). A similar preface preceded His injunction to obedience. His "friends" obey Him implicitly, and they also enjoy the Father's favor (John 15:14-15).

Fifth, another use of the word is seen in the Jewish wedding customs. A groomsman was called, "the friend of the bridegroom" (John 3:29). His function was to accompany the groom as he brought his bride home on the wedding day.

Friendship is seen at different levels. Most of us have many acquaintances, whom we know on a superficial level. Others are friends with whom we have many things in common. Fortunate is the person who has one, "bosom friend" who enters into the deepest concerns of his life. Only the Lord is the "Friend who sticks closer than a brother."

Gentleness of God

Reading: Psalm 18:25-36

"...thy gentleness makes me great" (Psalm 18:35. NAS).

David's success was attributed to the gentleness of God; his true greatness came also from God's gentleness. Seen in the spirit of kindness, fairness and compassion. The Apostle Paul emphasized that Christians should be known for a spirit of gentleness to all people. "Let your gentleness be evident to all. The Lord is near" (Philippians 4:4-5 NIV). "By the meekness and gentleness of Christ, I appeal to you. I, Paul, who am 'timid' when face to face with you, but 'bold' when away!" (2 Corinthians 10:1-2 NIV).

Let it be true of us that we are known by our gentleness in our relationships with others. "If every lily of the field, lifting its head, can say, Thy gentleness hath made me great; if every sparrow chirping on the eaves is only echoing that meadow music, then I do feel that you and I, who are of more value to God than the many sparrows, owe more than we shall ever understand to the abounding gentleness of heaven." —George Morrison

---

God's Smile Questioned

Reading: Proverbs 11:16-25

"Does it please you to oppress me, to spurn the work of your hands, while you smile on the schemes of the wicked?" (Job 10:3 NIV).

God smiles also when we think we have sacrificed to give ourselves in the work of church planting, all the while knowing there is no sacrifice involved only the joy of giving. Did not He say through Solomon that "There is he that scattereth; and yet increaseth; there is he that withholdeth more than is fitting but it tendeth to poverty." (Proverbs 11:24 KJV).

Bouknight reminds us that to seek to build a church just to help pay off the mortgage is the most godless of all reasons to set evangelism into our preaching. Too many mainline churches are not calling sinners to be redeemed; they are just rounding up respectable folks to help pay off the mortgage.

Vance Havner has been widely quoted in any number of sermons as saying, "We are building million dollar launching pads to send up firecrackers."

Dallas Willard in his work *The Renovation of the Heart* points this out so well: "For the productive character giving has an entirely different meaning. Giving is the highest expression of potency. In the very act of giving I experience my strength, my wealth, my power. The experience of heightened vitality fills me with joy. I experience myself as overflowing, spending alive, hence is joyous. Giving is more joyous than receiving, but not because it is a deprivation, but because in the act of giving lies the expression of my aliveness."

Green Apples

Reading: Job 10:1-12

"Your hands shaped me and made me. Will you now turn and destroy me?" (Job 10:8 NIV).

God must smile at our impatience. After spending five days in the hospital recently, I returned home with an appetite to eat. Went out back to check on my little dwarf apple tree and noticed two apples had fallen to the ground. Picked them up and ate them.

It reminded me of the days when I was a kid. My buddy and I climbed the apple tree high enough not to be seen by our mothers. We ate green apples that afternoon. And groaned all during the night. Did not seem to worry the moms; they knew where we were and what we had done. They smiled.

It was later that I realized God was saying: if you can't outsmart your mothers what makes you think you can outsmart me. After all, I will provide suitable apples for you to feast upon in my perfect timing. We are just like that in our desire to see the fruit of our labors. We want to plant and harvest in the same breath. The great temptation is to uproot the plant to see if it is growing.

Listen Up, Moses

Reading: Exodus 11:1-10

"This is what the LORD says…" (Exodus 11:4 NIV).

Suppose we dialogue with Moses before we read about the next plague recorded in Exodus eleven. Imagine saying, if you will, "Hey, Moses, your image isn't showing too good these days. You're supposed to be leading your brothers out of Egypt, but you keep getting into trouble with Pharaoh and his lot. Image is all important, Moses. Those Egyptians may be thinking highly of you at the moment, but they will turn on you, believe me. Another thing you are overlooking is your brothers. They are getting awfully testy about your perceived skills as a leader. Like I say, image or perception is where it's at these days. Then there is God. What do you suppose He thinks about His choice of you as His man to deliver His people out of bondage? You'd better watch, Moses, or God will sack you and get him a leader whose image guarantees success. God isn't going to be patient with you forever; He wants results. Right Now! Leaders are expendable, Moses. You can be replaced. Better get humpin'! Soon you'll be getting it in the neck from all sides: Pharaoh, your brothers and God."

Now our fanciful flight of imagination connects us with the culture of today that says image supercedes substance. Consider what part perception plays in the name of politics and advertising in the marketplace. Much is based on illusion, being deceived by a false perception or belief, rather than fact and reality. But now we read Exodus 11:4 and see that Moses is convinced of power, not based not on illusion, but on God. Moses is emphatic: "This is what the LORD says:". If we spent more time on the power that really counts, we'd have less time to engage in imaging and with less reason.

"Now I have given up everything else—I have found it to be the only way to really know Christ and to experience the mighty power that brought him back to life again, and to find out what it means to suffer and to die with him" (Philippians 3:10 TLB).

Silence

Reading: 3:1-8

"There is a time to keep silence, And a time to speak" (Ecclesiastes 3:1 NIV)

Every day it seems that we are being mugged by noise. If it isn't television, it's the telephone, the radio, or the stereo. On more than one occasion while in our automobile there's a loud rumble that signals an earthquake, only to learn that a car has pulled alongside with unabated noise coming from the radio. Our car rumbled with the beat. What to make of it?

Ravi Zacharius observed: It was Luther of old who once cried out, "Bless us, oh Lord; yea, even curse us, but please do not be silent." Secularization - the silencing of the supernatural - brings about an eerie silence. We don't want to silence the supernatural, that is in God's domain; however, we can't be chattering all the time, lest we miss the point of being silent.

We who live in a world of noise and the silencing of the supernatural must draw aside and take time apart to learn the spiritual value of silence, to let God speak to us through his Word. Admittedly, it's a temptation to want to be talking when we should be listening to God. There is a time for both, but we fail when we talk so much and listen so little. As Oliver Wendell Holmes Sr. wrote:

"And Silence, like a poultice, comes To heal the blows of sound."

Songs in the Night

Reading: Psalm 42:1-8

" ...God, my maker, who gives songs in the night." (Job 35:10 NIV).

During the day Job left no doubt how he felt about his suffering. He complained to God, but during the night he showed his inalienable trust in God

"By day the LORD directs his love ,And at night his song is with me". (Psalm 42:8 NIV).

Longfellow suggests:

And the night shall be filled with music,
and the cares, that infest the day,
Shall fold their tents, like the Arabs,
and as silently steal away.

It was in the night when Paul and Silas were in prison that they burst out in song, "praying and singing hymns to God." Paul wrote the Roman believers that the Gentiles would glorify God. "Therefore I will praise you among the Gentiles; I will sing hymns in your name" (Romans 15:9 NIV). Jesus is said not to be ashamed to call them brothers... "In the presence of the congregation I will sing your praise (Hebrews 2:12 NIV).

The black church gave voice in song to their deepest feelings about God. J. Cone writes: "The black spirituals . . . are historical songs which speak about the rupture of black lives; they tell us about a people in the land of bondage and what they did to hold themselves together and fight back." We are told that the people of Israel could not sing the Lord's song in a strange land. But, for the blacks, their being depended upon a song. . . Much has been said about the compensatory and otherworldly ideas in the black spirituals. While I do not question the presence of that theme, there is, nevertheless, another train of thought running through these songs. .. the emphasis on freedom in this world.

Be joyful for songs in the night for as Antoine de Saint-Exupery felt, "Night, the beloved. Night, when words fade and things come alive. When the destructive analysis of day is done, and all that is truly important becomes whole and sound again. When man reassembles his fragmentary self and grows with the calm of a tree."

Surgery

Reading: Psalm 118:19-29

"Rejoice in the Lord always. I will say it again; Rejoice! Let your gentleness be evident to all. The Lord is near" (Philippians 4:4 NIV).

After surgery, I woke up about noon with a poem tied to my big toe, compliments of Dr. James Buchanan. "Here lay one Tom Younger, Divestor of books and wisdom. Citizen of DeKalb County. Tried to move back to Oregon, but didn't get far."

Drs. C.B. Hathaway (anesthesiologist), and Bob Edwards (surgeon), had completed a hernia procedure and now I was under the watchful care of several gentle nurses. Earlier my doctor, Paul Rexroth, had stopped by, as well as Buchchanan, Hathaway, and Edwards, to wish me well. Alongside their professional manner, lay a spirit of friendship that made an otherwise painful day, a pleasure. Now I know that hernia isn't akin to cancer or heart disease, but nevertheless you are required to sign off on a slip of paper, indicating anything can happen, for medicine isn't a perfect science. Those people helping me that day weren't reaching down to me only because I needed their help, but were reaching out to a fellow human being. Auburn, Indiana is blessed with men and women in the medical field who know the difference between curing and healing. They cannot cure. Only God can do that, but they help heal by their love and concern.

Martin Luther called love "left-handed power." A greater right-handed force can defeat a lesser right-handed power, nothing can defeat left-handed power, the power of love, of forgiveness, of self-giving. The cross of Christ is the greatest example of left-handed power.

Dr. Oliver Wendell Holmes once observed: "Say not too much, speak it gently, and guard it cautiously. Always remember that words used before patients are like coppers given to children; you think little of them but the children count them over and over, making all conceivable imaginary uses of them." I have a lot of coppers to remember the "helping professions" by. I must include another doctor of encouragement of a different kind – Smith is the name. Last, not least, I'm grateful for our Great Physician, Jesus Christ. And for all of you. Your prayers, calls and cards, are all appreciated. Now remember, should you be going to a doctor soon and wish to argue with him, he has inside information. And remember to "Rejoice in the Lord always..."

The Poetry of Christ

Reading: Luke 12:22-34

"Consider how the lilies grow. They do not labor or spin. Yet I tell you, not even Solomon in all of his splendor was dressed like one of these. If that is how God clothes the grass of the field, which is here today, and tomorrow is thrown into the fire, how much more will he clothe you, O you of little faith!" (Luke 12:27,28. NIV).

I'm sitting in my office this morning looking out the window at numerous tulips standing tall in red splendor, a harbinger of another springtime. Jacques Barzun writes of the tulip: "The flower, an import from the Near East, had first been seen in Europe around the mid-16C and had been especially prized in Central Europe and the Netherlands...Owning a garden full became a status symbol and the desire to buy and grow tulips spread among the Dutch at every rank. By 1635 the demand had raised prices to vertiginous heights; a Haarlem merchant was reported to have given half his assets for a single bulb – not to resell but to show off." Soon the Dutch created a market for buying and selling bulbs, trading them much like we treat the stock market today; however, in two years the fever for buying and trading tulips collapsed.

However that may be, flowers lift our spirit as we drink in the beauty of God's creation. As Christopher Smart's poem observed, *"Flowers Are Great Blessings*"

For there is a language of flowers.
For there is a sound reasoning for all flowers.
For elegant phrases are nothing but flowers.
For flowers are peculiarly the poetry of Christ.
Quoted from: *God the Worker,* Robert Banks, p. 143.

The Use of Means

Reading: John 3:1-21

"The wind blows wherever it pleases. You hear its sound, but you cannot tell where is comes from or where it is going. So it is with everyone born of the Spirit" (John 3:5 NIV).

In the evening of September ,1931, perhaps the most significant evening in his Life. Lewis (C.S.) invited two close friends – Dyson and Tolkien – for dinner. They began discussing myth and metaphor. After dinner they strolled the Oxford campus, along beautiful Addison's Walk. This mile long path under magnificent beech trees cutting though open fields of flowers is often visited by deer. The three men stood in the dark and listened to the wind. Perhaps this came to have symbolic meaning for Lewis, who had been reading in the Gospel of according to St. John 3:5. : Twelve days after that evening. Lewis wrote to Arthur Greeves: "I have just passed on .to definitely believing in. I will try to explain this another time." And in other letters. "My long night talk with Dyson and Tolkien had a good deal to do with it" . . . And in other letters, "...the intellectual side of my conversion was *not* simple; Dyson and Tolkien were the immediate causes of my conversion."

Quoted from Dr. Armand M. Nicholi, Jr. *The Question of God* Page 91

How might God use you in a witness to someone? He uses even the simple words of reference to His mighty power and salvation.

When God Smiled

Reading: Job 23:1-12

"Does it please you to oppress me, To spurn the work of your hands, while you smile on the schemes of the wicked?" (Job 10:3 NIV).

Job is speaking to God. He mistook God's smile as a personal slight to him, but that wasn't the case at all. God knew Job had a personal relation with him; his friends didn't. He knew God, based upon a relationship by faith, even though he couldn't see clearly the reason for his suffering. Job's friends knew little about God however well meaning they were. Therein is the difference between Job and his friends. You cannot know God except you have a relationship with Him.

God's sense of humor was there. He smiled for He knew Job had it over his friends. Make no mistake; God's smile is in no way taking the wickedness of men lightly. After all He is the Mighty Judge who can torch men's wickedness and He will.

God smiled listening to Job talk about his trials that were ordered by God.

He knew that in His timing, He would step forth and restore Job in ways Job never dreamed.

Wonderfully Significant

Reading: Mark 14:1-9

"When she poured this perfume on my body, she did it to prepare me for burial. I tell you the truth, whenever this gospel is preached throughout the world, what she has done will also be told, in memory of her" (Matthew 26:12 NIV).

A World of Difference:

But often in the world's most crowded streets,
But often, in the din of strife,
There rises an unspeakable desire
After the knowledge of our buried life;
A thirst to spend our fire and restless force
In tracking out our true, original course;
A longing to inquire
Into the mystery of this heart which beats
So wild, so deep in us – to know
Whence our lives come and where they go.

Matthew Arnold The Buried Life

As we live life, we can't see around every bend in the road – whether we're looking ahead or in the rear view mirror – but we can trust a loving heart that beats for God, that gives itself in self-sacrifice to others, as Mary did to Jesus in her act of anointing him with expensive perfume. Mary's comfort came from a huge sense of love for Jesus. His comment about the significance of her act, it seems to me, surely amazed her, and shocked the disciples. Mary's heart manifested a sense of eternity and purpose – nothing was too excessive for the sake of the Savior. The disciples, for all intents and purposes, were still given to opportunism. They were utilitarian in spirit – walking by sight, not by faith, looking only to the present, not to the future. We can thank Mary for yet another lesson on the cross given by Jesus. He used Mary's act of love to further explain a previous statement "Self-sacrifice is the way, my way, to finding yourself, your true self" (Matthew 16 The Message). What action might we take today on behalf of someone else that would be of wonderful significance, reflecting self-sacrifice, casting its shadow ahead into eternity?

Words

Reading: Psalm 119:71-80

"I know, O LORD, that your laws are righteous..." (Psalm 119:75 NIV).

The Psalmist hated falsehood but loved the law of the Lord; praised God for His righteous laws which he followed. He reveled in the fact that the Word of God is righteous. (119: 7, 75, 123, 138, 144, 172.) He knew God was dependable, unshakable as heaven and earth, inexhaustible. He found the Word of God wondrous to explore. (119: 18, 27, 129) and a breadth unparalleled.

Eliphaz, one of Job's friends exclaimed as he contemplated the Word of God "A spirit glided past my face, and the hair on my body stood on end." (Job 4:15). Yes, one is left to wonder how Eliphaz could be so wrong in his assessment of Job and his condition of suffering. All of which serves as a reminder that we can treasure something dearly and yet be mistaken because of a lack of our own understanding.

Don't Kill the Goose

Reading: Titus 2:1-15

"Similarly, encourage the young men to be self-controlled. In everything set them an example by doing what is good" (Titus 2:6,7 NIV).

After only a few days on our church staff, we were talking ministry; he, the new and junior staff member; I, the old and gnarly, senior pastor. Like a wild stallion never ridden, my latest charge was a true "Son of Thunder." No ordinary fellow. God's hand was upon him, and I could see good days for the church were ahead. The only question I had was how could I give him the gift of "becoming" and not extinguishing the flame of his youth.

During our conversation that day, my friend said: "I'd like to spend a lot of time at your feet, learning everything I can about ministry." That didn't sound out of reason to me, but then he continued: "It may take a month."

"Are you serious?" I asked, "Really? A month? Do you think it'll take that long?" He assured me that he was a quick learner.

It was my choice; should I laugh or cry? I've had many a laugh since as have my friends when I tell the tale. Imagine; a month to learn all you need to know! Surely I must write a book and entitle it: *All You Need To Know About Ministry in Less Than a Month.*

My young charge "learned" all he needed to know about ministry from me in less than thirty days, and we labored happily, side by side for another three years – an electric three years. He reminded me of Benjamin Franklin whose experiment with electricity, once knocked himself out. Franklin was trying to kill a turkey with an electric shock, but he was stunned, not the bird.. Upon regaining consciousness Franklin said, "I meant to kill a turkey, and instead, I nearly killed a goose."

After a novice learns everything he can from you in less than thirty days, give him his chance. Let him be himself and make mistakes, even fail, and, oh yes, pray daily that he'll not kill the goose!

Churches

Reading: Acts 20:28

"Keep watch over yourselves and all the flock of which the Holy Spirit has made you overseers. Be shepherds of the church of God which he bought with his own blood." (Acts 20:28 NIV).

The task of being Christ's church in this day is not automatic simply because we meet for worship. Many churches die each year, while others simply wait for someone to pronounce them dead. Many times it is because they have abandoned the preaching of the true gospel. But often the symptoms of death for a church can be summed up in seven words: "We've never done it that way before." It is estimated that 85% of America's Protestant churches are either stagnating or dying.

We've been privileged to pastor six churches in our time all of which have enjoyed 50 to 100 years of ministry.

Several characteristics may go with age: resistance to change; desperate nostalgia hoping that tomorrow will be yesterday; thrashing about trying to catch up with the times, but don't know how; hanging on to traditions because of fear of abandoning them would seem like turning one's back on God;

and an outright hatred of change. Pray for the shepherds of the churches.

The Blessings of Generosity

Reading: 2 Corinthians 8:1-15

"I do want you to experience the blessing that issues from generosity" (Philippians 2:17 The Message).

William Bennett observed that "Generous giving sometimes makes us act foolishly. But what is foolish for the head may be wise for the heart." Cultivating a lifestyle that believes giving is better than receiving leads to a blessed life. We experience inner peace and double edged joy when we give. A retired pastor bought a used car and agreed to pay $3,000. A friend, choosing to keep his identity secret, heard about the deal and paid for half the amount on behalf of the pastor. The pastor himself, a generous person, found the tables turned on him. His friend was blessed.

It is God who enables us to give. A man once gave a check for $60,000 to me for a college I served. I thanked him profusely for his generosity. He responded "God made it possible for me to give." According to the Bible great harvests come from great times of sowing.

We're spared the entrapment of selfishness, an insidiously evil characteristic. Selfishness says, calculate the cost, give out of your abundance, give to get.

We're relieved of keeping short accounts with God. He keeps the records. No one has ever out-given God. The Bible says, "A generous man will prosper; he who refreshes others will himself be refreshed" (Proverbs 11:25). A gift given in love multiplies beyond our comprehension.

A Good Man

Reading: John 3: 1-21

"Jesus declared, 'I tell you the truth, no one can see the kingdom of God unless he is born again.' 'How can a man be born when he is old?' Nicodemus asked. 'Surely he cannot enter a second time into his mother's womb to be born.' Jesus answered, 'I tell you the truth, no one can enter the kingdom of God unless he is born of water and the Spirit. Flesh gives birth to flesh, but the Spirit gives birth to spirit. You should not be surprised at my saying, You must be born again" (John 3:3-7 NIV).

Cornelius in the book of Acts was a Roman Centurion stationed at Caesarea. The headquarters of the government was in Palestine. A God-fearing man; he was known for his loyalty and courage. He was also engaged in charity. He loved his fellow man and was a man of prayer. He did not know the God to whom he prayed; but, according to the light he had, Cornelius lived close to God. That poses a question: Does a good man need a Savior? Yes, he did need a Savior for good works and being a good man wasn't a qualification to receive eternal life. He, like good men and bad, was a sinner and needed to trust Christ his sin-bearer for eternal life. Many a man has stumbled over his goodness and missed eternal life because they thought themselves good enough to get to heaven on their own merit. Peter spoke to Cornelius about Christ. "...everyone who believes in him receives forgiveness of sin through his name" (Acts 10:43 NIV).

Happiness

Reading: Matthew 25

"His master replied, 'Well done, good and faithful servant! You have been faithful with a few things; I will put you in charge of many things. Come and share your master's happiness!'" (Matthew 25:23 NIV).

She is 92 years old, petite, well poised, and proud. She is fully dressed each morning by eight o'clock, with her hair fashionably coifed, and her makeup perfectly applied, in spite of the fact she is legally blind.

Today she has moved to a nursing home. Her husband of 70 years recently passed away, making this move necessary. After many hours of waiting patiently in the lobby of the nursing home, she smiled sweetly when told her room was ready. As she maneuvered her walker to the elevator, an employee provided a visual description of her tiny room, including the eyelet curtains that had been hung on her window. "I love it," she stated with the enthusiasm of an eight-year-old having just been presented with a new puppy.

"That does not have anything to do with it," she gently replied. "Happiness is something you decide on ahead of time. Whether I like my room or not, does not depend on how the furniture is arranged. It is how I arrange my mind. I have already decided to love it. It is a decision I make every morning when I wake up. I have a choice. I can spend the day in bed recounting the difficulty I have with the parts of my body that no longer work, or I can get out of bed and be thankful for the ones that do work. Each day is a gift, and as long as my eyes open, I will focus on the new day and all of the happy memories I have stored away...just for this time in my life. (Unknown)

Happiness is a choice. What will you choose today?

Money

Reading: 1 Timothy 6:1-10

"For the love of money is a root of all kinds of evil. Some people, eager for money, have wandered from the faith and pierced themselves with many griefs" (1 Timothy 6:10 NIV).

We can't hold enough in our hand, count it, weigh it, nor find two people to agree on what is enough. As if that were not enough, our definition of what is enough money changes at different points in life, I've observed over the years several things about people and money:

1: Few are seldom satisfied with what they are paid.

2. Many think if they were paid 10% more, they could make it.

3. Most feel a pay raise helps for only about three months.

4. Not a few think they are worth more than they are paid.

5. Then there are those who fret that others who, in their opinion, are less worthy and are getting paid more.

6. Very few are content and appear not to fret about money. And they are not necessarily those whom we characterize as rich.

Perhaps we can understand better the concept of enough by considering three questions:

1. Does money define our worth? If we think it does, we need to find another way of defining what we are worth.

2. Can money be a useful tool; as something we use to get something else? Yes, we use money to get things: cars, boats, houses, the pleasure of a vacation, etc. We also use money to get opportunity in the future: a college education, children, investing for our old age, investing in the Lord's work, etc.

3. Is it proper to look at money as a gift? First reaction is to say, "not if I earned it!" But look at it this way: God gave us our ability and talent. Look at it as His gift to us. Gifts prompt us to say, "Thank you, God!" Such a view will remove the problem of money becoming our master, wasting time worrying about it, or envying others who have more than we.

Seeing Him Who Is Invisible

Reading: Hebrews 12:1-13

"Keep your eyes on Jesus, who both began and finished this race we're in. Study how he did it. Because he never lost sight of where he was headed" (Hebrews 12:2 The Message).

Gorch Fock wrote to his wife: "If you should hear that our cruiser was sunk and none were saved, do not weep. The sea in which my body sinks is nothing but the hollow of my Savior's hand and nothing can snatch me from it." To know Jesus Christ as Lord and Savior, is to know Him who stands beyond that wall with outstretched hands.

Do you share this vision of Christ? Do you hold on to Him as the One who is always with us, yes, even goes with us whether it be sudden or lingering death?

Moses' source of endurance was his vision of Christ. "He had his eye on the One no eye can see, and kept right on going" (Hebrews 11:27 The Message). When skies all around you are dark, lift up your eyes to the One who is invisible and you'll find the power to endure. No greater example is to be found than that of our Master, Jesus Christ. He was radiant with joy. He resolutely moved through Gethsemane and endured the agony of Calvary, His face aglow with the vision of His Father's face.

Dare we practice that same presence? Yes, we can. Paul assures us, we can endure all things through Christ who strengthens us. (Philippians 4:13).

We Are Not Alone

Reading: Psalm 139:1-10

"The Lord himself goes before you and will be with you; he will never leave you nor forsake you. Do not be afraid; do not be discouraged" (Deuteronomy 31:8 NIV).

Carlyle asked Wilberforce if he had a creed. Wilberforce said he did and that as he grew old, the more uncompromising his creed became. But there was one thing that astounded him; that was the slow breakthrough his creed seemed to make in the world. Carlyle thought about Wilberforce's observation a few moments and then said: "Ah, but if you have a creed you can afford to wait," And if you can afford to wait, you can afford to serve. Is there any place in life's darkest hour, for desperation? —(*The Weaving of Glory* by George H. Morrison)

In one of Wordsworth's poems, there is a bird swept from Norway by a storm. It battles against the storm with desperate effort, eager to return to Norway. It struggles in vain, thinking the gale will carry it to death. Instead the bird is slanted backward to England. How many of us have been swept away by the storm, thinking all is lost; only to discover that "the wind blows where it pleases. You hear its sound, but you cannot tell where it comes from or where it is going." Suddenly , you discover that you are far richer, where there are green pastures and still waters.

We tend to become frantic when we lose control of life's detours, thinking that being in control of our circumstances is the most important ingredient to peace. Fact is, the issue is not our control at all, but God's care and oversight.

"Jehovah himself is caring for you! He is your defender. He protects you day and night. He keeps you from all evil and preserves your life. He keeps his eye upon you as you come and go, and always guards you" (Psalm 121:5-8 TLB).

Resentment

Reading: Job 1: 1-22

"Resentment kills a fool, and slays the simple" (Job 5:2 NIV).

Can you imagine the resentment many of Job's peers must have engaged in, what with Job's success as a farmer and businessman? Many a person has been dashed against the rocks because of resentment and envy leading to anger. Think of those farmers who looked askance at Job and envied his position. Eliphaz and his other friends may have been smitten with such resentment themselves.

John Osborne revolutionized modern English drama. He writes about "Angry Young Men", who identified with the lower classes in English society. The play is filled with resentment and suspicion. Osborne's play gave voice to a generation of young English people who view the English establishment as dominated by snobbery and hypocrisy. (Den Zeff, *World Book Encyclopedia*) It is in the nature of fallen man to succumb to resentment rather than to follow the Scriptural admonition to rejoice in another person's success.

In the Ravensbruck Extermination Camp, Germany, 1944, a woman who had harbored Jews as a member of the Dutch Resistance grieved the enormity of the evil she faced. Thousands around her – her sister Betsie among them – were being brutalized and killed. Only fragments of the Bible, shared with her fellow captives, kept her sane and alive. At last she found in Revelation 3:8 meaning in the midst of horror: "Because you have limited strength, have kept My word, and have not denied My name, look, I have placed before you an open door that no one is able to close." Resentment gave way to trusting God.

Road Kill

Reading: Job 38:1-11

"So Job opens his mouth with empty talk. Without knowledge he multiplies words" (Job 35:16 NIV).

So Job's friend, Elihu, accuses Job.

Most of what comes from the information highway is road kill, observed John Updike.

I get a lot of mail sent by well meaning friends packaged neatly via email. Most of it is useless prater disguised as an attempt to keep in touch. It does not do anything for me except clutter my mind with unworthy thoughts and is a waste of time. Fortunately I have a delete button that saves a lot of time and energy in order to devote myself to more worthy pursuits. Much of it is passed on as humorous, to reflect the issues of life we all have to deal with. Some of it comes in first hand, face to face order. Often it is a violation of our need for silence. I would rather spend time listening to good music or engaging in worthy conversation with friends. Something to reflect the goodness of God. It is a good thing that Job did not have to contend with email. Poor fellow. He was plagued enough by sorry rhetoric coming from his friends.

Make no mistake, Job was said to have 'opened his mouth with empty talk; without knowledge he multiplies words." We come forth self righteously at times in the midst of road kill.

Mirth

Reading Genesis 21:1-7

"He will yet fill your mouth with laughter and your lips with shouts of joy" (Job 8:21 NIV).

Life would be sterile were it not for mirth and laughter. They go together. Garrison Keilor said, "Humor, a good sense of it, is to Americans what manhood is to Spaniards and we will go to great lengths to prove it. Experiments with laboratory rats have shown that, if one psychologist in the room will laugh at something the rat does, all of the other psychologists in the room will laugh equally. No body wants to be holding the joke."

We are blessed when friends make us laugh. Not laughing at friends, but with them, admiring their joyful exuberance. Sometimes we are gleeful at another person's expense, which is our loss. Engaging in a low level of reveling is debilitating as N. F. Simpson says: "Each of us as he receives his private trouncings at the hands of fate is kept in good heart by hearing of the moth in his brother's parachute and the scorpion in his neighbor's underwear."

But Florence King observed: "Any discussion of the problems of being funny in America will not make sense unless we substitute the word wit for humor. Humor inspires sympathetic good-natured laughter and is favored by the 'healing-power' gang. Wit goes for the jugular, not the jocular, and it's the opposite of football; instead of building character, it tears it down."

Does Christian mirth differ from worldly? John Henry Newman contended that it did; that Christian mirth is subdued. "In the world feasting comes first and fasting afterwards; men first glut themselves, and then loathe their excesses. They take their fill of good, and then suffer; they are rich that they may be poor; they laugh that they may weep; they rise that they may fall. But in the Church of God it is reversed; the poor shall be rich, the lowly shall be exalted. Those that sow in tears shall reap in joy, those that mourn shall be comforted, those that suffer with Christ shall reign with Him..."

Conspicuous Yet Silent

Reading: Luke 9:18-27

"The Son of Man must suffer many things and be rejected by the elders, chief priests and teachers of the law, and he must be killed and on the third day be raised from the dead" (Luke 9:22 NIV).

Ours is a conspicuous, but not silent "tell all age" of the Oprah and Dr. Phil talk shows. Their number is legion; battalion numbers of people want to talk about sordid sufferings, and armies of people want to hear about them. We yearn for salient attention and are willing to go to any means to find a forum to tell all, or as we say, "to let it all hang out." Most sensational topics have to do with, in one way or another, the subject of suffering. The effect our "tell all" society is having upon itself is, to make money, entertain, attract attention, and dig the hole of agony a little deeper, using the latest "fix-it-yourself," tools.

Jesus suffered conspicuously before the whole world, yet was mostly silent in His reference to His sufferings. He agonized with innumerable indignities on His way to Calvary, yet spoke of them no more than was absolutely necessary. When we suffer, our first reaction is, we want to talk. "Why? Why me? Why should I suffer, Lord?" Then, we want to gabble to the whole world of our misery. Lewis Smedes comments, "Most of us look at suffering and wonder, why? Jesus tells us to look at suffering and wonder, why not?"

It seems to me, there is still place for silence while suffering. Real friends will pick up on our distress and offer the right amount of comfort and prayer support. Often when hard times come down on us, and we think it's all over, we'll discover as the Apostle Paul did, "As it turned out, it was the best thing that could have happened. Instead of trusting in our own strength or wits to get us out of it, we were forced to trust God totally – not a bad idea since he's the God who raises the dead" (2 Corinthians 1:8&9 The Message).

The Restraint of Power

Reading: 1 Corinthians 13

"Love cares more for others than for self" (1 Corinthians 13:4 The Message).

Earl Palmer, Pastor of the First Presbyterian Church in Seattle, wrote an original parable on the kite, as a way of illustrating that power does best when it's restrained. It's a marvelous parable. One of his points is that the kite soars best when it's attached to the string held by someone on the ground. Palmer likens love to the string that restrains the kite. And love is not a theory; it's an event.

I planned to tell this story in a sermon one Sunday, having no idea that a great event of love would unfold that very morning. The event involved our youth pastor, Chad, who was celebrating his twenty-third birthday. Chad began the service, as always with a few announcements; but as he addressed the congregation, a chorus of people sitting halfway to the front began singing Happy Birthday to him. He was in complete shock, for the twenty-six people comprised his fiancé, her mother and dad; Chad's mother and dad, and Chad's brothers, sisters, aunts, uncles and cousins. Most of them had come to Auburn, Indiana that morning from Grand Rapids, Michigan and the rest from Cedarville, Ohio.

What an event of love! Chad soaring high like a kite in the euphoria of his budding youth ministry, with twenty-six loved ones hanging on to the string! An event we don't often hear about these days.

Before the two families had jumped into their vans and raced three hours to get to the church on time, they had called Chad to wish him a happy birthday, leaving him with no other impression than that he was loved, if only from a distance.

Love draws people together, giving pleasure to the lover and the one loved.

Every Tub On Its Own Bottom

Reading: Hebrews 4:1-13

"Nothing in all creation is hidden from God's sight. Everything is uncovered and laid bare before the eyes of him to whom we must give account" (Hebrews 4:13 NIV).

My Dad gave me an unforgettable lesson about being accountable when I was a kid. One day after school, I hit a ball through a neighbor's window. Thinking that my fellow team members ought to share the blame and help pay damages for this remarkable feat – would have been a home run had there been playing fields in those days – I chose to debate the issue with my dad. He listened a few minutes and then said: "Son, every tub must rest on its own bottom." Off we went to the lumber yard for glass. It was a lesson on accepting responsibility for what we do. Although my dad paid for the glass and I didn't, I remember to this day the principle of accountability and of grace.

One important way God works to hold us accountable for our actions is the teachings in the Bible. "God means what he says. What he says goes. His powerful Word is sharp as a surgeon's scalpel, cutting through everything, whether doubt or defense, laying us open to listen and obey. Nothing and no one is impervious to God's Word. We can't get away from it – no matter what" (Hebrews 4:13 The Message).

Wounded Heroes

Reading: 2 Corinthians 4:1-12

"We always carry around in our body the death of Jesus, so that the life of Jesus may also be revealed in our body" (2 Corinthians 4:10 NIV).

Larry LaSueur, CBS radio correspondent, accompanied Allied soldiers in "Operation Overlord," the invasion of Normandy in France, June 6, 1944, World War II. He scrambled on shore of "Omaha Beach," hunkered down behind a stone hedgerow to escape the searing fire of Hitler's coastal batteries. He heard groaning near by, a badly wounded American soldier lay in shock from shrapnel that had torn into his thigh. LaSueur comforted the lad: "It's a clean wound, son. Stay put until help arrives. This will be your ticket to Britain, or perhaps, home to the States – out of the war for good."

But struggling above the noise of battle and through intense pain, the GI whispered, "But you don't understand, sir, I didn't come here to be wounded."

No one enters the Christian life expecting to be wounded. However, he soon learns he's in a fight and in this struggle no one escapes without being wounded in some way or other. "For our struggle is not against flesh and blood, but against the rulers, against the authorities, against the powers of this dark world and against the spiritual forces of evil in the heavenly realms" (Ephesians 612).

You may be suffering wounds even now, by some disappointment in marriage, by an unfair practice affecting your work. You may be waging war against a crippling bout of loneliness. Perhaps you're drained by the devastating effects of a child's rebellion. How shall you handle it? You didn't expect a wound of this sort. Like the struggling GI fighting against his fate we also struggle against our battles. But don't despair. Find encouragement in Peterson's paraphrase, "So we're not giving up. How could we! Even though on the outside, where God is making new life, not a day goes by without his unfolding grace. ,But these hard times are small potatoes compared the coming good time, the lavish celebration prepared for us. There's far more here than meets the eye. The things we see now are here today, gone tomorrow. But the things we can't see now will last forever" (2 Corinthians 4:16-18 The Message).

In Their Midst

Reading: Psalm 46

"Do not take me away, O my God, in the midst of my days; your years go on through all the ages" (Psalm 102:24 NIV).

I listened carefully on the last Sunday of the year as one person after another recounted their walk with God during the year. Many thanked God for a smooth running year, giving God the glory for it all. Other testimonies included some aspect of life amidst difficulties, disappointments, uncertainty and disease. Thc loss of loved ones, the prospect of complex eye surgery, the decision on how to treat cancer all were in the mix of praising God. Yes, praising God in difficult times. There was the quiet calm of those who identified with David: "Though I walk in the midst of trouble, you preserve my life; you stretch out your hand against the anger of my foes, with your right hand you save me." Elsewhere the Psalmist wrote: "There is a river whose streams make glad the city of God, The holy dwelling places of the Most High. God is in the midst of her, she will not be moved..." (Psalm 46:4,5 NASU). The certainty of and confidence that God is in our midst inspires hope. Nothing changes; Jesus is in the midst. He was in the midst of scholars in the temple; in the midst in the upper room; in the midst of the churches in Revelation; in the midst of the four and twenty elders in glory. Jesus, who is the same yesterday and today will be the same tomorrow. "For where two or three have gathered together in My name, I am there in their midst." NASU

Index

About the Author

Tom Younger was a graduate of Taylor University, Fort Wayne, Indiana and Baptist Bible Seminary, Johnson City, New York. He ministered five years in Arcanum, Ohio, followed by seventeen years at Immanuel Baptist Church, Fort Wayne, where twelve new churches were planted under his leadership. He later pastored churches in Walnut Creek, California and Auburn, Indiana. He also served as president of Western Baptist College in Salem, Oregon and as a trustee of Cedarville University, Cedarville, Ohio. Tom went to be with his Lord in January, 2003. His widow, Davina, lives in Salem, Oregon.

Tom also authored the book, *Vision Inspired Leadership,* published in 2003.

Notes

[1] *How Majestic is Thy Name* (Green Forest, AK: New Leaf Press, 2001), 28.

[2] *How Majestic is Thy Name* (Green Forest, AK: New Leaf Press, 2001), 30.

[3] *How Majestic is Thy Name* (Green Forest, AK: New Leaf Press, 2001), 26.

[4] *How Majestic is Thy Name* (Green Forest, AK: New Leaf Press, 2001), 52.

[5] *How Majestic is Thy Name* (Green Forest, AK: New Leaf Press, 2001), 36.

[6] Philip Yancey, *Soul Survivor* (New York: Doubleday, 2001), 263.

[7] *How Majestic is Thy Name* (Green Forest, AK: New Leaf Press, 2001), 38.

[8] *How Majestic is Thy Name* (Green Forest, AK: New Leaf Press, 2001), 48.

[9] *How Majestic is Thy Name* (Green Forest, AK: New Leaf Press, 2001), 6.

[10] *How Majestic is Thy Name* (Green Forest, AK: New Leaf Press, 2001), 62.

[11] *How Majestic is Thy Name* (Green Forest, AK: New Leaf Press, 2001), 16

[12] Dallas Willard, *Renovation of the Heart* (Colorado Springs, CO: NavPress, 2002), 135.

[13] *How Majestic is Thy Name* (Green Forest, AK: New Leaf Press, 2001), 44.

[14] Philip Yancey, *Soul Survivor* (New York: Doubleday, 2001), 206.

[15] Philip Yancey, *Soul Survivor* (New York: Doubleday, 2001), 129.

[16] William Barclay, *The Gospel of John* (Edinburgh, Scotland: The Saint Andrew Press, 1956), 168.

[17] William Barclay, *The Gospel of John* (Edinburgh, Scotland: The Saint Andrew Press, 1956), 169.

[18] William Barclay, *The Letter to the Romans* (Edinburgh, Scotland: The Saint Andrew Press, 1957), 57.

[19] William Barclay, *The Gospel of John* (Edinburgh, Scotland: The Saint Andrew Press, 1956), 89.

[20]Helmut Thielicke, *The Waiting Father* (Cambridge, England: James Clarke & Co., Ltd., 1978), 55.

[21]Helmut Thielicke, *The Waiting Father* (Cambridge, England: James Clarke & Co., Ltd., 1978), 54.

[22] Soren Kierkegaard, *Works of Love* (New York: Harper & Row, 1962), 286.

[23] William Barclay, *The Letter to the Romans* (Edinburgh, Scotland: The Saint Andrew Press, 1957), 175.

[24]Helmut Thielicke, *The Waiting Father* (Cambridge, England: James Clarke & Co., Ltd., 1978), 18.

[25]Soren Kierkegaard, *Works of Love* (New York: Harper & Row, 1962), 261.

[26] *How Majestic is Thy Name* (Green Forest, AK: New Leaf Press, 2001), 46.

[27]Helmut Thielicke, *The Waiting Father* (Cambridge, England: James Clarke & Co., Ltd., 1978), 31.

[28]Helmut Thielicke, *The Waiting Father* (Cambridge, England: James Clarke & Co., Ltd., 1978), 34.

[29] William Barclay, *The Acts of the Apostles* (Edinburgh, Scotland: The Saint Andrew Press, 1955), 143.

[30] *How Majestic is Thy Name* (Green Forest, AK: New Leaf Press, 2001), 34.

[31] *How Majestic is Thy Name* (Green Forest, AK: New Leaf Press, 2001), 54.

[32] William Barclay, *The Acts of the Apostles* (Edinburgh, Scotland: The Saint Andrew Press, 1955), 2.

[33] *How Majestic is Thy Name* (Green Forest, AK: New Leaf Press, 2001), 40.

[34] *How Majestic is Thy Name* (Green Forest, AK: New Leaf Press, 2001), 10.

[35] Soren Kierkegaard, *Works of Love* (New York: Harper & Row, 1962), 11.

[36] *How Majestic is Thy Name* (Green Forest, AK: New Leaf Press, 2001), 32.

[37] Soren Kierkegaard, *Works of Love* (New York: Harper & Row, 1962), 262.

[38] *How Majestic is Thy Name* (Green Forest, AK: New Leaf Press, 2001), 42.

[39] Dallas Willard, Renovation of the Heart (Colorado Springs, CO: NavPress, 2002), 118.

**Scripture used in this book taken from the following Bible Translations:

KJV – *King James Version.* Oxford University Press, Inc., 1967.

NAS – *New American Standard.* The Lockman Foundation, 1977.

NIV – *New International Version.* International Bible Society, 1973, 1978, 1984.

NKJV – *New King James Version.* Thomas Nelson, Inc., 1979, 1980, 1982.

THE MESSAGE: The Bible in Contemporary Language, 2002 by Eugene Peterson.

TLB – *The Living Bible.* Tyndale House Publishers, 1971.

**Brief quotations and facts throughout the book have been obtained using the following computer software. *Microsoft Bookshelf 2000* (Microsoft Corporation, 1987-1999).

Printed in the United States
16029LVS00004B/37-153